ISLAMIC ART OF ILLUMINATION

Classical Tazhib from Ottoman to Contemporary Times

ISLAMIC ART OF ILLUMINATION

Classical Tazhib
From Ottoman to Contemporary Times

SEMA ONAT

NEW JERSEY ● LONDON ● FRANKFURT ● CAIRO

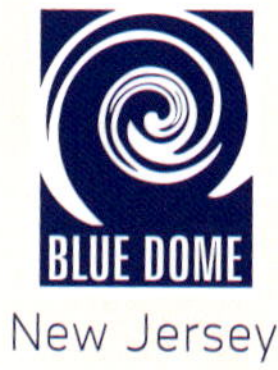

New Jersey

25 24 23 22 4 5 6 7

Published by Blue Dome Press
335 Clifton Avenue, Clifton
New Jersey 07011, USA

www.bluedomepress.com

Library of Congress Cataloging-in-Publication Data Available

ISBN 978-1-935295-82-2

Art Director Engin Çiftçi
Graphic Designer Murat Arabacı
Photographer Murat Şimşek

Front cover: Sema Onat's work showing the whole process of making classical illumination. The first segment of the design shows the gold sections, including the branches and leaves, the chain-pattern, and other places designated to be shiny in the background design. The next segment displays the contour lines and the painting of the motifs with various colors. The larger segment shows the light-toned flower colors applied on a dark color background. Then the flowers are toned and, after making the needle-pointed ornamentation, the illumination of the design is completed.

Back flap: Completed gilded illumination work by Sema Onat

Front flap: Detail from the illuminated family insignia in the tughra form by Sema Onat. Like all the tughras of the Ottoman sultans, this family insignia consists of three vertical strokes and the accompanying three "S-shaped" lines, contrasting with wide intersecting ovals at the bottom. The inner areas of the calligraphy are painted with elaborate patterns of spring blossoms on a gilded background.

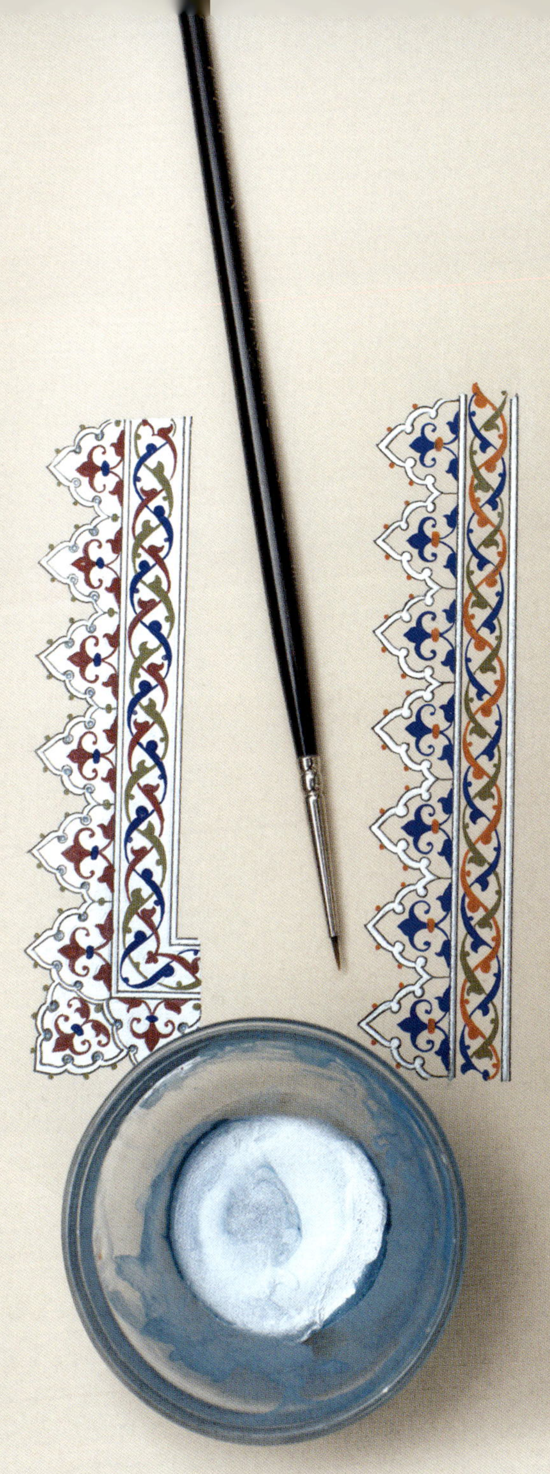

Contents

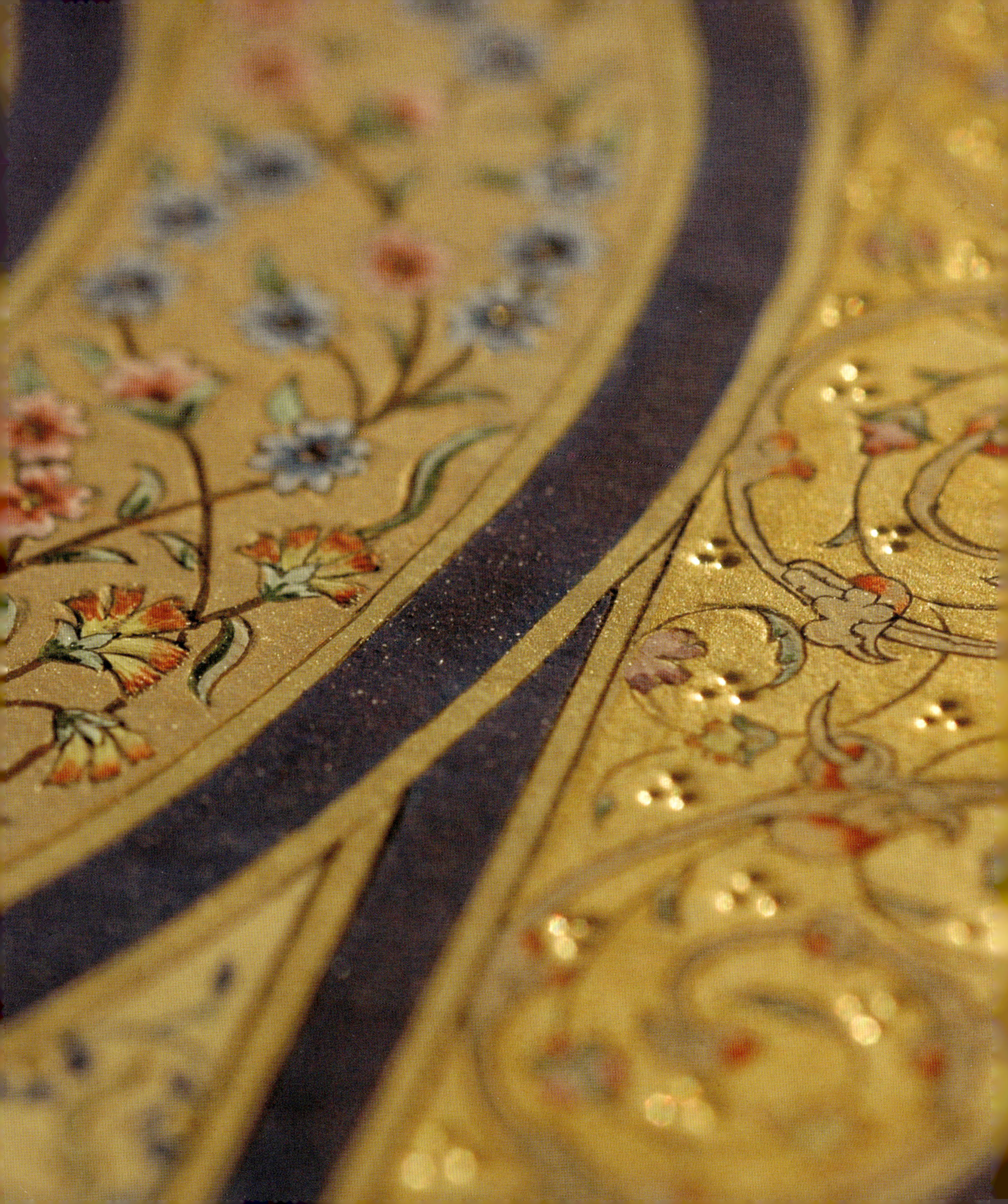

Introduction

Art has existed in every period of human history. Even in the most primitive ages, human beings felt the need to express themselves. The branches of art that emerged from this need developed in very diverse forms depending on the social and cultural characteristics of specific societies all over the world.

Illumination art is one of the major means by which the treasures of rich art heritage from across the globe are preserved and conveyed to future generations. Classical Islamic art of illumination is a result of the accumulated knowledge of local environments and societies, incorporating Turkish, Persian, and Arabic traditions. Illumination held a central place in the traditional arts of the Ottomans who developed their own unique style in the art.

Various definitions of art have been made in many sources. According to Ilhan Ozkececi and Bilge Ozkececi, art is a form of personal human expression. It is the quest of figuring out the veiled reality of natural phenomena and then giving shape to this cognizance about the reality of things and events around us in a form that can be perceived by the five sensory organs. According to Inci A. Birol, it is conveying with symbols the things and events people see and feel while watching the world they live in with the eye of the heart. In my opinion, art is expressing, in an aesthetic way, the reflections in a person's inner world of their perceptions in the external world using their imagination and ability. The traditional Islamic art of illumination thus reflects the inner world of an artist's perceptions of the world around them.

Illumination (*tazhib*) is the art of decorating various works by using gold and various earth-based paints. In the strictest definition of the term, the word *tazhib* (from Arabic *tadhhib*) means "gilding," due to the early illumination artists' use of gold fill and gilding in their works. Therefore, an illuminated work referred only to those decorated with gold. In time, the illumination artists started to use colors like green, red, navy blue, and turquoise along with gold. While the use of gold was one of the most captivating features of the traditional Turkish art of illumination, the use of these varying colors added richness and depth to the art.

Detail from an illumination work by Ayşe Koç

Manuscript Illumination

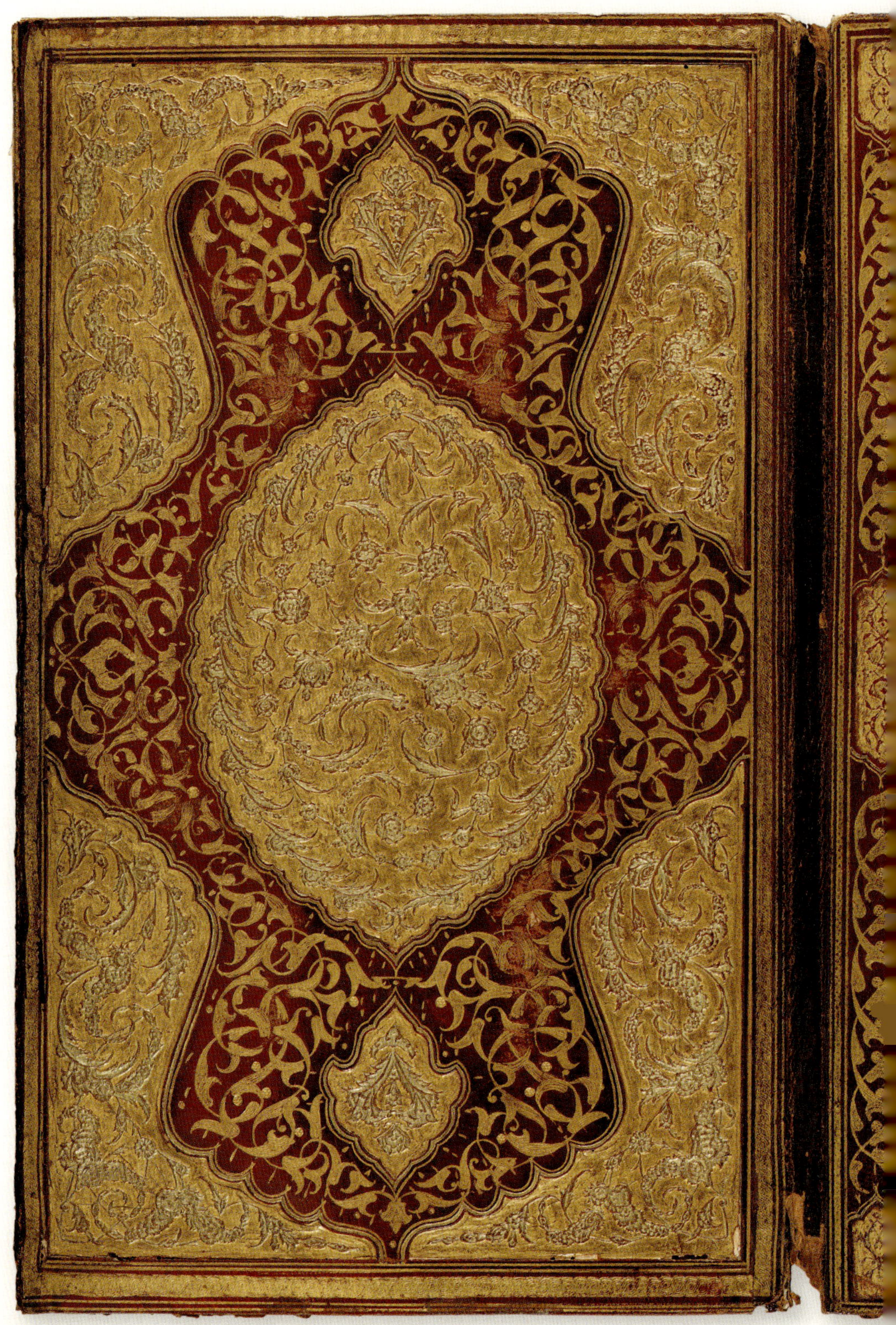

Decorative leather book bindings with flaps represent one of the most important components of manuscript illumination. The covers of Qur'an manuscripts bound in fine leather bindings have long been decorated in rich illumination.

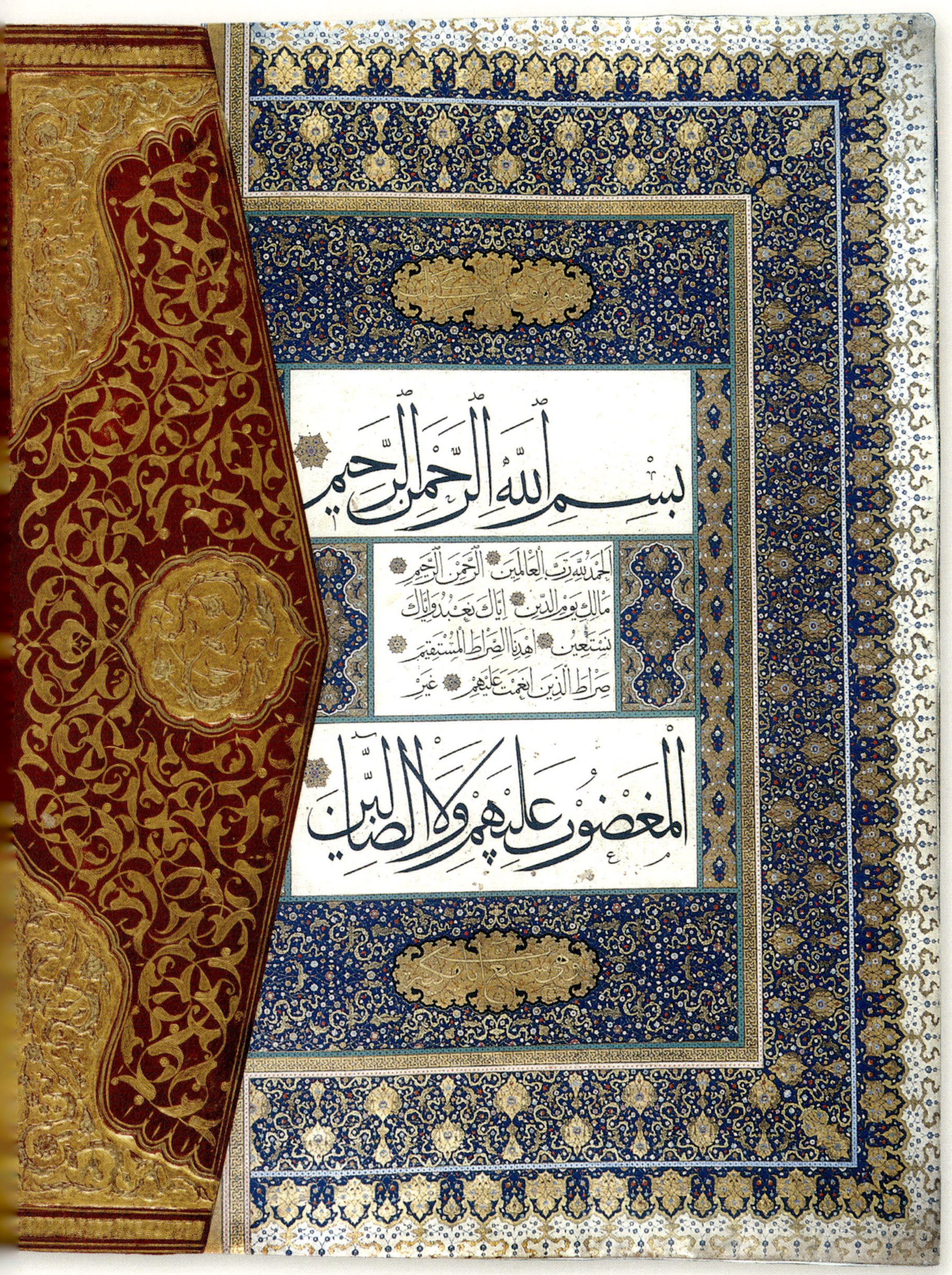

The Qur'an manuscripts usually open with illuminated pages called *sarlawha*. This is the right side of the double-page *sarlawha* design by the 16th century renowned Ottoman calligrapher Ahmad Karahisari. Topkapi Palace Museum

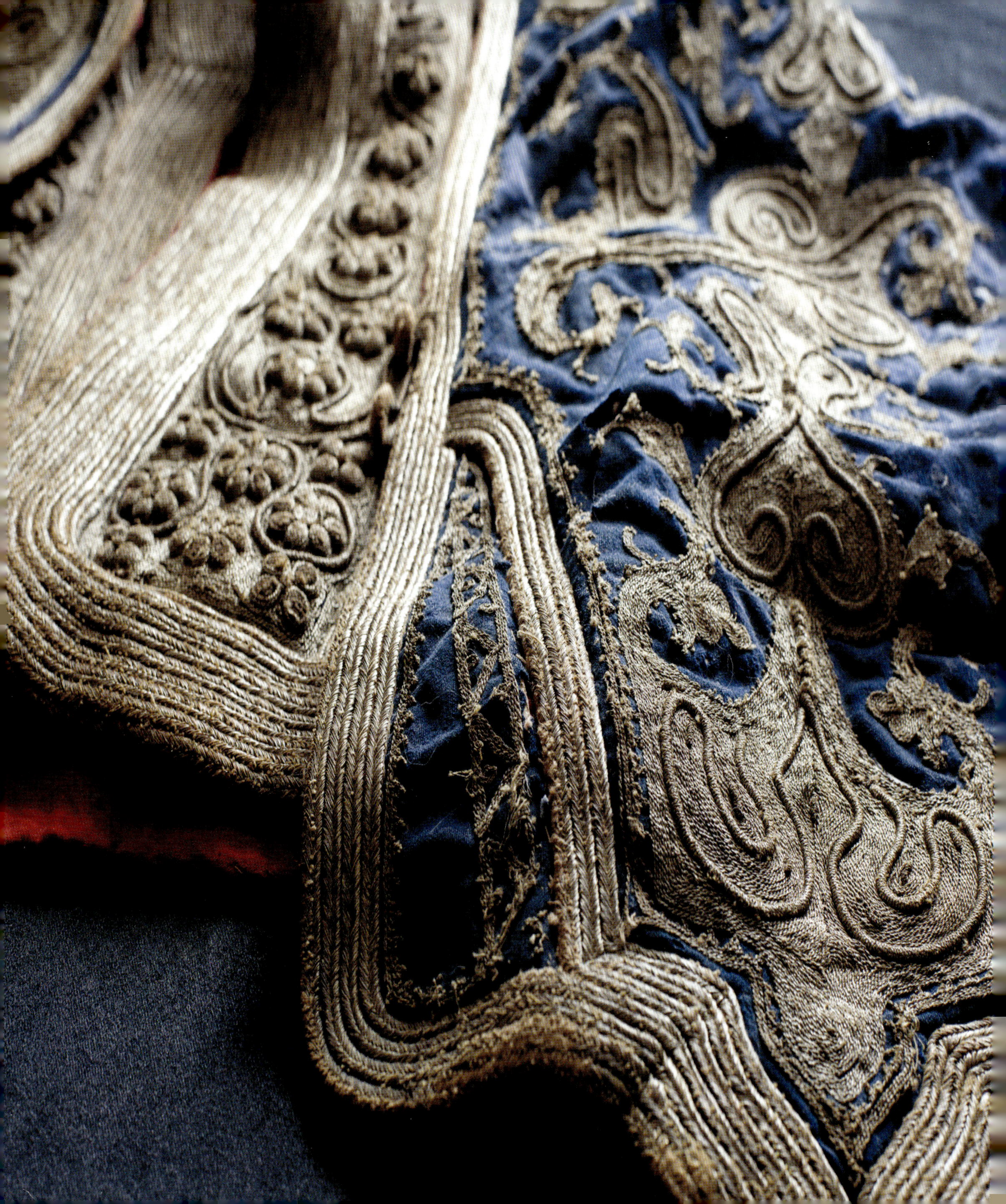

Textile

Throughout Islamic history, Qur'an manuscripts played a crucial role in the development of the traditional art of illumination—and also the art of calligraphy. Though calligraphy (*khatt*) was applied mostly in religious texts, specifically Qur'an manuscripts, and thus can be included under the category of traditional book arts, the mediums upon which illumination art were applied are not limited to handwritten books, but include a variety of objects, from small decorative pieces to architectural surfaces.

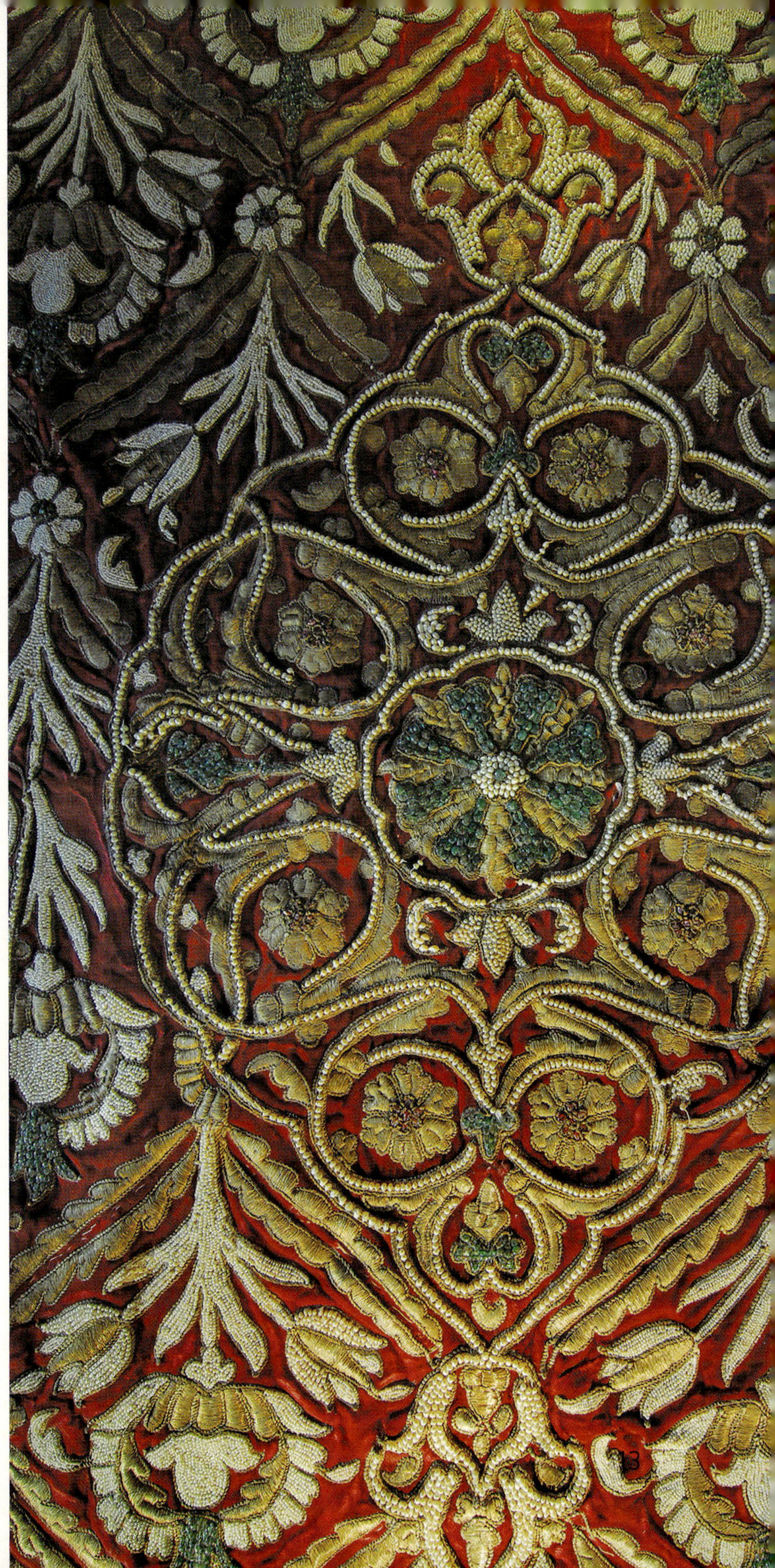

Detail from a traditional long-sleeved Ottoman jacket ending at the waistline. It has stylized foliate and floral motifs embroidered with silver thread.

Textile detail from the Audience Hall, Topkapi Palace Museum.
Ottoman sultans would accept high-ranking statesmen, foreign envoys, and scholars in the Audience Hall. The cushions of this hall are lavishly decorated with precious stones and gold upon classical Ottoman floral illumination patterns.

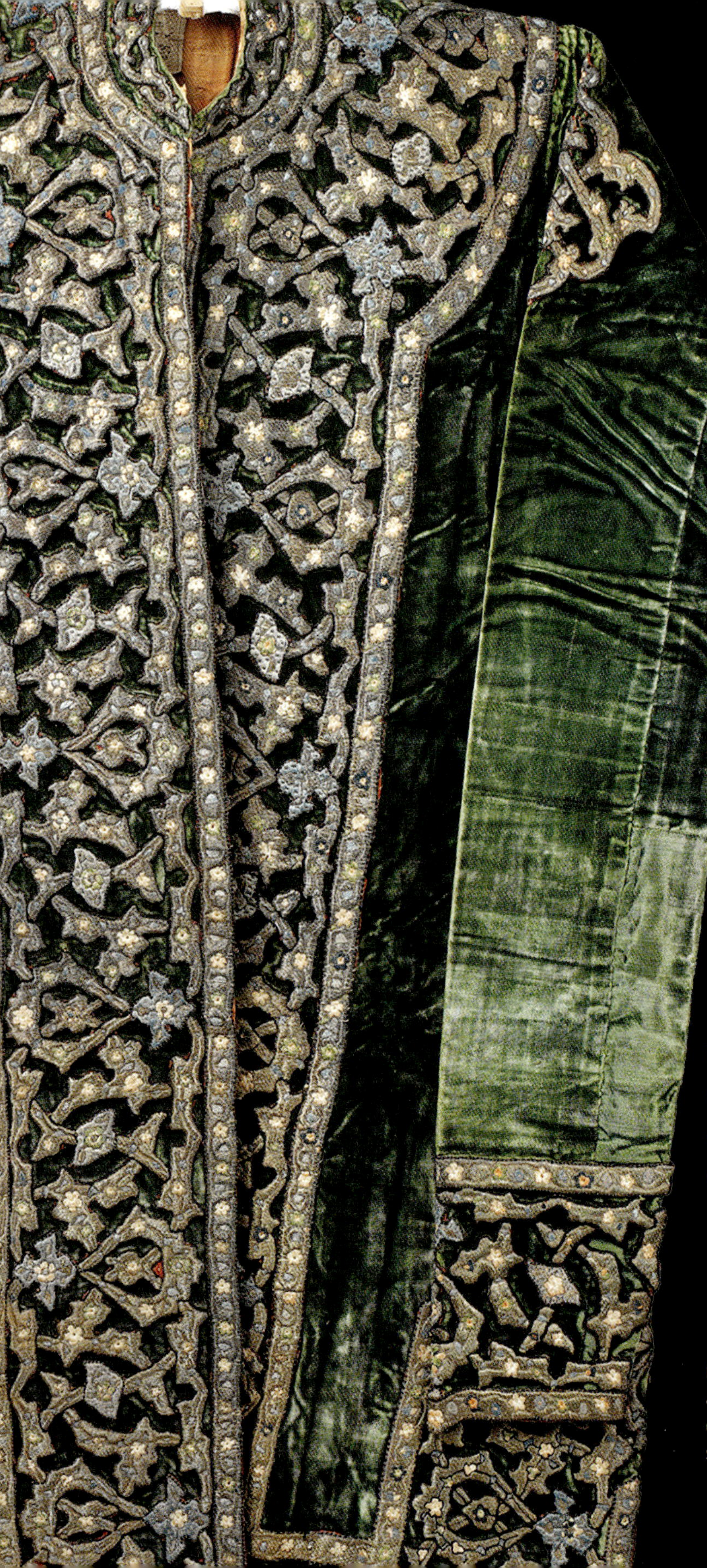

Royal Caftans

During the Ottoman period, illumination was applied to many articles including pictures, royal edicts and insignia, tiles, chests, ever-basin sets, candle hangers, and even costumes prepared for the Sultan and his family. Over time, the use of illumination spread to include tent poles, gun holsters and cases, parade helmets, shields, quivers, and bows and arrows. These illuminated works differ from Ottoman miniatures (*taswirs*) or manuscripts illustrated with figural decoration. They are illuminated mainly with floral and geometric designs due to the prohibition on pictorial representations of human and animal figures, especially in religious manuscripts.

Today, along with the Qur'an manuscripts, illumination has extensively been applied on decorative papers, book covers, carpets, textiles, ceramic tiles and plates, glass and wood panels, metal works and architectural surfaces.

Long-sleeved royal caftan with a colorful illumination design embroidered on the collar, rims and sleeves. Topkapi Palace

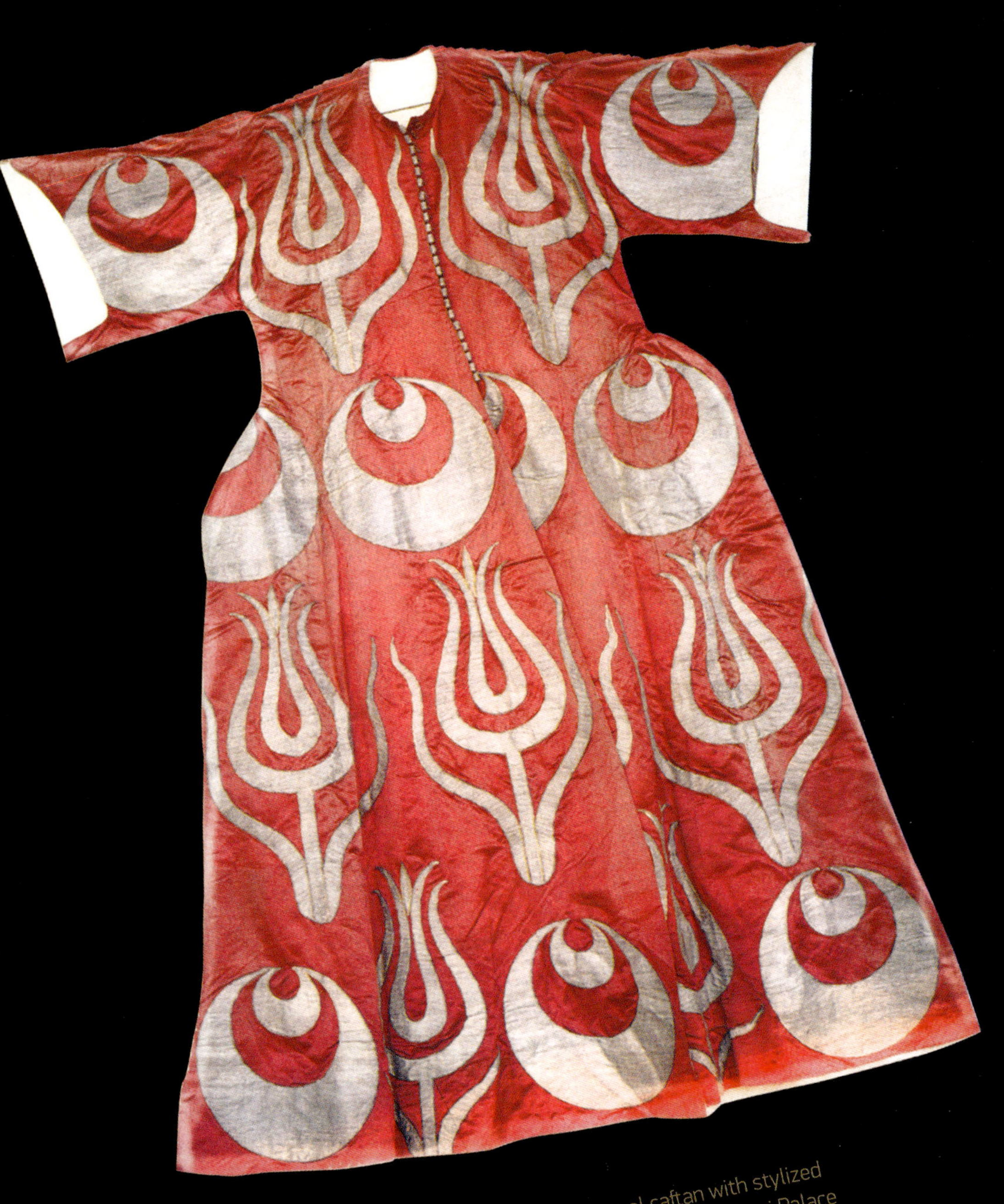

Short-sleeved royal caftan with stylized tulip and crescent motifs. Topkapi Palace

Chintamani Pattern

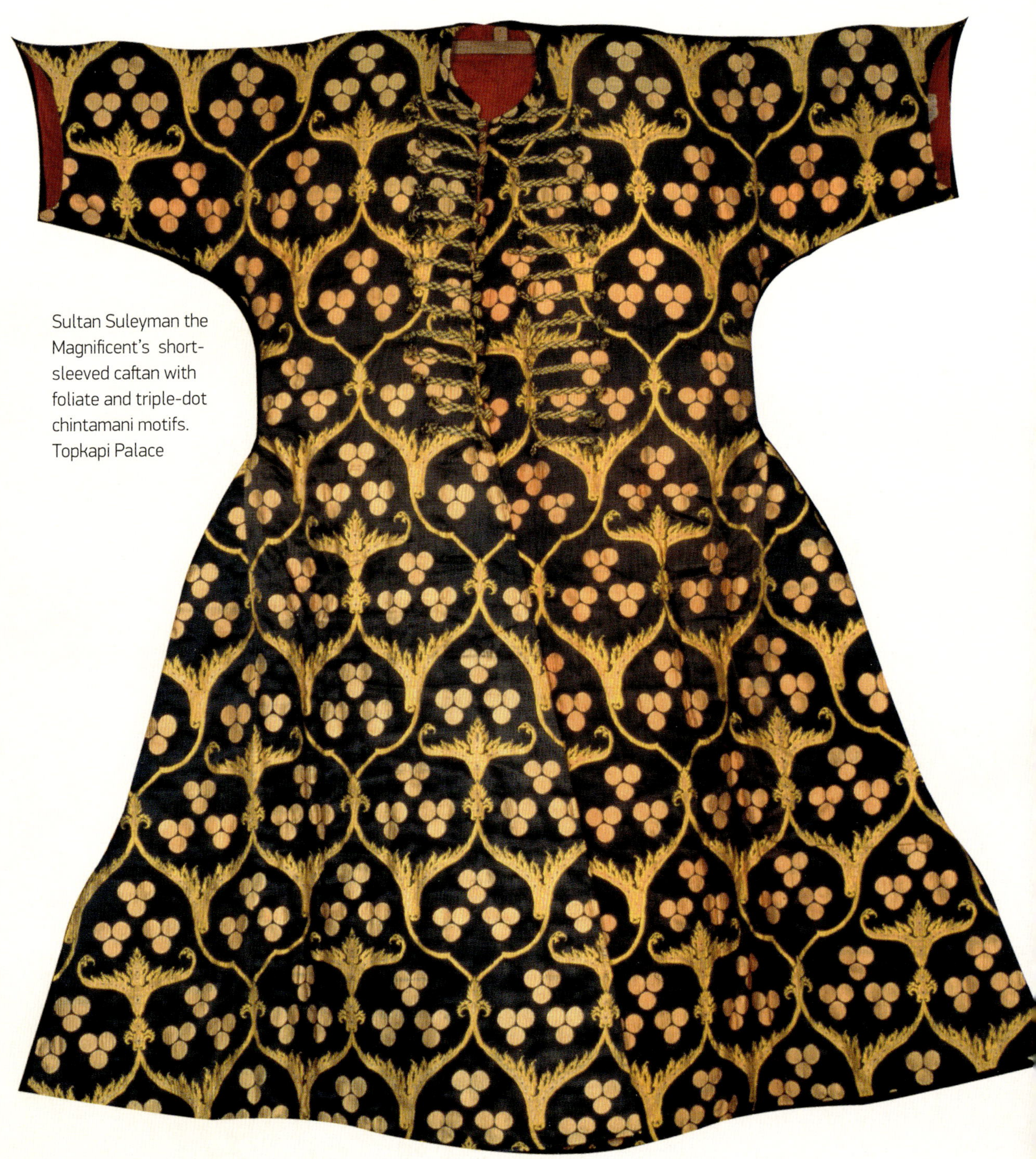

Sultan Suleyman the Magnificent's short-sleeved caftan with foliate and triple-dot chintamani motifs. Topkapi Palace

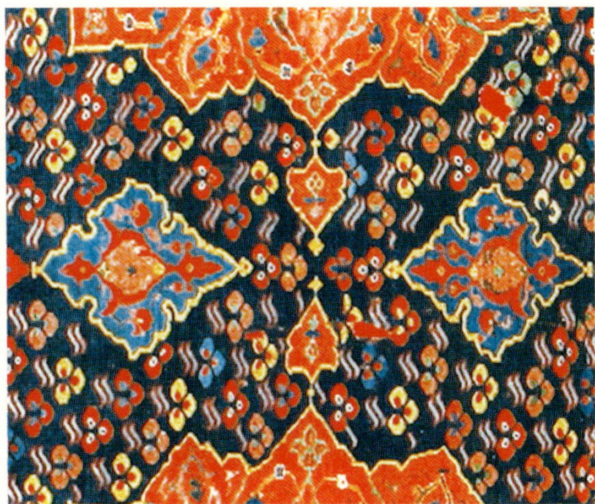

Detail from a 16th century Ottoman carpet with shamsa and chintamani motifs. The Museum of Turkish and Islamic Arts

It is possible to see similar refined Chintamani motifs used in both carpets and textiles. Chintamani is the Chinese-inspired triple-dot motif with auspicious royal associations, often combined with wavy lines to form tiger-skin patterns as seen above.

The handwoven runner carpet on the right has three borders. The first border is a red straight line. The third border has a red base and a blue line with a serrated edge. The main border with a yellow base has geometricized floral motifs along with a blue zigzagging line.

Chintamani patterns with three dots fill the main brown base. The blue contour with hooks around the tiger stripes makes the motif look like a crab.

Runner carpet with chintamani pattern, 18th century.
The Museum of Turkish and Islamic Arts

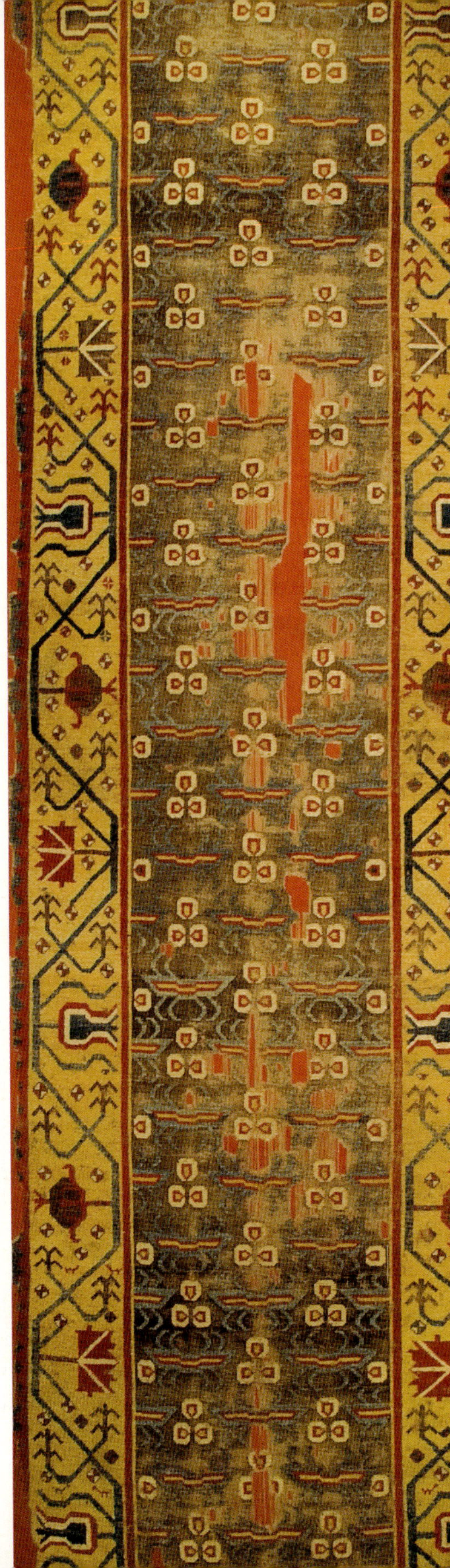

Metalwork

The copper candle hanger on the right was originally the property of the Bayezid Mosque in Istanbul. It is decorated with pierced motifs and it has a grooved brim. The dome shaped upper part is divided into twelve segments with pierced motifs and there are two knots on top. The inscriptions at the bottom are the name of Sultan Bayezid II, as well as praises and prayers for him. The front surface opens with a two-wing door and there are seven candle sockets inside. There are oval shaped decorations and plant motifs on side surfaces.

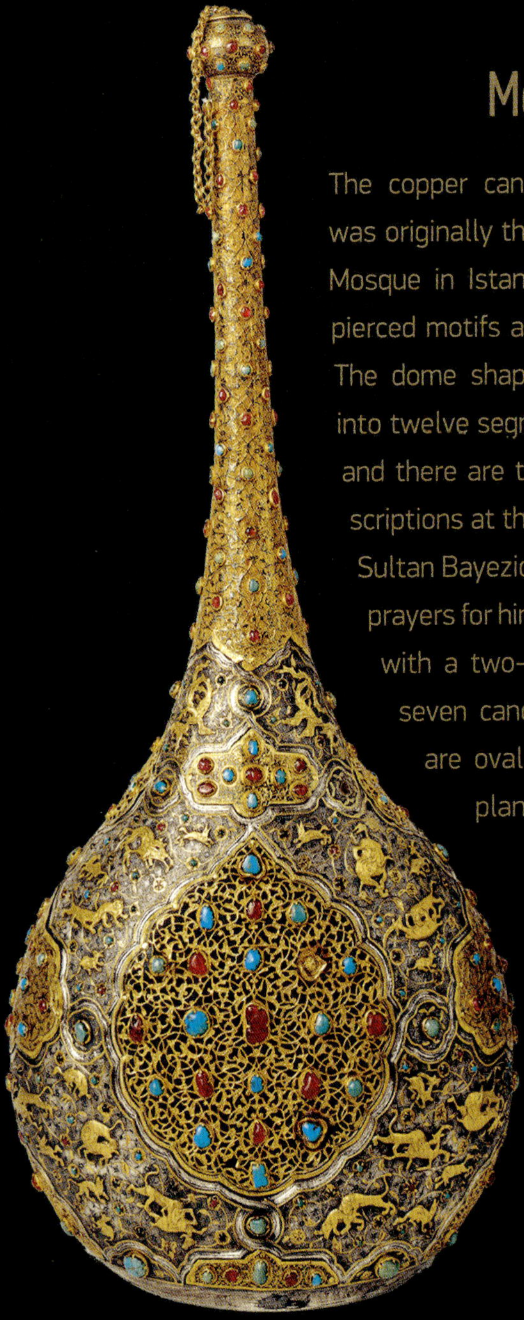

Rosewater flask, richly illuminated and encrusted with precious stones. Topkapi Palace Museum

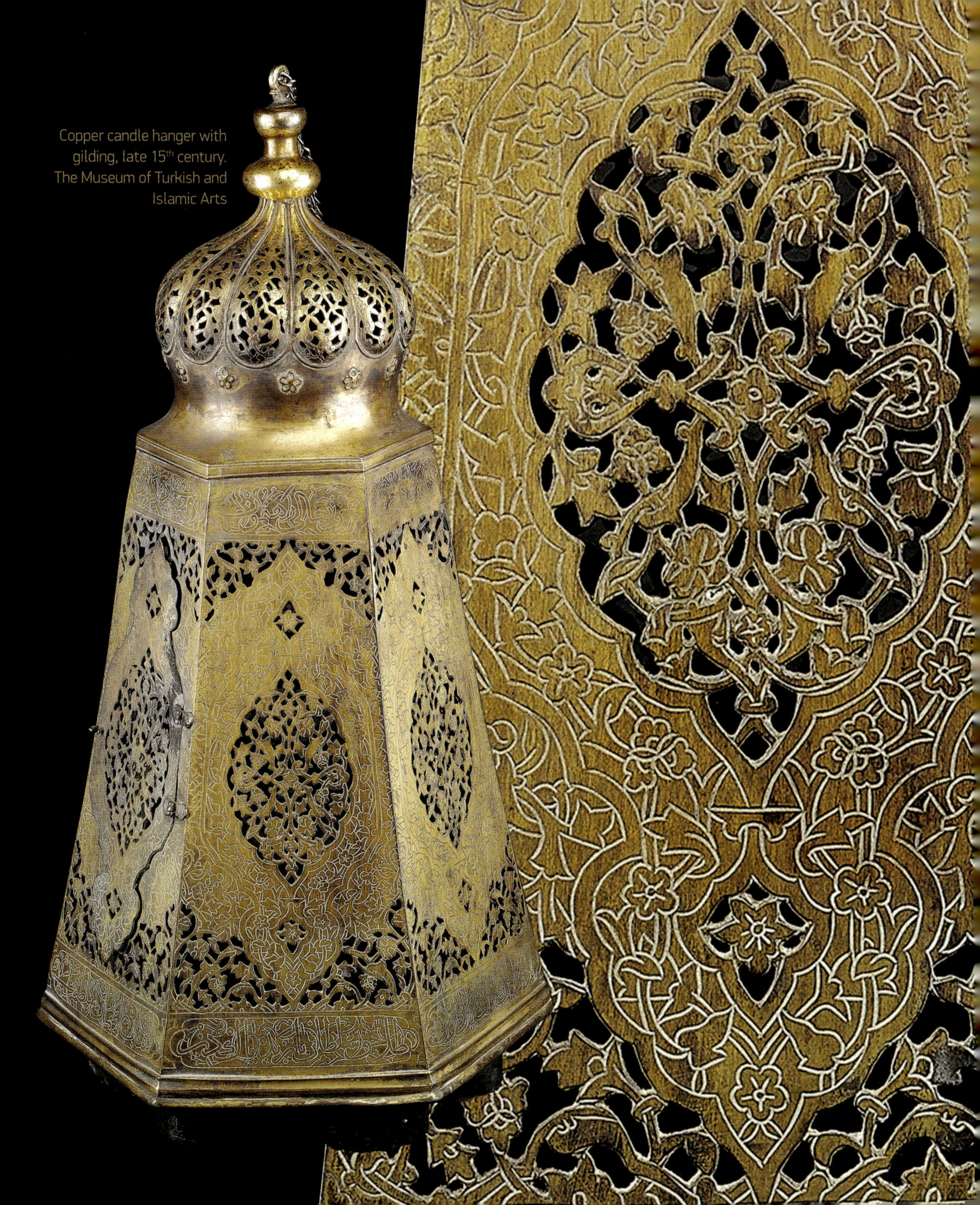

Copper candle hanger with gilding, late 15th century. The Museum of Turkish and Islamic Arts

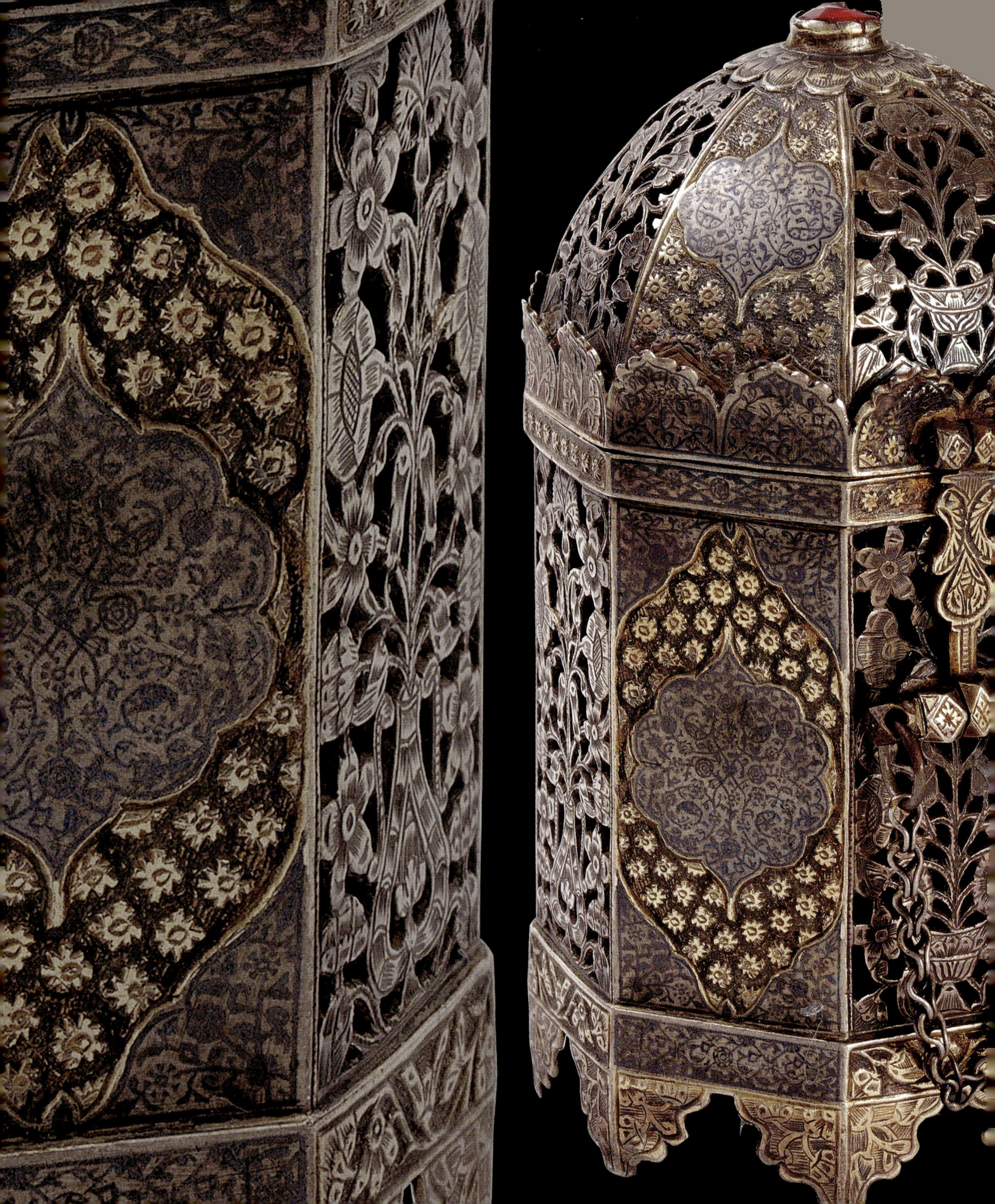

Silverware

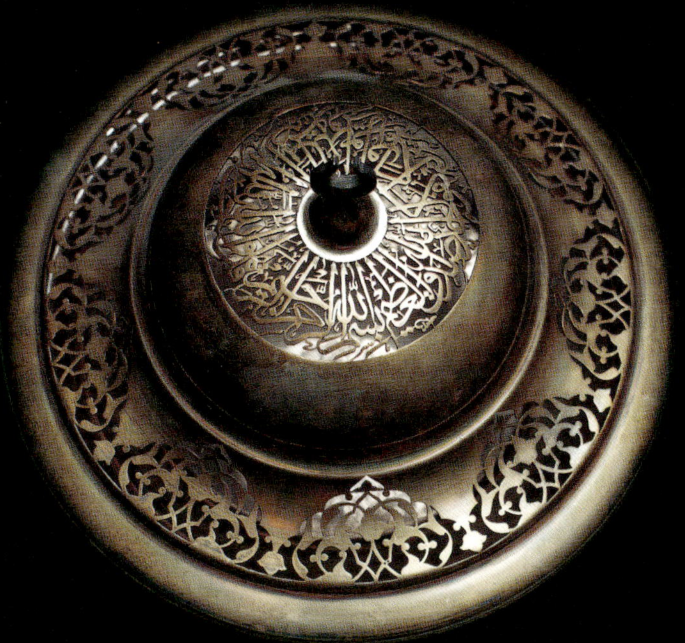

Silver plate with a repeating illumination pattern translated into the cut-out design.
This openwork decoration on the lid has an elegant combination of Arabic calligraphy on its dome shaped upper part and repeating Rumi motif along its rim.

The art of engraving patterns with a sharp steel-tipped graver on articles made of soft metals such as gold, silver, brass, or copper, was known as "penwork." Silver objects were far more frequently engraved than those made of other metals. Gold was too expensive to be used in large quantities or for large items, while cheaper metals such as brass and copper were more liable to oxidization and decay. Thus, penwork was almost exclusively the preserve of silver objects. The finest examples of classical Ottoman illumination motifs were drawn on the silver ewers, bathing bowls, sugar bowls, plates, and trays.

Richly decorated silver case containing the Noble Prophet's strands of hair. Pavilion of the Sacred Relics, Topkapi Palace.
This ornate silver case with openwork, deep incisions, surface shading, and engraved black patterns (niello) demonstrates the Ottomans' elegant taste in illumination and decorative arts.

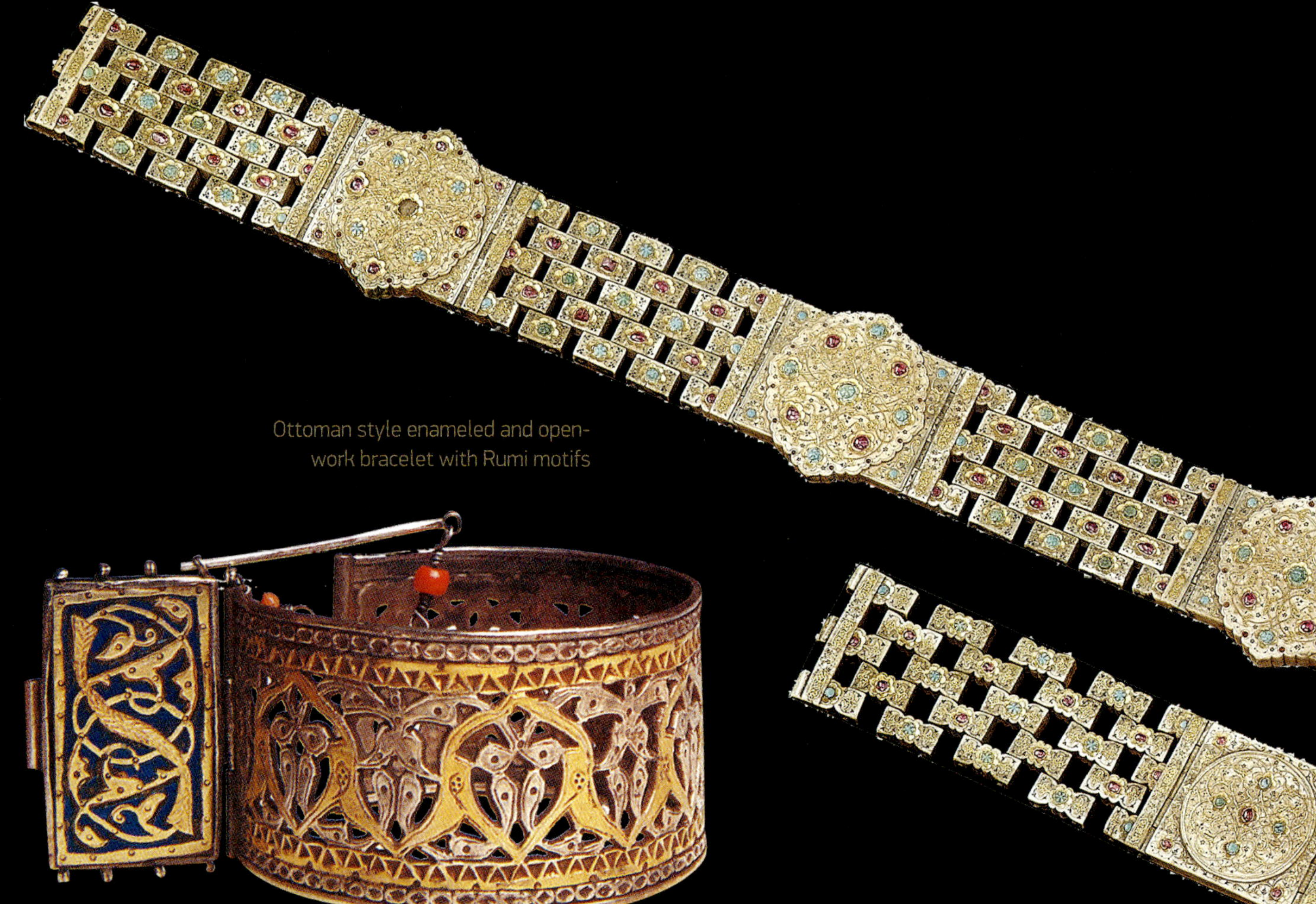

Ottoman style enameled and open-work bracelet with Rumi motifs

Jewelry

The ivory belt that is composed of five square plates has oval studs on them. These oval studs slightly protruding from the sides of the plates are decorated with turquoises, rubies, and gold stands. The square plates are connected with small rectangular pieces. The same gems on these rectangular pieces maintain a harmonious composition. The other ivory belt composed of four plates with round studs has the same properties. Both the oval and round studs are richly illuminated.

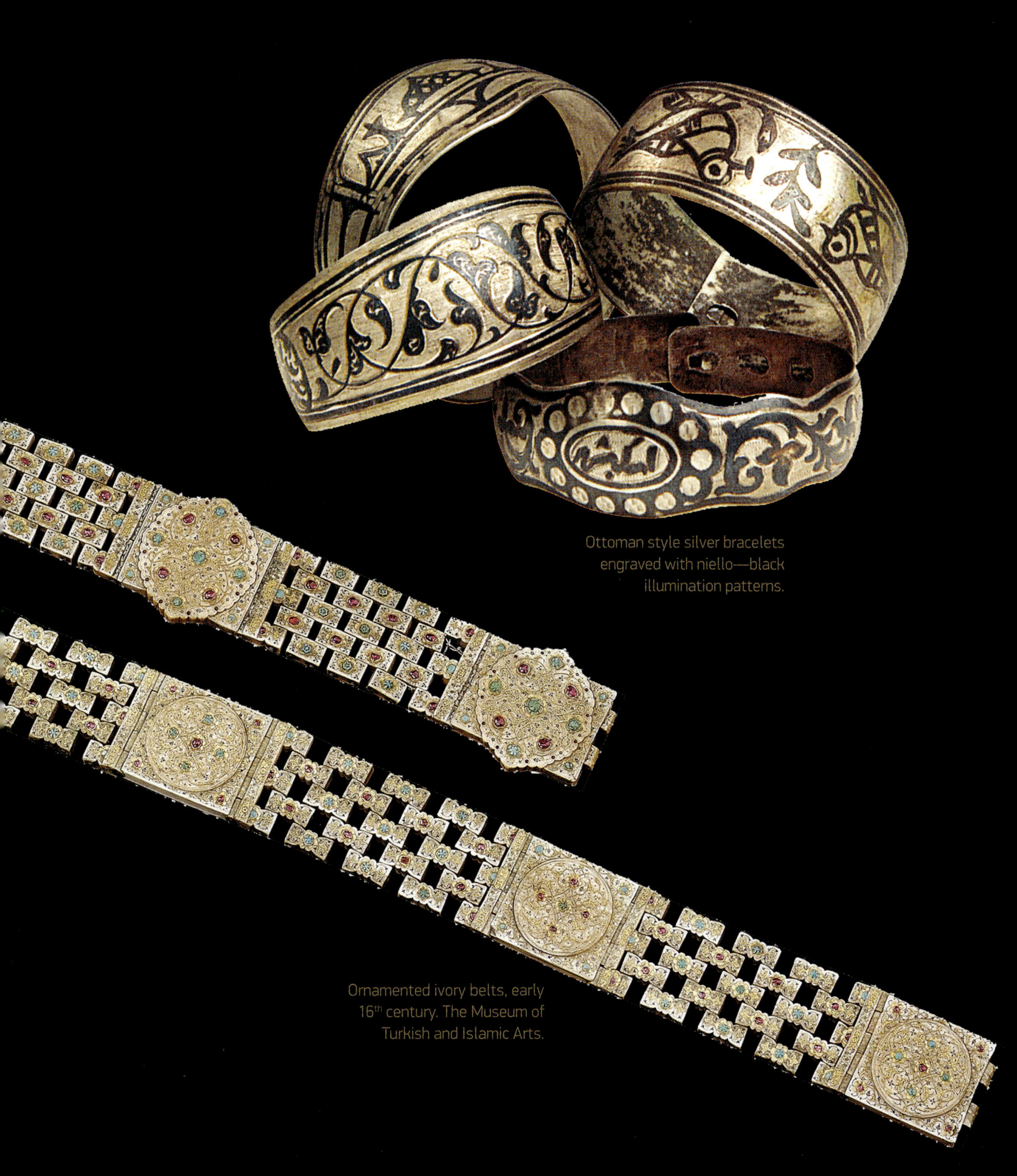

Ottoman style silver bracelets engraved with niello—black illumination patterns.

Ornamented ivory belts, early 16th century. The Museum of Turkish and Islamic Arts.

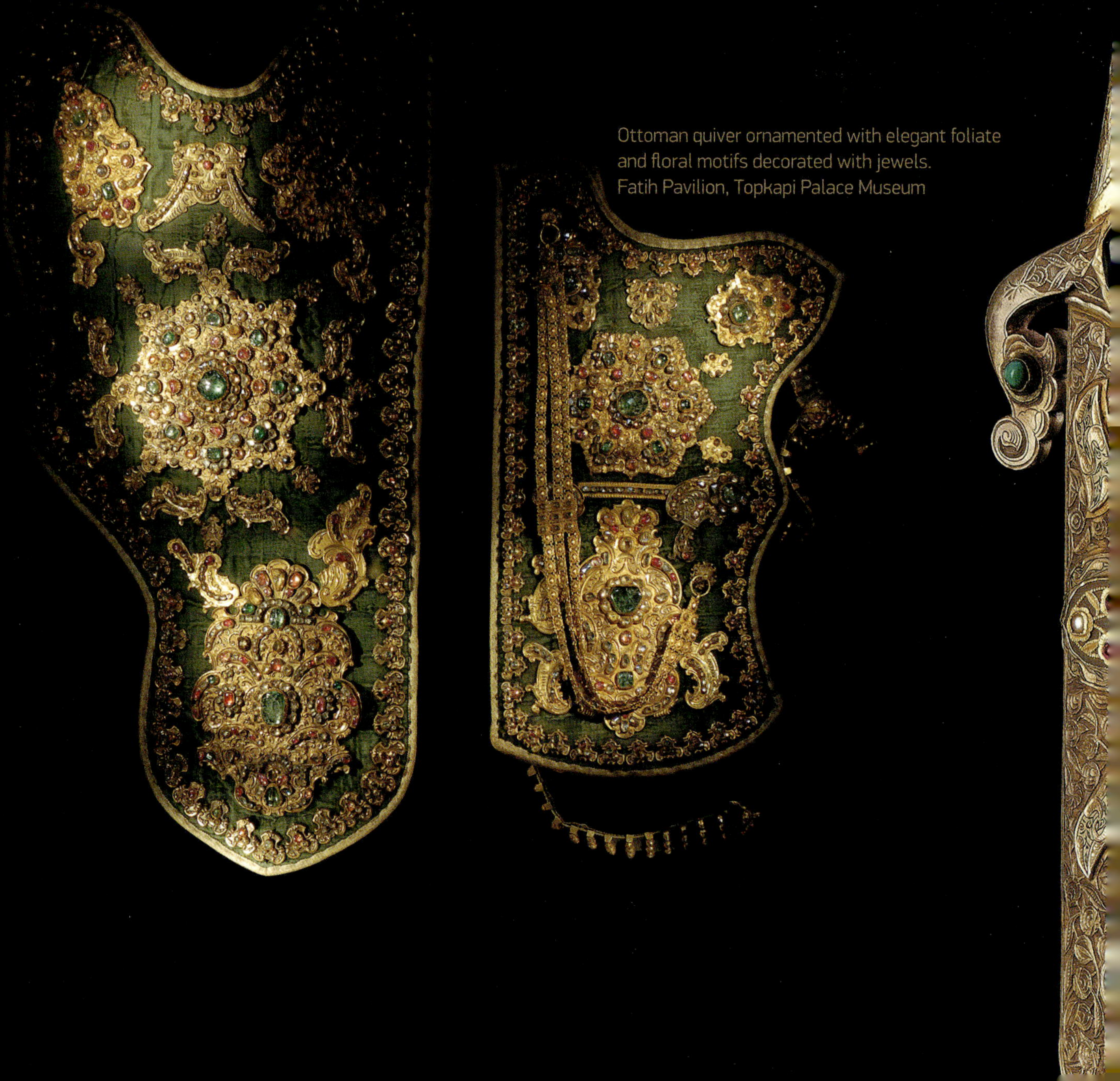

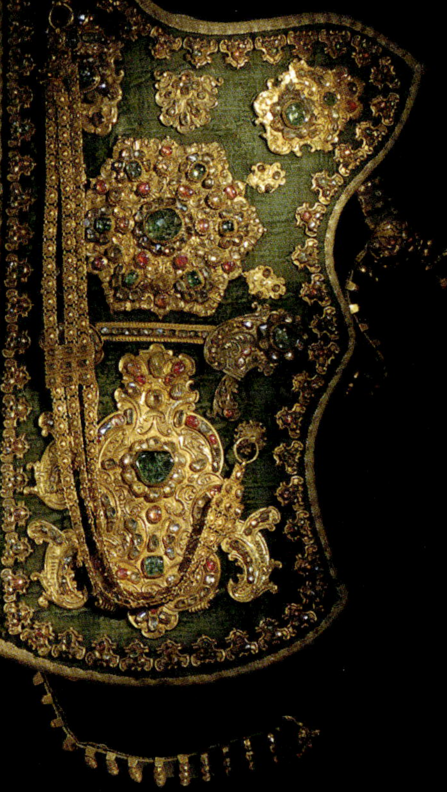

Ottoman quiver ornamented with elegant foliate and floral motifs decorated with jewels.
Fatih Pavilion, Topkapi Palace Museum

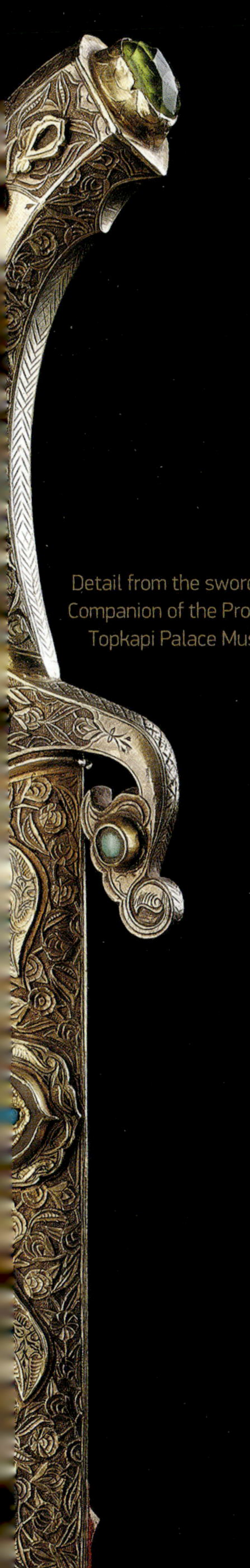

Detail from the sword of a Companion of the Prophet. Topkapi Palace Museum

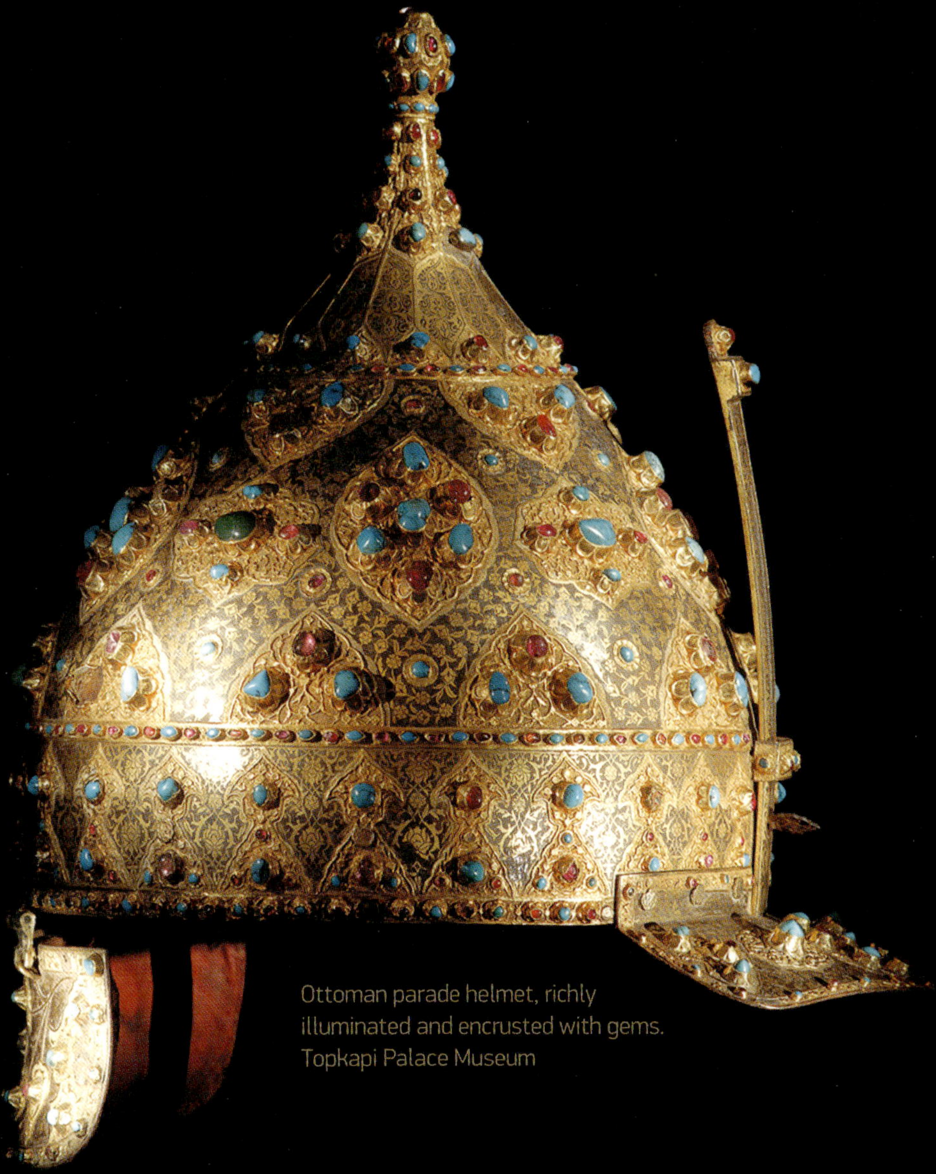

Weaponry

The hilt of the Companion's sword is gilded silver cast in a hexagonal form. Both sides of the hilt have applied plates, gilding, and foliate and floral designs. The cross guard is also ornamented with foliate and floral motifs and is encrusted with a large gem. The curved arms of the cross guard have spiral foliate forms, and they are encrusted with turquoise. The curved pommel is inlaid with a topaz. The scabbard is richly decorated with foliate and floral motifs.

Ottoman parade helmet, richly illuminated and encrusted with gems. Topkapi Palace Museum

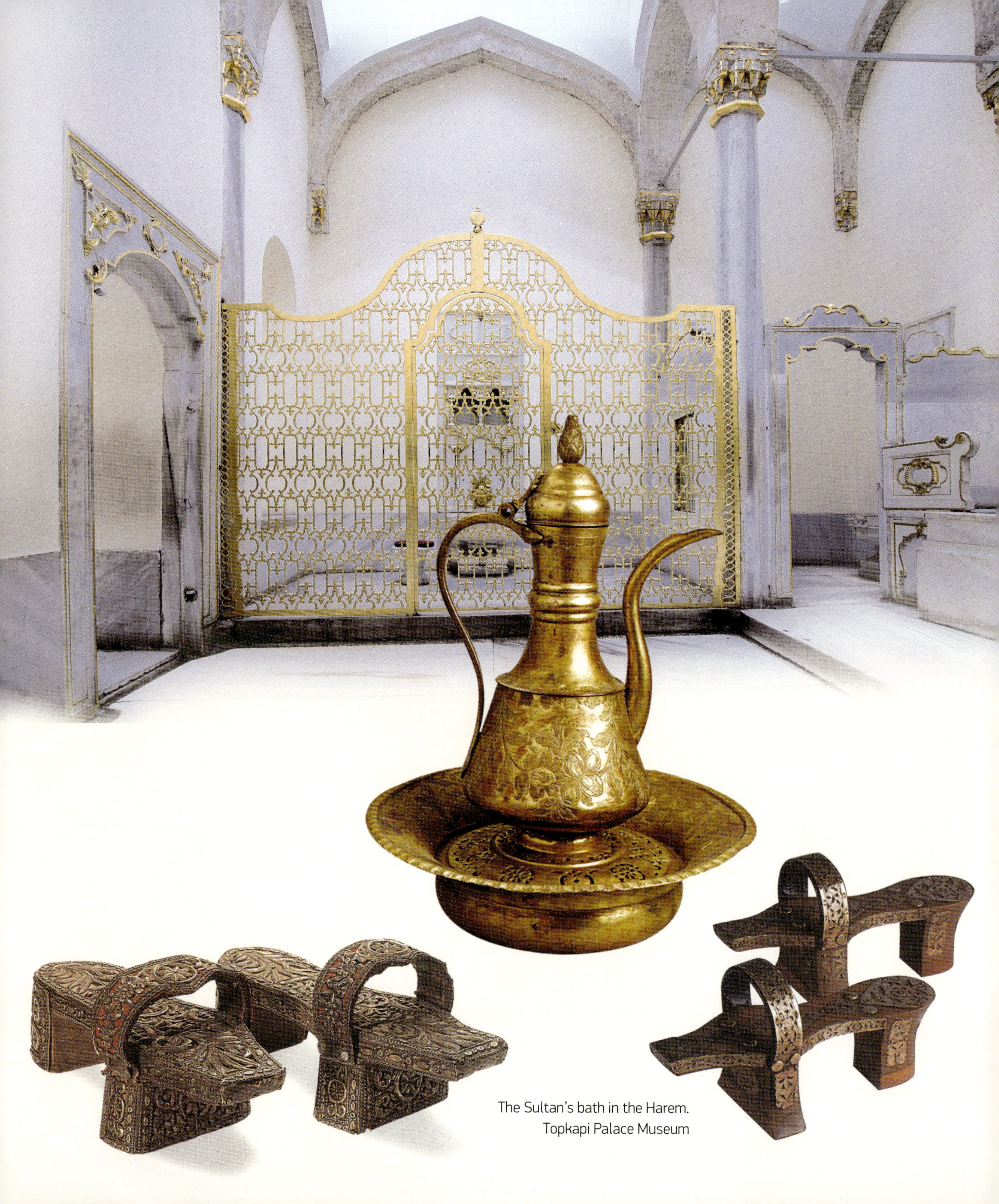

The Sultan's bath in the Harem.
Topkapi Palace Museum

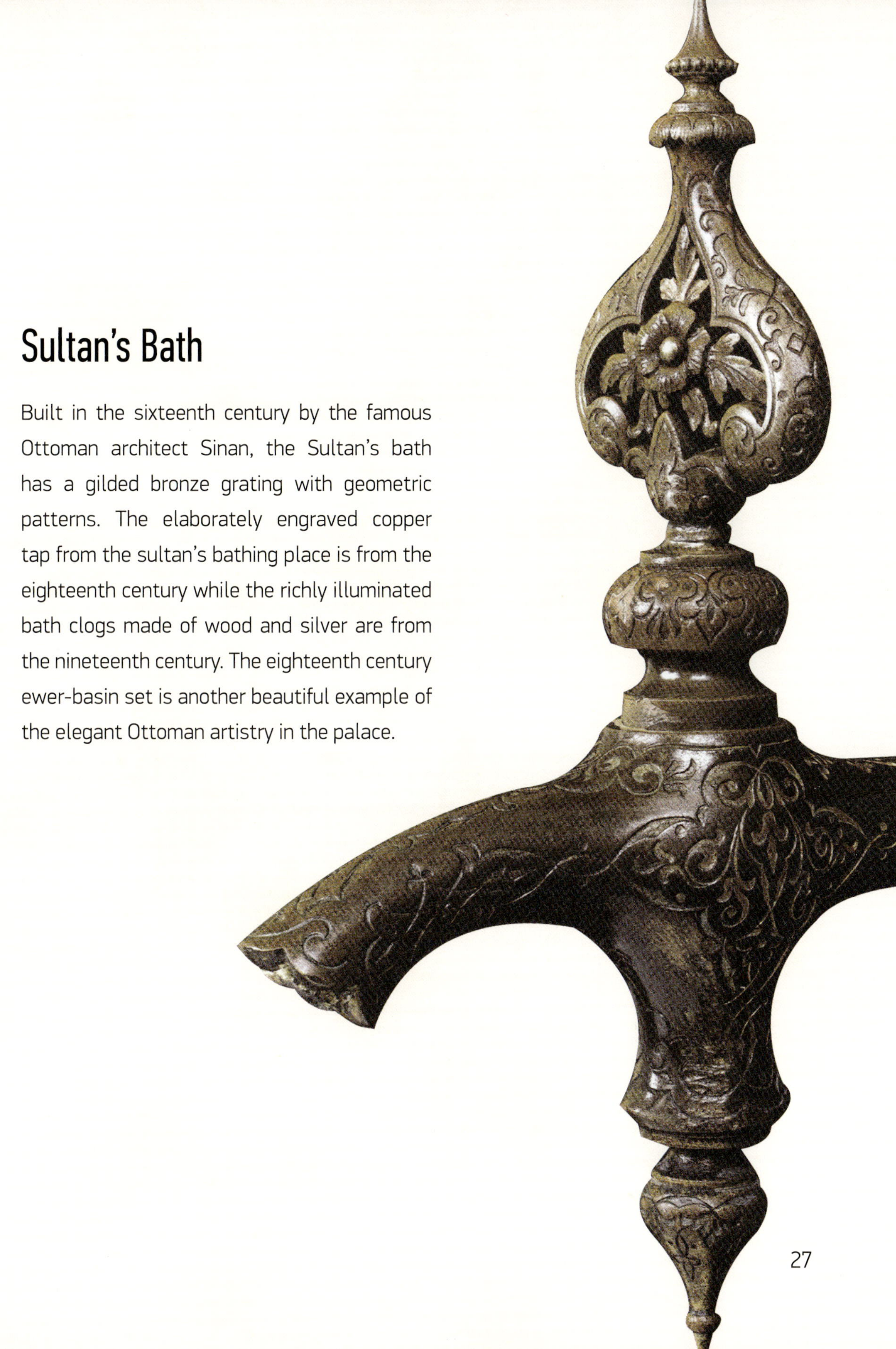

Sultan's Bath

Built in the sixteenth century by the famous Ottoman architect Sinan, the Sultan's bath has a gilded bronze grating with geometric patterns. The elaborately engraved copper tap from the sultan's bathing place is from the eighteenth century while the richly illuminated bath clogs made of wood and silver are from the nineteenth century. The eighteenth century ewer-basin set is another beautiful example of the elegant Ottoman artistry in the palace.

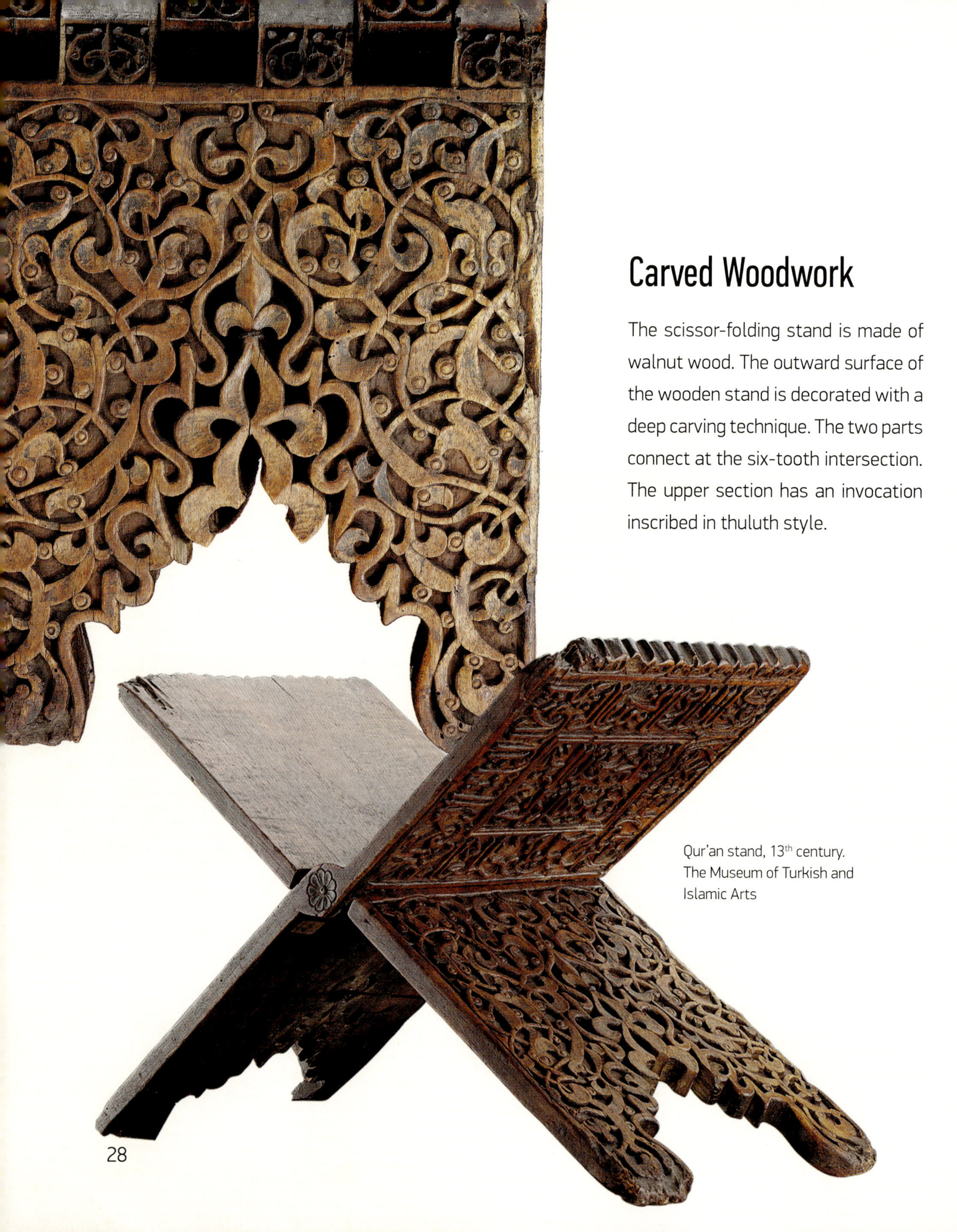

Carved Woodwork

The scissor-folding stand is made of walnut wood. The outward surface of the wooden stand is decorated with a deep carving technique. The two parts connect at the six-tooth intersection. The upper section has an invocation inscribed in thuluth style.

Qur'an stand, 13th century.
The Museum of Turkish and Islamic Arts

The pair of window wings, which is from Sheikh Necmeddin Ishakoglu's tomb in Konya, is made of walnut wood and decorated with a rich carving technique. In the central panels, the wooden wings have three medallions with stylized plant motifs that are constituted of bands of Rumi leaves. The medallion in the middle has a floral badge. The inscription on the upper panels can be translated as "There is no honor greater than piety, and there is no beneficence better than abandoning passion and passing desires." On the lower panels, a thin band forms stylized crests on a base of foliate motifs.

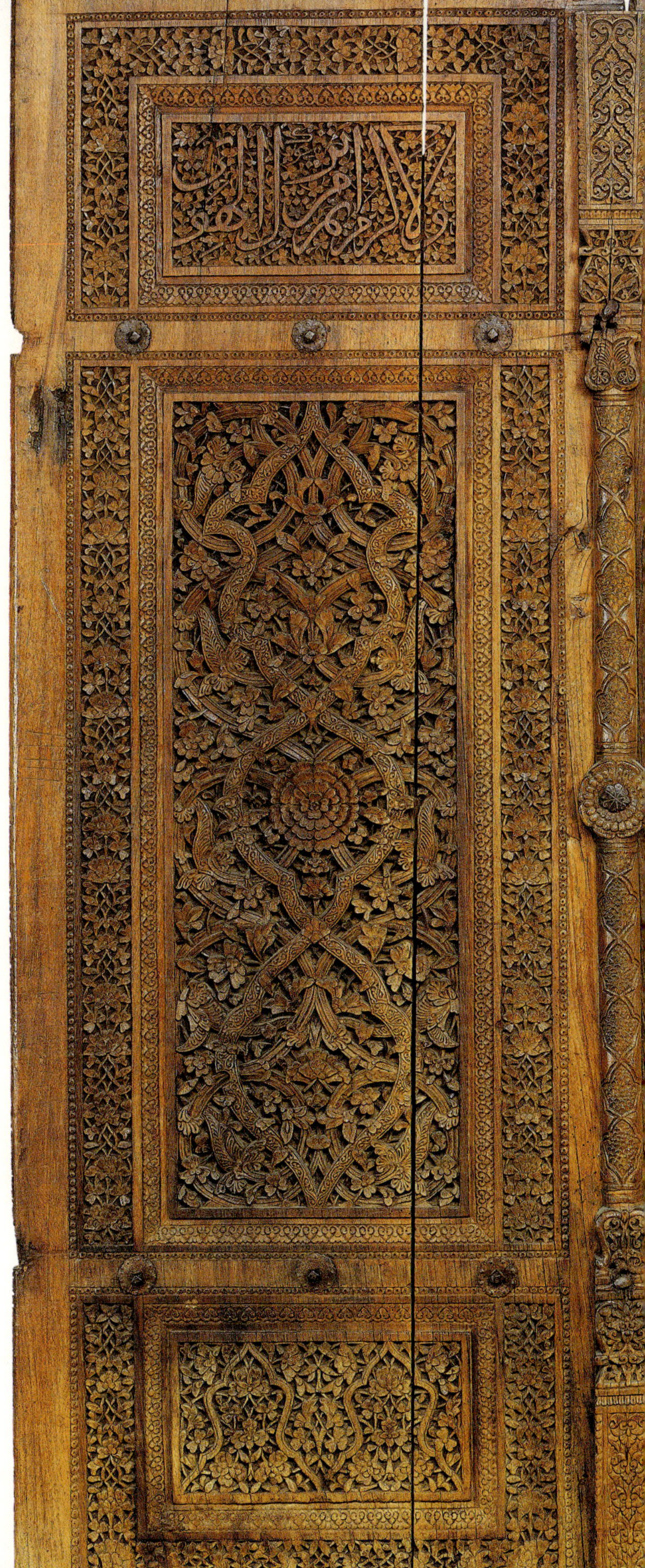

Window wings, early 14th century.
The Museum of Turkish and Islamic Arts

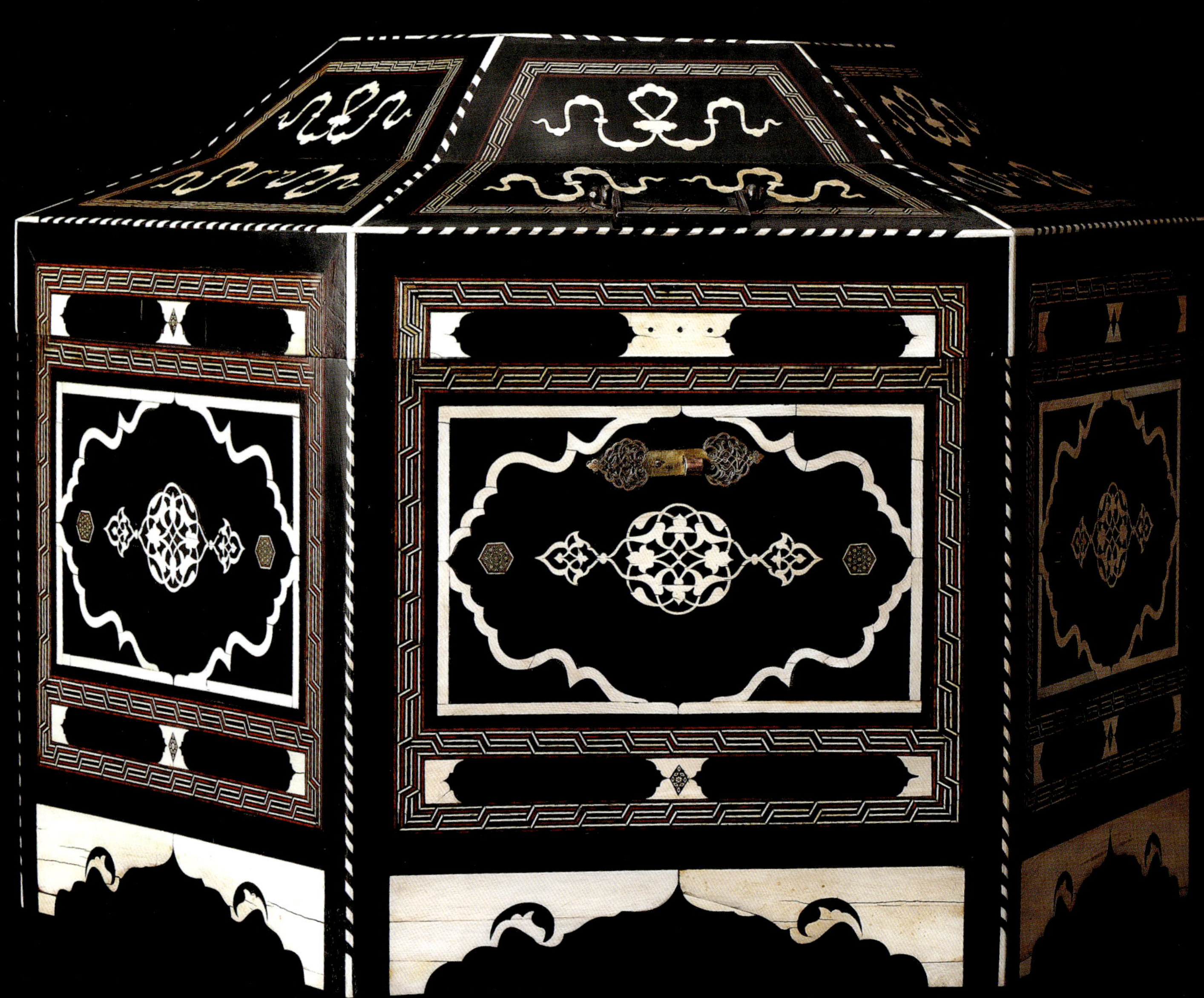

Protective case for the Qur'an. Museum of Turkish and Islamic Arts. The pyramidal cover has six sides and the body is shaped as a hexagonal prism. The body and the cover are decorated with ebony frames and inlaid with ivory. The inlaid wood of the cover is decorated with the ivory cloud motifs while the hexagonal body has elaborate Rumi shamsa motifs within rectangular chain patterns.

Furniture with Elaborate Inlays

Mother-of-pearl and other inlay materials such as ivory and tortoiseshell are specifically used in geometric illumination patterns. After the designed illumination composition is carefully engraved on walnut, oak or ebony wood panel, mother-of-pearl or other materials are finely cut to fit the selected places in the composition. After the completion of the embedding process with hot glue, fine levelling is done and the entire work is then polished.

Mother-of-pearl inlay was applied to objects as diverse as the protective cases for the Qur'an to the inkwell sets of calligraphers, and from desks and chairs to the doors and corners of Sultanate kiosks and pavilions.

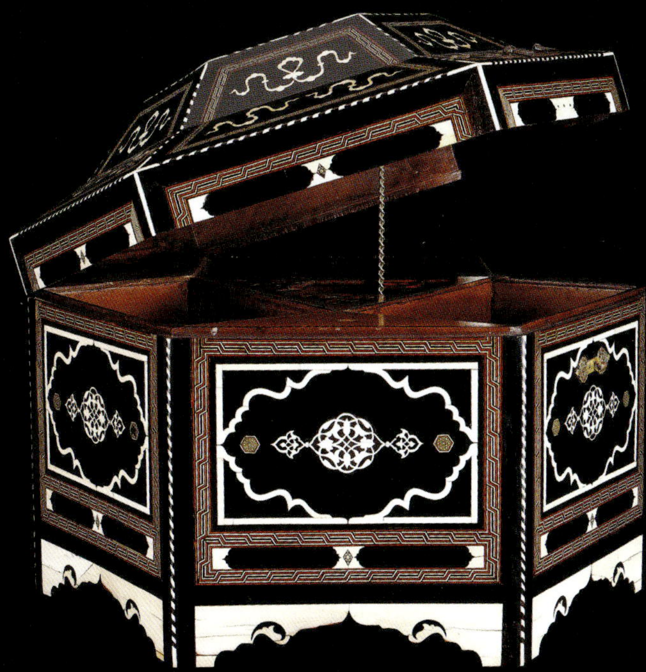

The protective case has three partitions for the parts (juz) of the Qur'an to be kept.

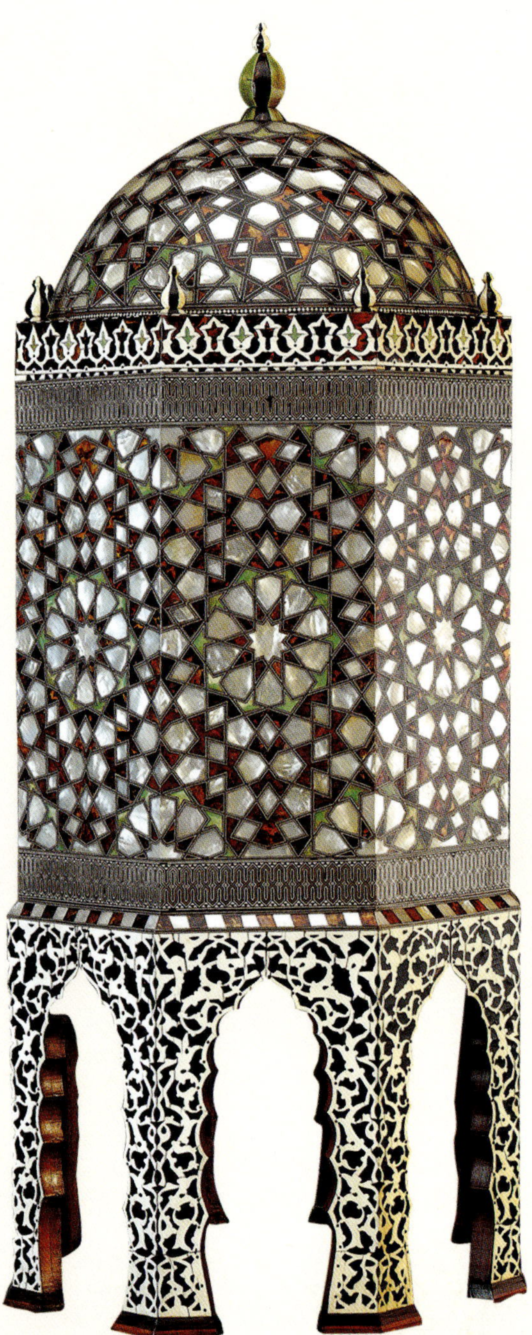

Protective case for the Qur'an, early 17th century.
The Museum of Turkish and Islamic Arts

Mother-of-Pearl Inlay

The body of the protective case is in the form of an octagonal prism supported by eight arched feet. The inlaid wood of the dome-shaped lid and body are richly decorated with ivory, mother of pearl, turtle shell, ebony, and wires. The ten-cornered stars on the body and the top make up a composition based on the principle of infinity together with the other geometric figures. The brim is surrounded with palmette motifs with ivory contouring applied on a turtle-shell base. The feet consist of ornamentations of Rumi leaves and curves applied with coating technique to the ebony.

Mother-of-pearl window wings surrounded by wall recesses with glazed Iznik tiles with floral patterns.
Privy Chamber of Ahmed I, Topkapi Palace
The window wings, cabinet doors, and the drawers of the chamber are beautiful examples of the elaborate Ottoman mother-of-pearl artistry in the palace.

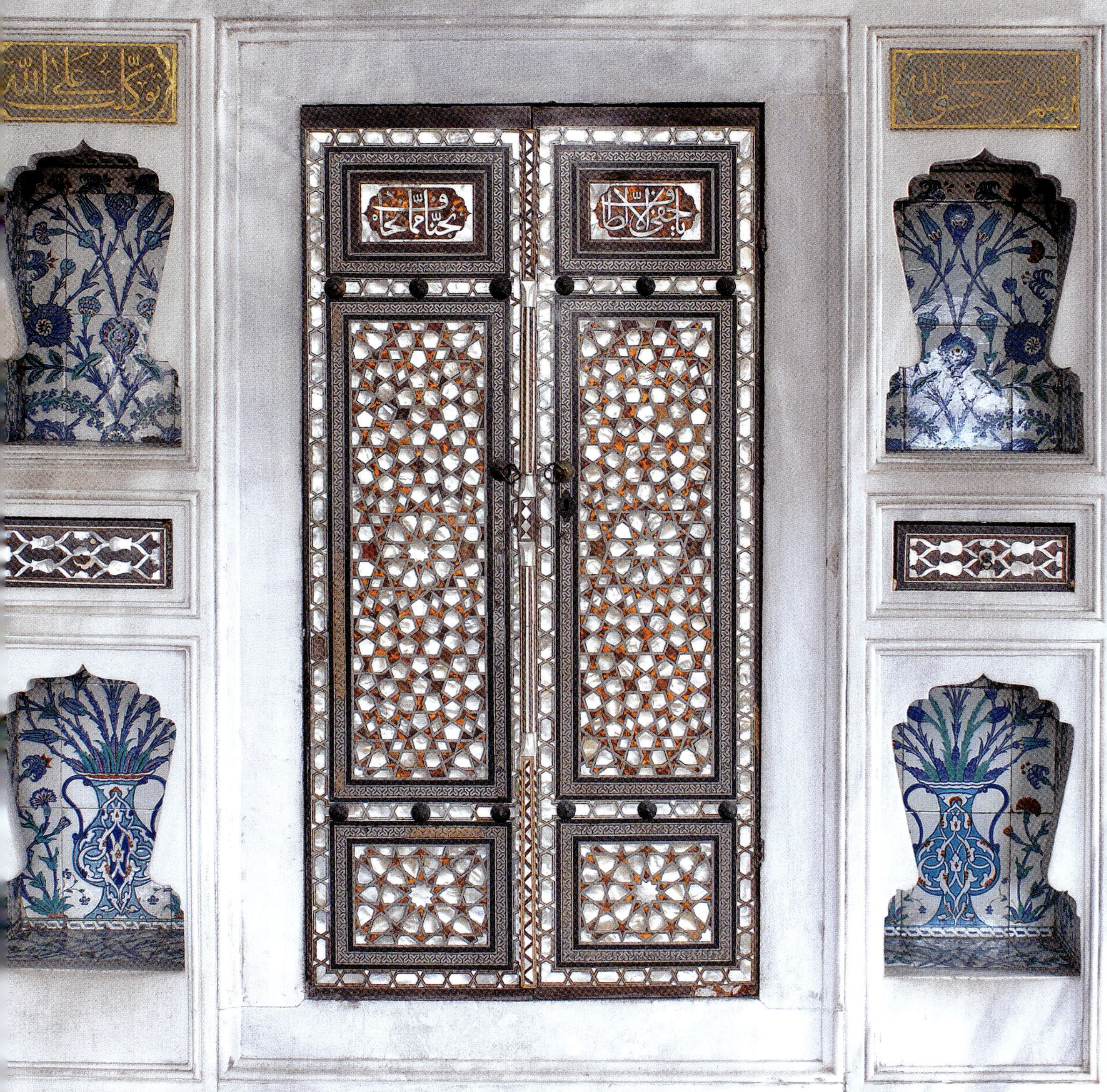

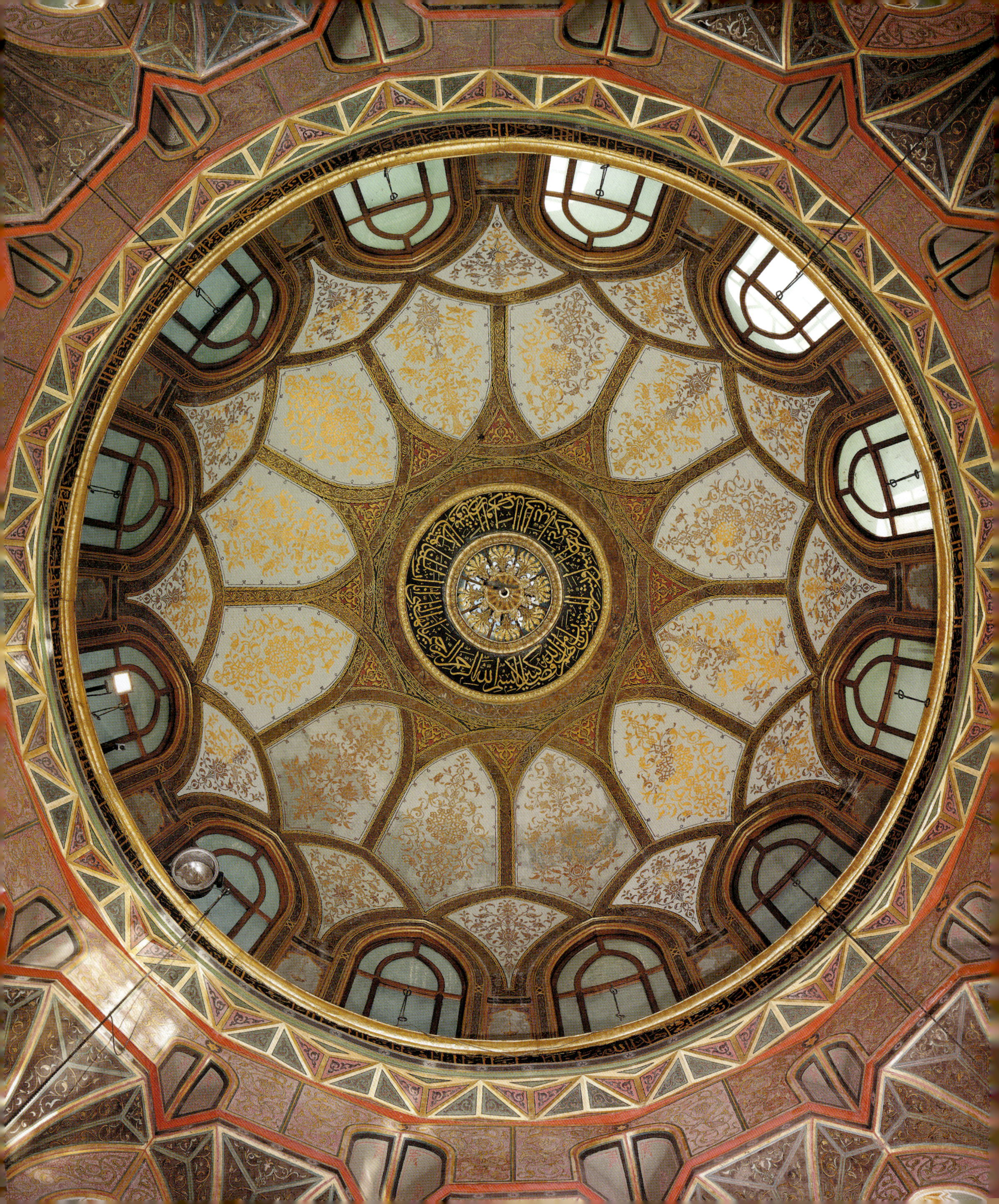

Illumination in Interior Decoration

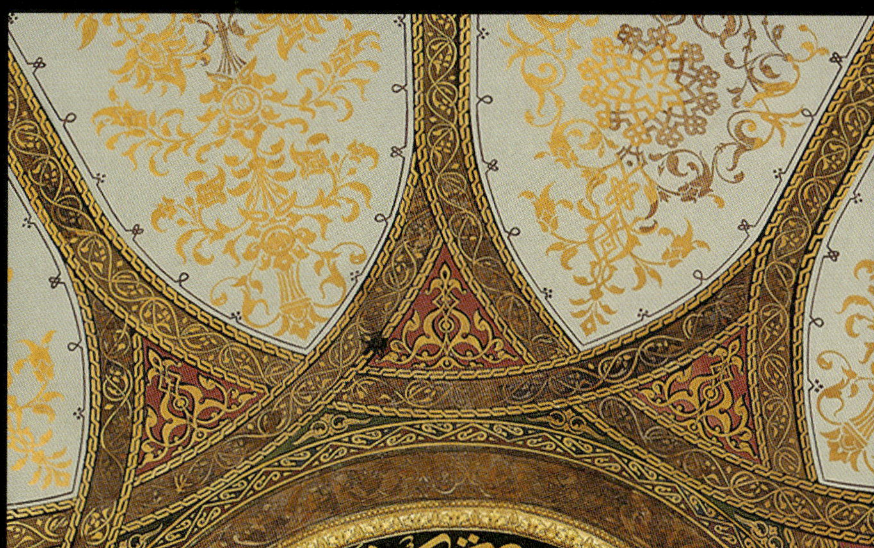

Detail from the ceiling decorations of the Privy Chamber

Ceiling decorations of the Privy Chamber (Throne Room). Topkapi Palace. Qur'anic verses are inscribed in the center of the dome while gilded penwork of foliate and floral motifs are illuminated in the ceiling decorations of the chamber. Rich gilded ceiling decoration is characteristic of the Ottoman style.

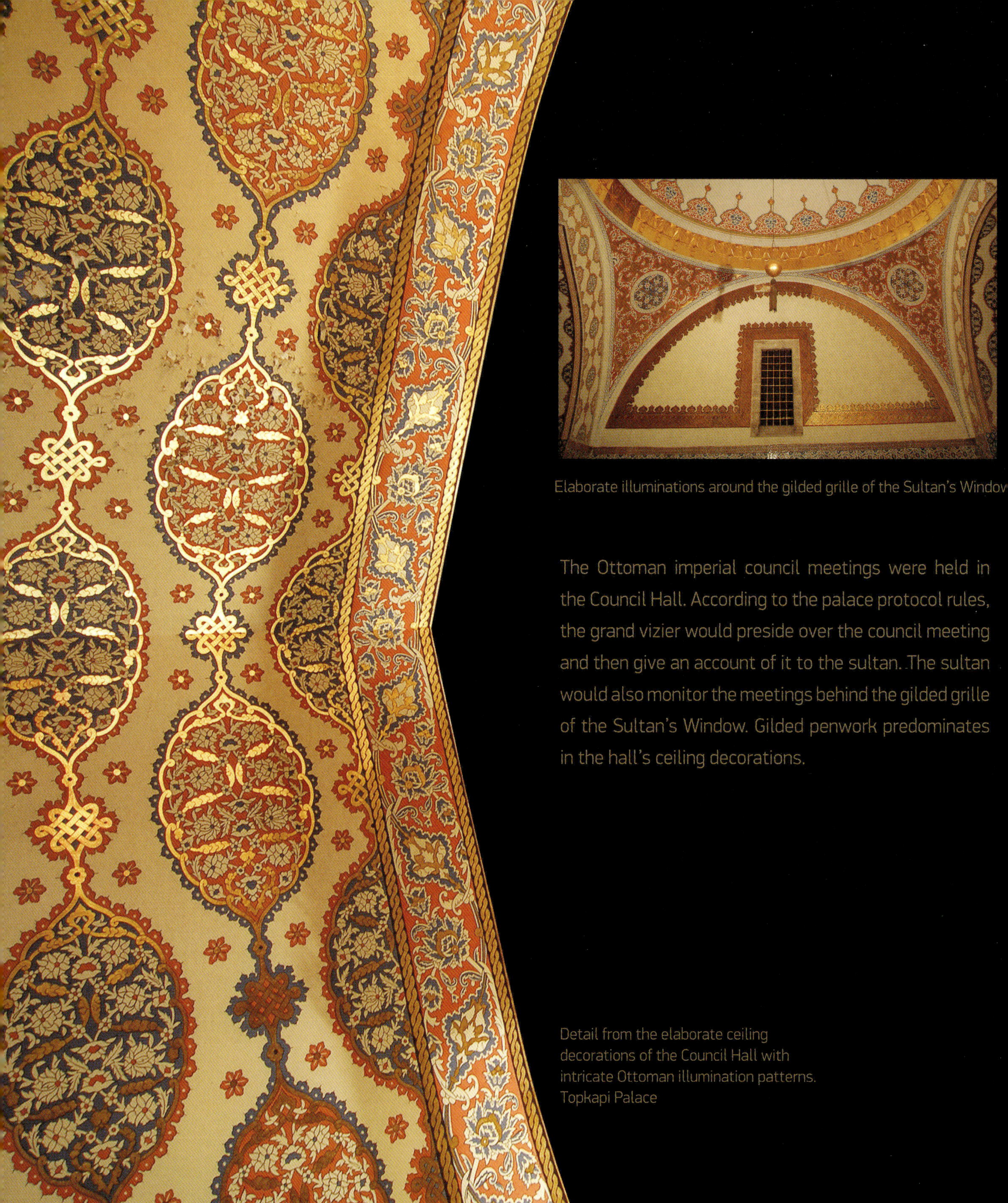

Elaborate illuminations around the gilded grille of the Sultan's Window

The Ottoman imperial council meetings were held in the Council Hall. According to the palace protocol rules, the grand vizier would preside over the council meeting and then give an account of it to the sultan. The sultan would also monitor the meetings behind the gilded grille of the Sultan's Window. Gilded penwork predominates in the hall's ceiling decorations.

Detail from the elaborate ceiling decorations of the Council Hall with intricate Ottoman illumination patterns. Topkapi Palace

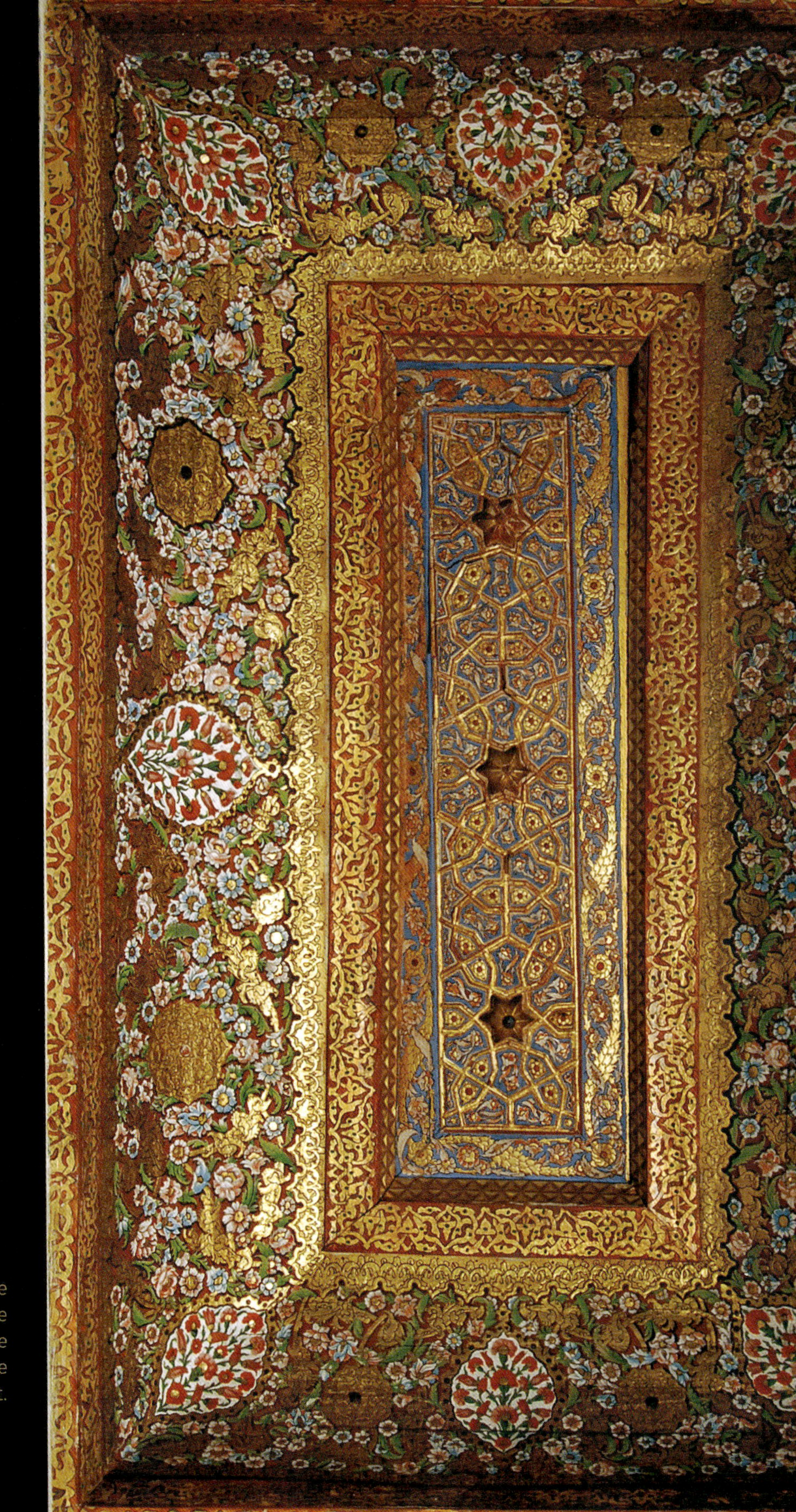

Ceiling decorations of an alcove of the Revan Pavilion, Topkapi Palace
The decorations on the ceiling are particularly splendid examples of the Ottoman illumination art.

Iznik Ceramics

The Ottomans were known for their high quality ceramics, used for both tiles and vessels, most notably Iznik ware. Iznik was very famous for its exquisite Ottoman-style tiles and ceramics. It was also known for the development and use of a bright red pigment, "Iznik red," in both tilework and pottery.

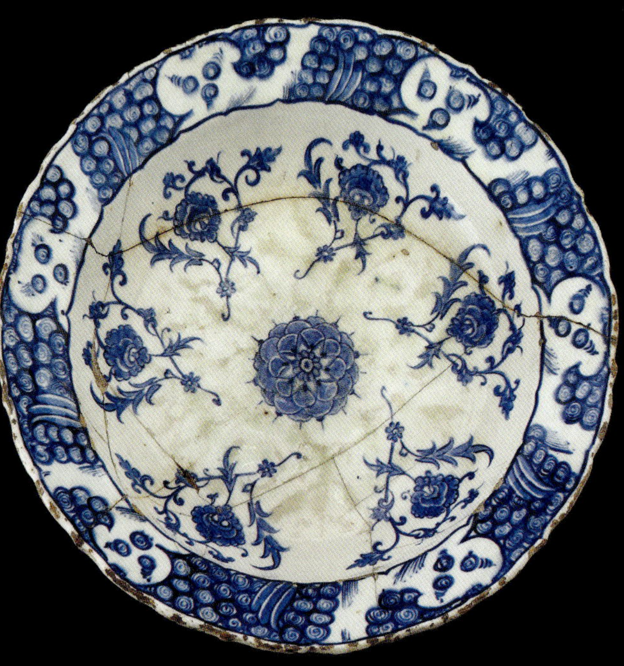

Iznik ware plate, 16th century. The Museum of Turkish and Islamic Arts
The glazed ceramic plate has a white base and blue decorations. The large multi-levelled panch motif at the center is surrounded by elaborate foliate and floral motifs.

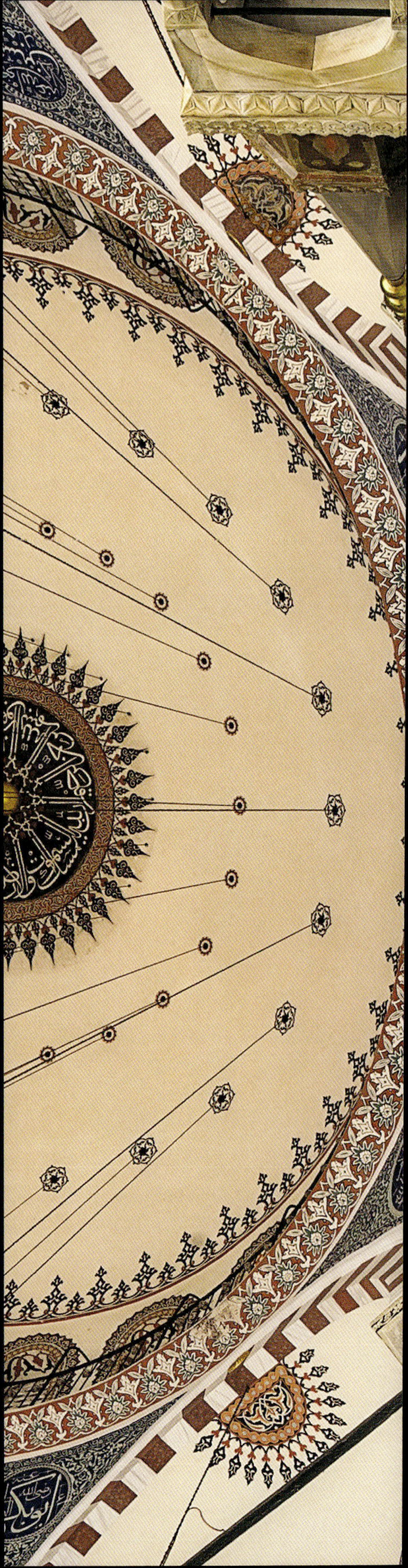

The captivating Iznik ceramics of the prayer niche. Rustem Pasha Mosque

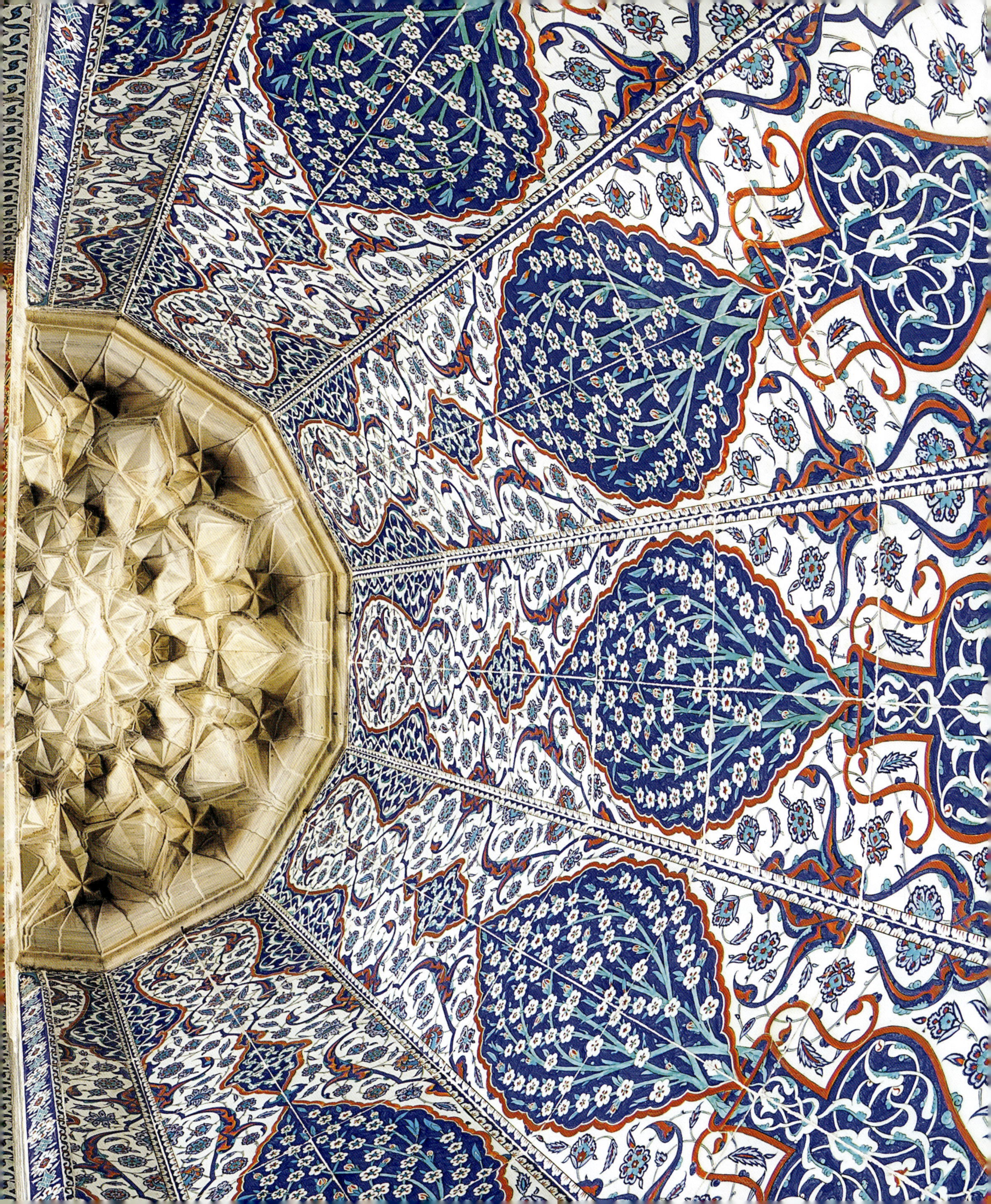

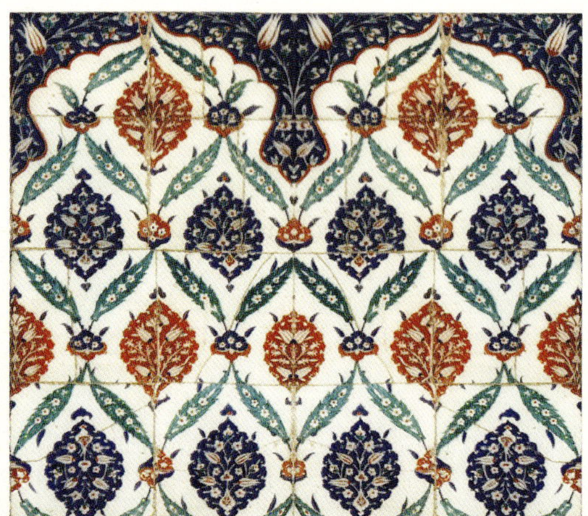

The beautiful blue tiles that give the Blue Mosque its nickname

Marble Carving

Enchanting illumination motifs are applied to the pulpit, walls, and domes of the interior decorations of the Sultanahmet Mosque.

The mosque is also known as the Blue Mosque because of its magnificent interior decoration of over 20,000 glazed blue tiles. A myriad of designs with floral patterns in these beautiful blue Iznik tiles truly give the "Blue" Mosque its nickname.

The pulpit of Sultanahmet Mosque has exquisite marble carvings of geometric, foliate, and floral designs. In marble carving, illumination motifs were carved with a steel instrument—the chisel with a diamond point. The use of different types of steel instruments, some deep-cutting, some more superficial, add greatly to the decorative quality of the illumination work and make its appearance much more attractive.

The marble pulpit of the Sultanahmet Mosque is decorated with exquisite carvings of geometrical, foliate, and floral designs with gilding.

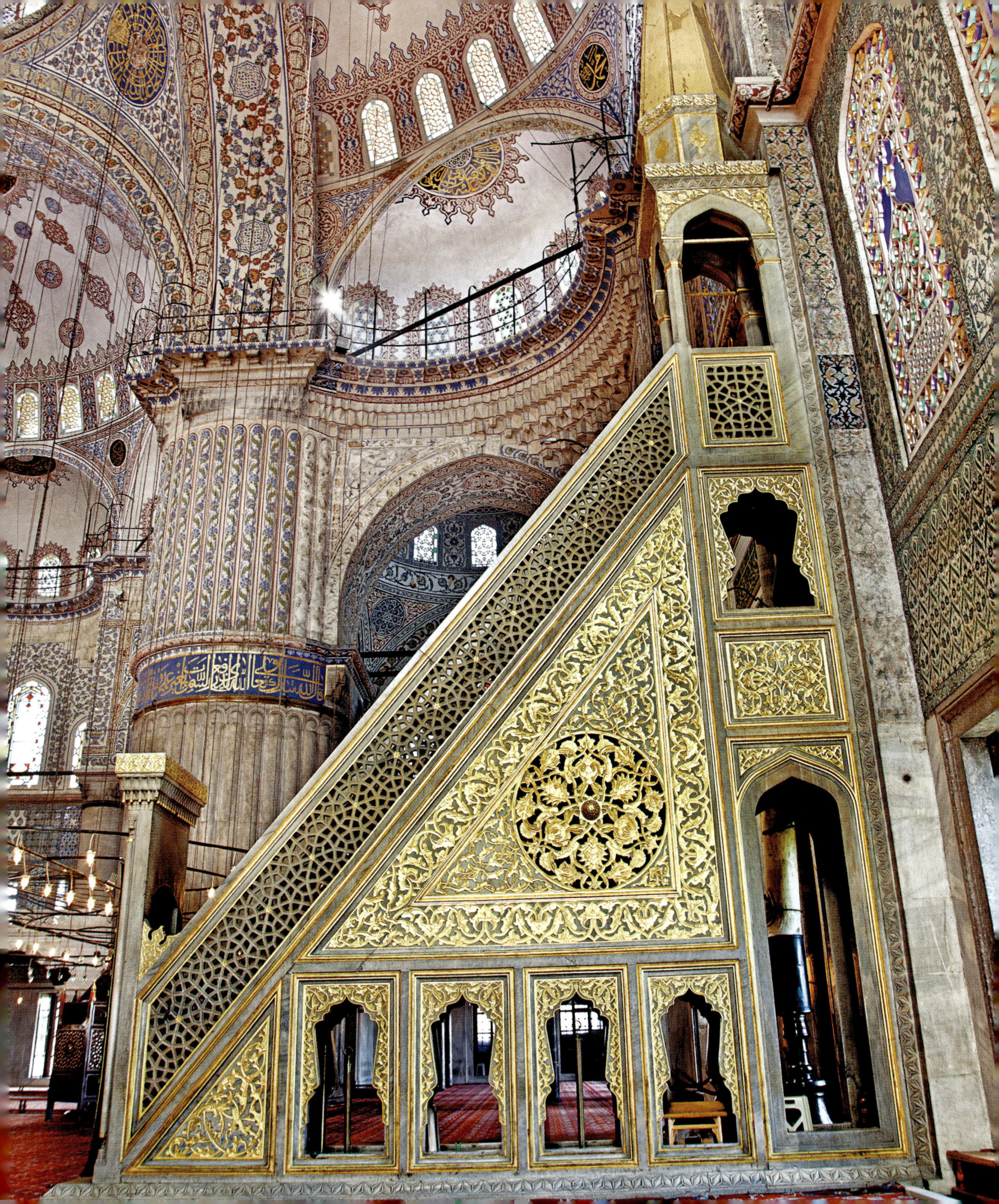

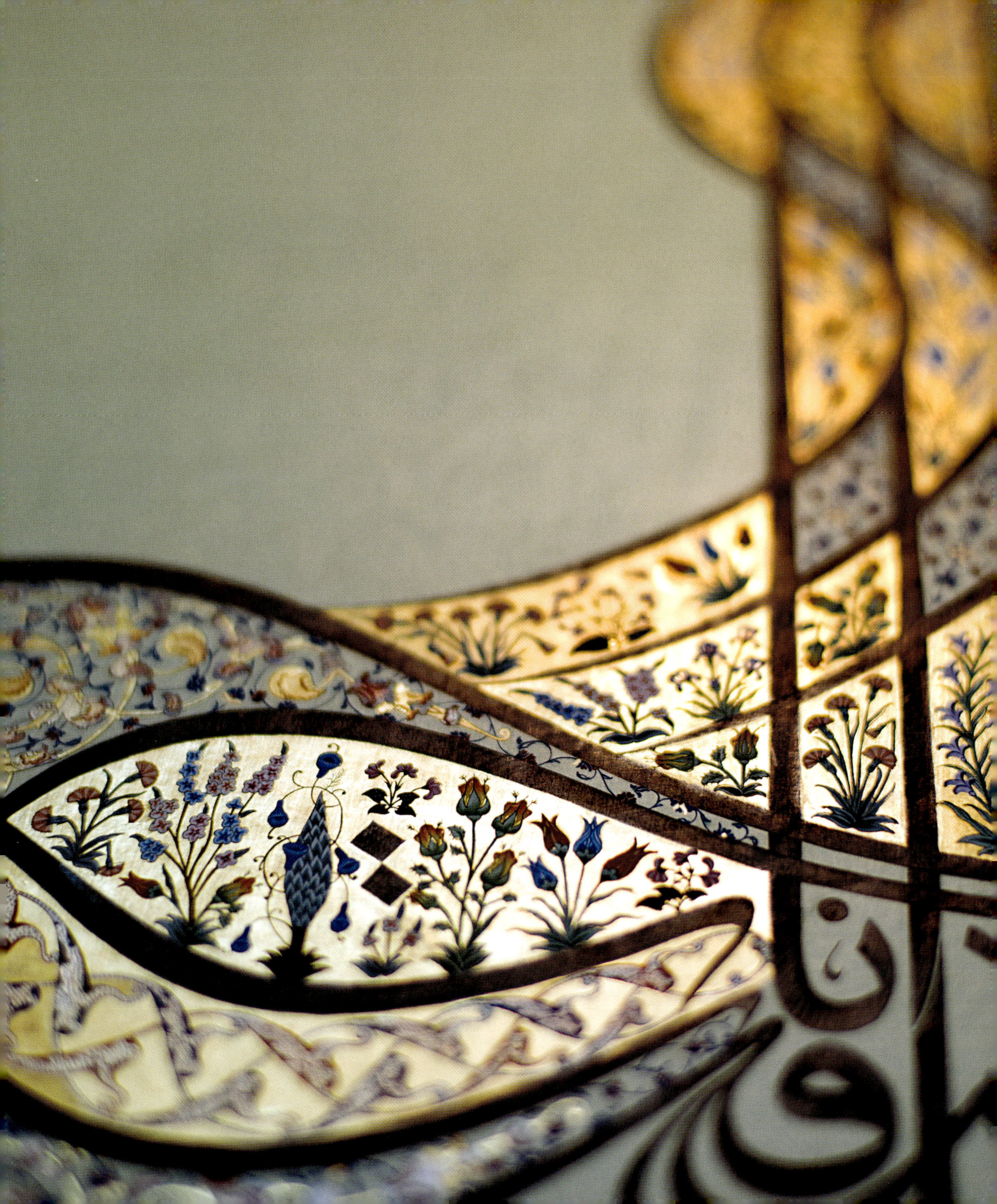

Part One

A Short History of Turkish Illumination Art

History of the Classical Turkish Tazhib

Arabic calligraphy showing the name of God surrounded b
the Sazyolu style floral design and illumination by Sema On

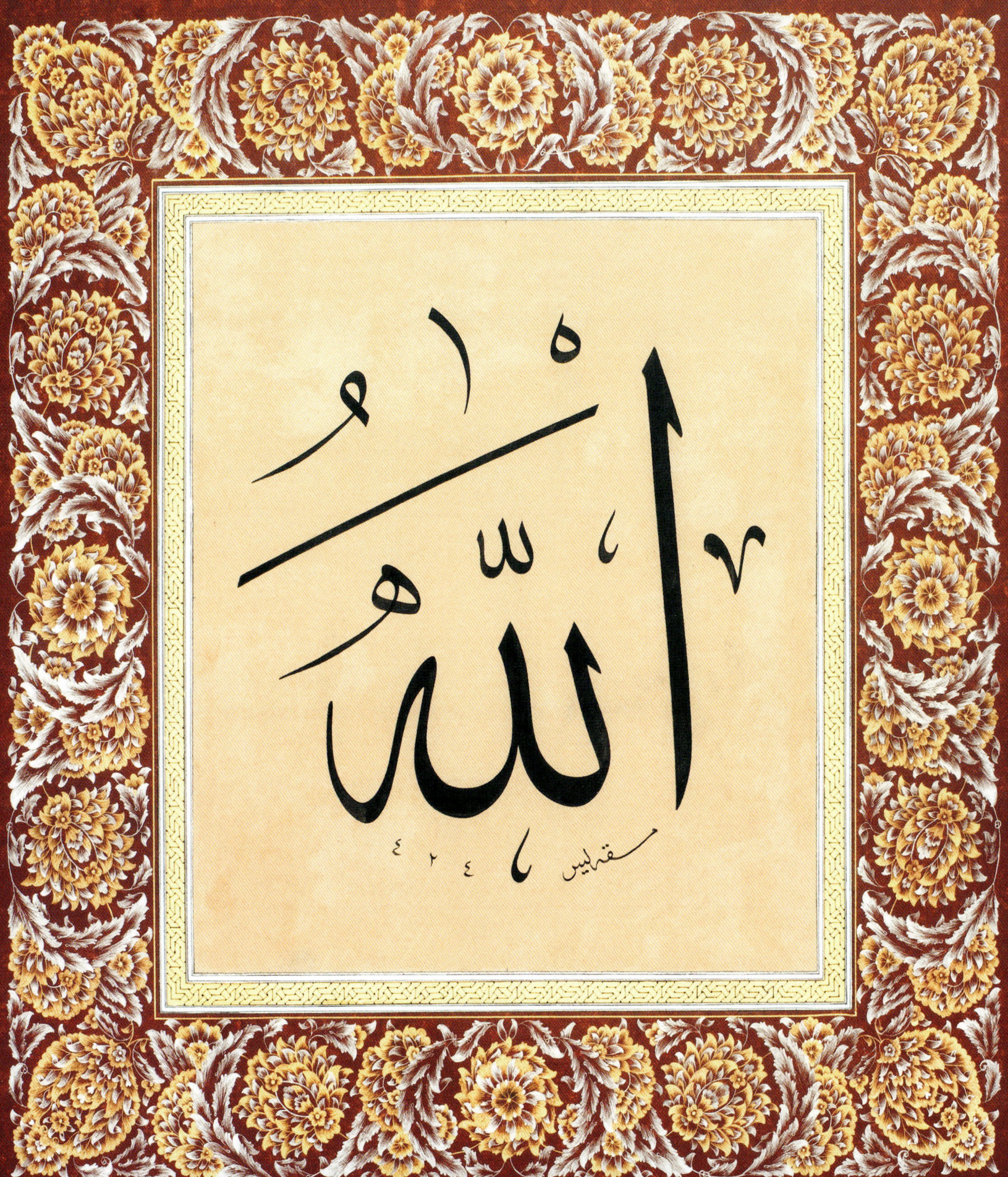
الله

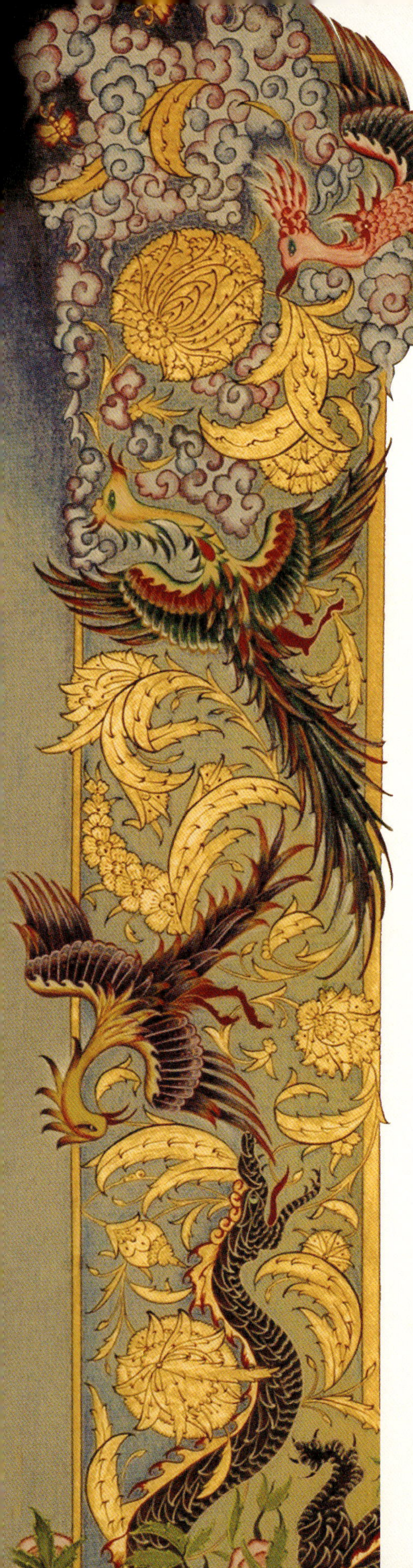

The foundation of the art of illumination was laid before the advent of Islam in Turkish history. The first examples of this art appeared with the transfer of the figures and motifs the Uygur Turks had on wall paintings to book adornments. The background of the adornment was blue during this period. Red, white, gold gilt, purple, and light and dark green colors were also used in the illuminations. The main motifs were simple tree pictures and spiral branches adorned with leaves.

During the time of the Seljuk Turks (13th and 14th centuries), the art of illumination moved from Central Asia to Asia Minor. Geometric designs were dominant in adornment during this period. Also established in this period, the tradition of palace adornment workshops were continued during the Ottoman period. Perfect works in the art of illumination were produced in adornment workshops set up during the reign of Sultan Mehmed the Conqueror, in particular. The influence of Persian illumination artists was also seen during the period of Sultan Bayezid II (reigned 1481–1512).

After the reign of Sultan Mehmed II, the second strongest time for the Ottoman art of illumination was the 16th century. Classical Turkish illumination began to appear during this period. Important advances and innovations were seen in art during the reign of Sultan Selim I. Going beyond book adornment, the art of illumination began to be used extensively as composition in other branches of art like weaving and ceramics.

The art of illumination experienced its richest period during the age of Sultan Suleyman the Magnificent (reigned 1520-1566). This was considered the "Golden Age" for Ottoman illumination art. Rich workmanship was seen in royal edicts and insignias as well as book covers, titles, heads of Qur'anic chapters, and end pages; gold was used abundantly. Navy blue dominated illumination. Ottoman Artists Shah Kulu and his student, Karamemi, put their mark on this period. Shah Kulu of Baghdad produced a new school with his

Illumination of Sazyolu style flowers, simurg, and dragon by Ayşe Koç

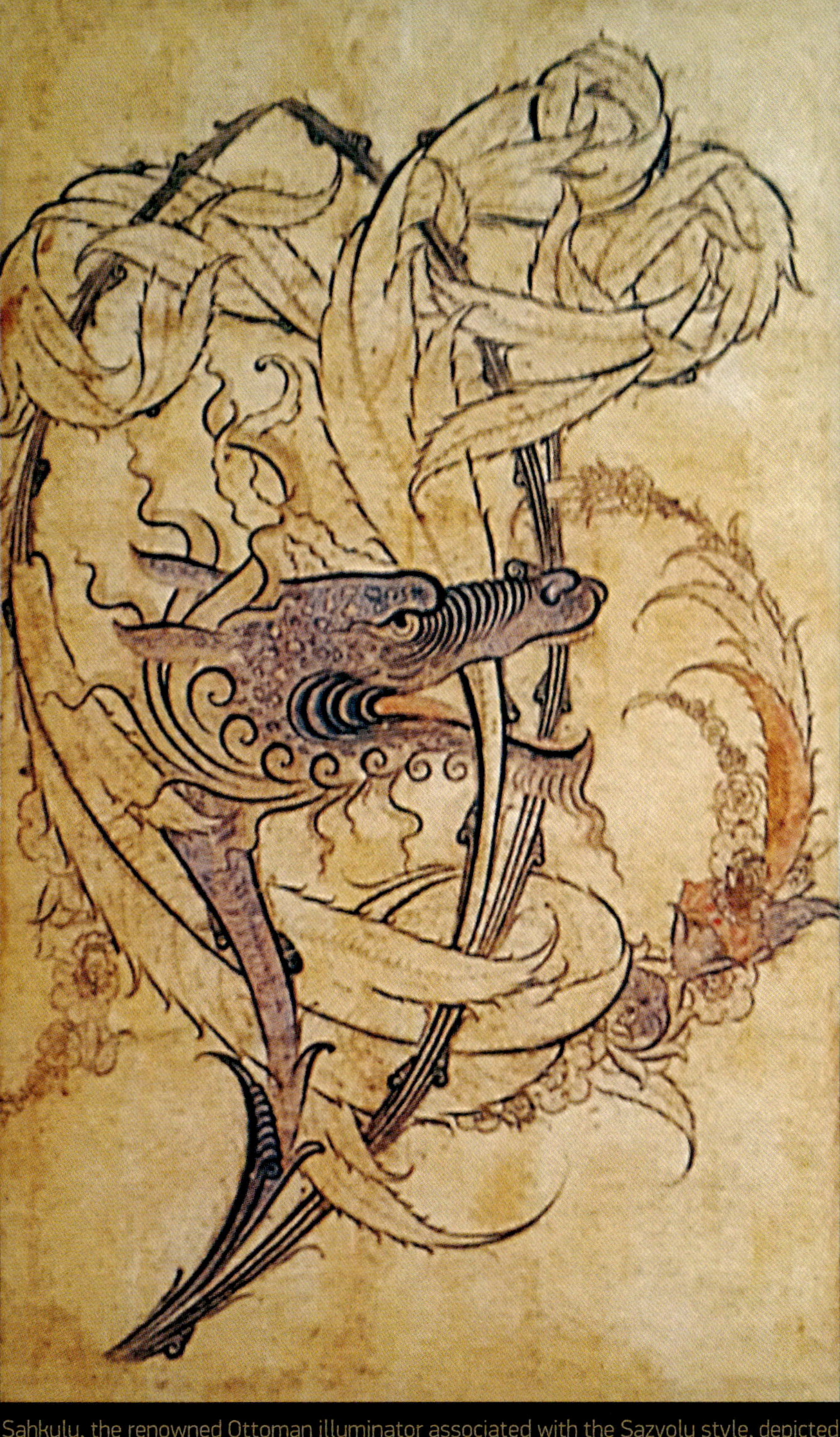

Sahkulu, the renowned Ottoman illuminator associated with the Sazyolu style, depicted here a fantastic world filled with twisting leaves, inhabited by a dragon.

“Sazyolu” (reed) style. The new naturalistic style Karamemi developed spread to other art branches and survived for many centuries.

The best Ottoman illumination was heavily concentrated in Istanbul, the capital of the empire. Hundreds of imperial artistic societies, called Ahlu’l Hiraf (the “Community of the Talented”), were administered at the Topkapı Palace under the royal family’s patronage. These artistic societies attracted the empire’s most talented artists to the capital and the sultan’s court from all over the vast Ottoman territory. The adornment workshops (*naqqashhanas*) the artists and artisans worked in functioned as an academy. In these adornment workshops, the masters who oversaw them carried the title of “bash naqqash” (head artist), and they were generally illumination artists, showing the central place illumination art held in the Ottoman arts. Since the time adornment workshops were first set up until the present, famous illumination artists, along with many adornment artisans, were trained and many masterpieces produced. Male illumination artists are called “mudhahhib” and female illumination artists are called “mudhahhiba,” while a work adorned with illumination is referred to as a “mudhahhab.”

The influence of Western art could be seen in Turkish illumination art during the Tulip Period (1718-1730). With the influence of French Rococo, the classic form was almost completely abandoned and large flowers and bouquets were amply used. This style continued until the end of the 19th century. The school named “Madrasatu’l Khattatin,” which was opened in 1914, ensured the liveliness of traditional arts like calligraphy, illumination, water marbling, binding, paper coating, collage and gold leaf. After 1928, the school took the names “School of Calligraphy” and “School of Eastern Ornamental Arts,” respectively, and these were tied to the Fine Arts Academy in 1936. Just as ornamental artists are trained academically by the fine arts faculty today, they are also trained with a hands-on approach in special classes in art centers like in Topkapi Palace and other art workshops. In these art centers, pupils receive the license (*ijaza*) from a master illuminator to practice the art independently upon reaching a certain maturity in the art.

Karamemi’s illumination of flowers in Sultan Suleyman the Magnificent’s collection of poems, called *Muhibbi Diwan*

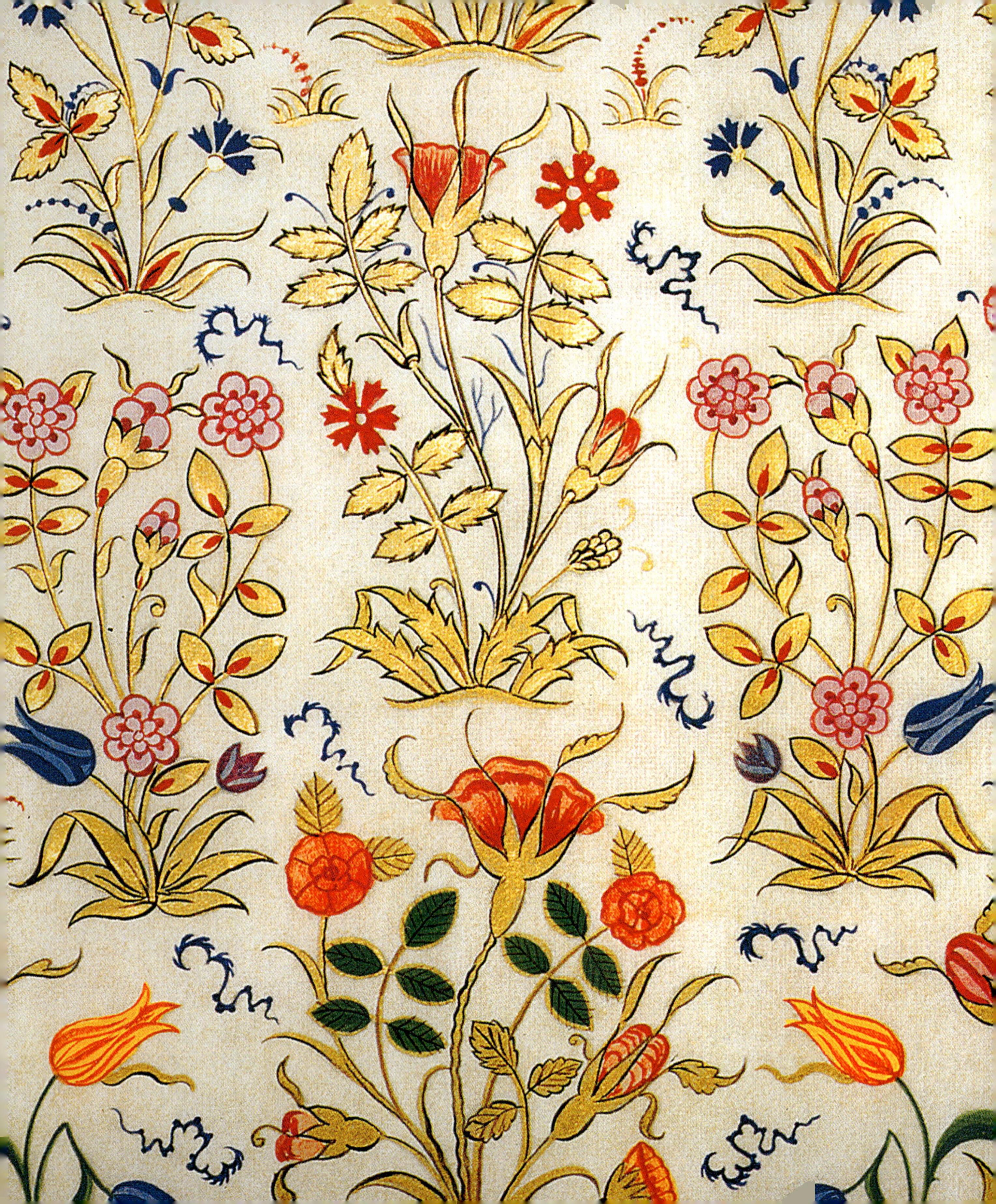

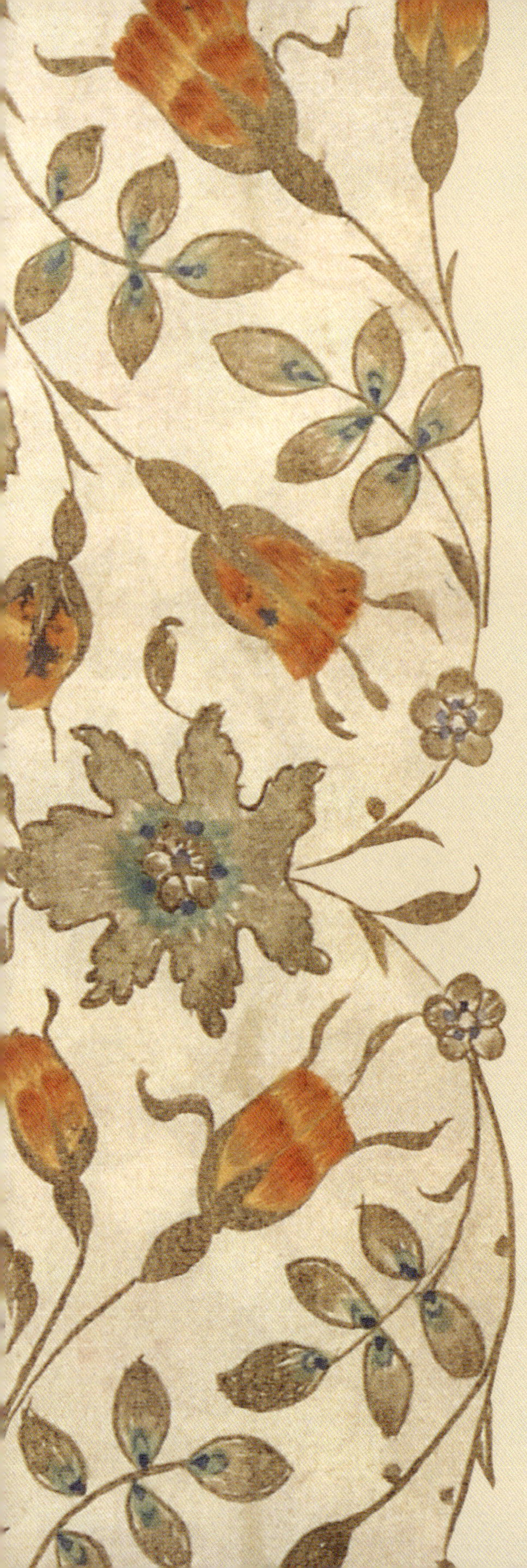

It would not be correct to limit the art of illumination, which came down from the Uygur Turks, to just one civilization. The art of illumination was influenced by other cultures, art circles, and artists that were prominent during the same period, and it influenced them as well. For this reason, it is possible to see traces of many civilizations in the art of illumination.

The ornamentation motifs and compositions designed by illumination artists were used in all art branches, from ceramics to weaving and from jewelry-making to wood-engraving. The reason for the unity of style seen in Turkish arts is that the compositions worked in these arts were born in the same center under the patronage of the sultan, royal family members, and other elites. However, even with this unity of style, all Turkish works carry a unique identity.

Karamemi's illumination of semi-naturalistic spring flowers

Prominent Artists in the Art of Illumination

The handing down of the ornamental arts from generation to generation was done by means of training in the master-apprentice method. In the past, young people who wanted to receive this training would begin their work with a good master. The apprentice would be evaluated by the master according to the patience, good manners, loyalty, ability and success he showed, and through masterful works he made as an accomplished artist the apprentice would receive his license from the master. This document, called an *ijazatnama*, was a kind of certificate of accomplishment showing that the master was convinced that the student had been sufficiently trained. The apprentice who received his certificate now had permission to put his signature on the works he made after this. The importance of this tradition, which was valid for calligraphers, craftsmen and ornamentation artists in the past, has been maintained by partial application in some circles today.[1]

There have been many master illumination artists since the time the art of illumination first appeared. However, the names of only some of these artists are known today. The reason for this is that there was no tradition of signing illumination works.

However, Shahabaddin Qudsi, a famous fifteenth century Ottoman illumination artist, wrote his name on the edge of works he made. Ottoman Sultan Mehmed the Conqueror

1 For further reading, see Birol, *Türk Tezyini Sanatlarında Desen Tasarımı* (Pattern Design in Turkish Decorative Arts), p. 20.

brought Baba Naqqash to head the ornamentation workshop he established at Topkapi Palace. Baba Naqqash produced masterpieces at the palace and trained many students.

Shah Kulu, a famous illumination artist from the period of Sultan Suleyman the Magnificent, pioneered the "Sazyolu" (reed) style. His student, Kara Mehmed Chelebi, who was popularly known as Karamemi, later became the chief illuminist at the ornamentation workshop in the sultan's palace. He introduced the "Haliç work" style to Ottoman illumination.

From the second half of the 16th century, the art of illumination began to lose its speed of development. The main illumination artists of this period were Sürahi Mustafa, Baruthaneli Abdullah, Dervish Mehmet, and Velican. Like Shah Kulu, Velican came from Tabriz and produced works in the *Sazyolu* style.

The 18th century is a time when the art of illumination was influenced by the West. Abdullah Bukhari, Yusuf Misri, and his student, Ali Üsküdari, can be considered some of the famous illumination artists of that time. Ali Üsküdari produced many great works and trained many students. He worked at the palace during the reigns of sultans Ahmed, Mahmud II, Osman III, and Mustafa III. He was a great artist who dissolved the Western influence in the classic style during a period when Turkish ornamentation began to disappear through Westernization.

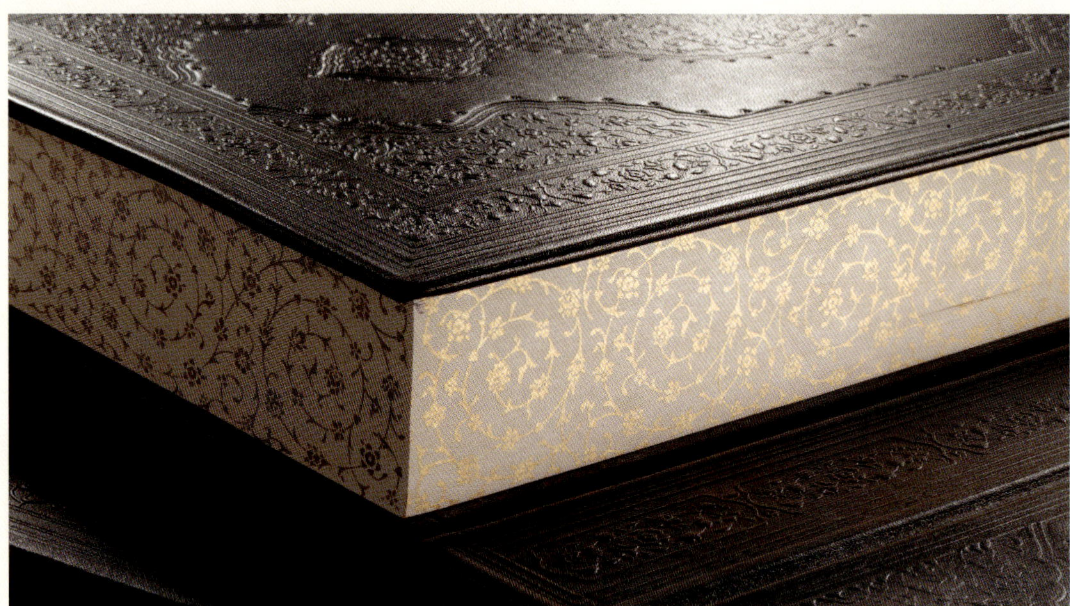

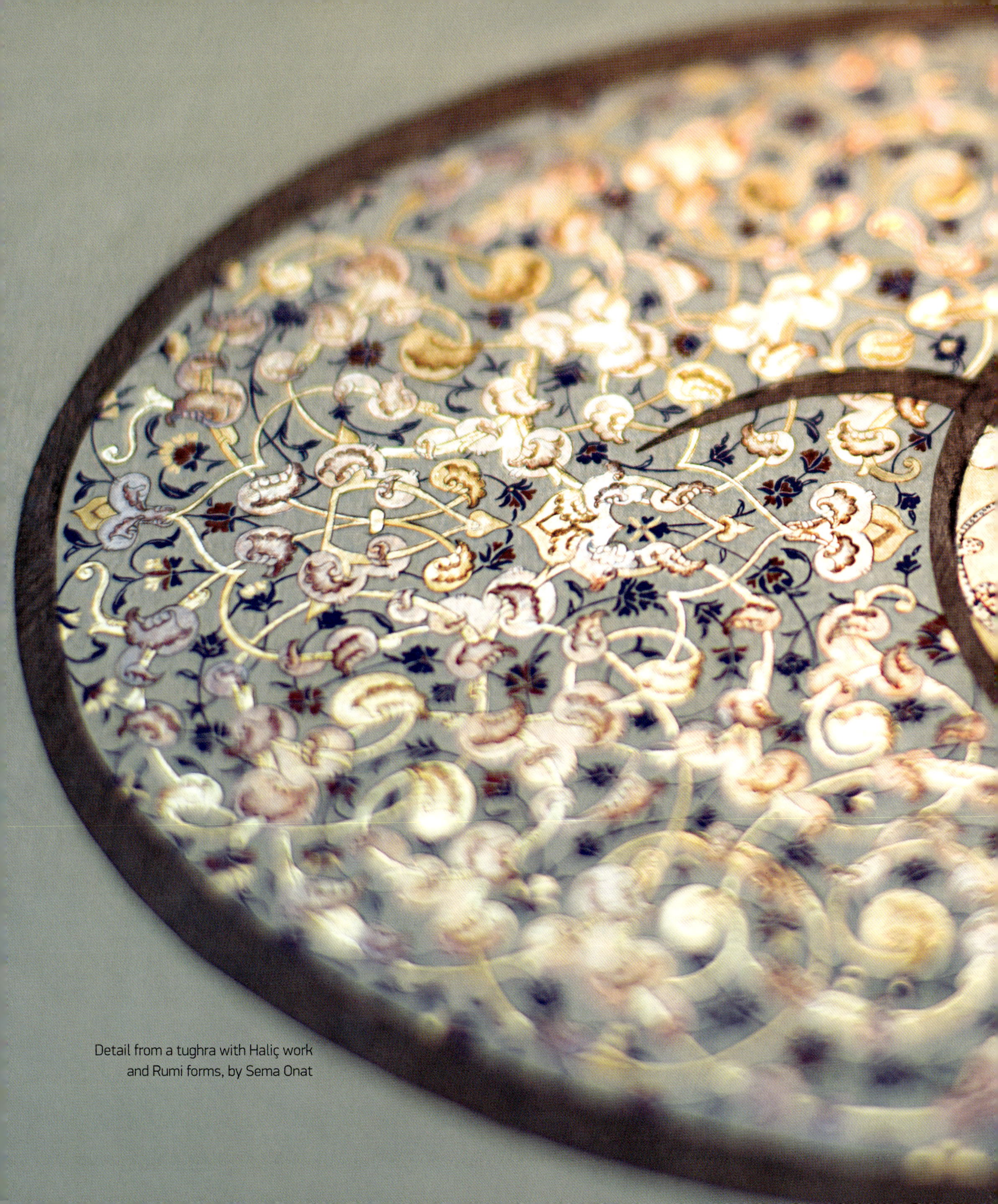

Detail from a tughra with Haliç work and Rumi forms, by Sema Onat

The art of illumination declined significantly during the 19th century. The artists of this period produced Rococo style works. Hajji Hasan Salih was one of the illumination artists for Sultan Abdulmecid and Sultan Abdulaziz. During Abdulhamid II's reign, Tevfik Efendi, Lalelili Şakir's student Nureddin Efendi, Hüsnü Efendi, Bahaeddin Efendi, and Hakkı Bey were among the masters.

However, in contrast to the western-influenced Rococo adornment, since the 1950s, there has been a revival of the classical understanding. Rikkat Kunt, Muhsin Demironat and A. Süheyla Ünver can be considered to be among the famous illumination artists of the contemporary age.

Modern Period Artists

The leading contemporary illuminators Rikkat Kunt and Muhsin Demironat have produced classical works, mostly of picture ornamentation. Their role in performing the illumination art in a way that remains faithful to the classical understanding today is great.

Ms. Rikkat Kunt began to work with Feyzullah Dayıgil, a ceramic ornamentation teacher at the State Fine Arts Academy in Istanbul, with the encouragement of Necmeddin Okyay (1883-1976), who was also a professor at the same academy. She learned the classic illumination art concepts from the Ottoman sources, especially by examining ceramics from the 16th-18th centuries in the Historic Peninsula of Istanbul. Consequently, she served to kindle new life into illumination designs—by looking to the classical past.

Rikkat Kunt was invited to Portugal to restore an Ottoman period hand-written book embellished with miniatures, which was found in the Gulbenkian Museum in Portugal's capital, Lisbon, and which had been damaged by a disastrous flood in 1968. She had to return after 2.5 months due to the bad effects of the city's atmosphere on her health. However, this extremely valuable hand-written work of the early 16th century was officially sent to Istanbul by the Portuguese government with a request for the restoration to be completed. Ms. Kunt successfully completed this task and returned the book.

A predecessor of Rikkat Kunt, Muhsin Demironat is one of the esteemed illuminators who produced works in the classical style. With the encouragement of Necmeddin Okyay, Demironat chose Ali Üsküdari, the unequaled 18th century master of this art, to be his spiritual master. By studying Üsküdari's work, he produced perfect works in the same vein.

Muhsin Demironat remained so much under the influence of Ali Üsküdari that alluding to his master, he signed many of his works as "Muhsin-i Üsküdari." He made his first major professional work by illuminating the wide margins of the Qur'anic chapter of al-An'am, which was written in the cursive *naskh* script by the calligrapher Hajji Kemal Akdik. This splendid work was personally taken by Kemal Efendi to the Egyptian King Fuad in 1933.

Today, there are many artists who continue the tradition of classical Turkish illumination art. Modern illuminators use the illumination on its own or with calligraphy and miniatures. With traditionalism gaining importance, illumination motifs can be found on clothing items, in accessory designs, in spatial decoration, and in various other decoration areas.

Ali Üsküdari's flower illuminations.
Istanbul University Library

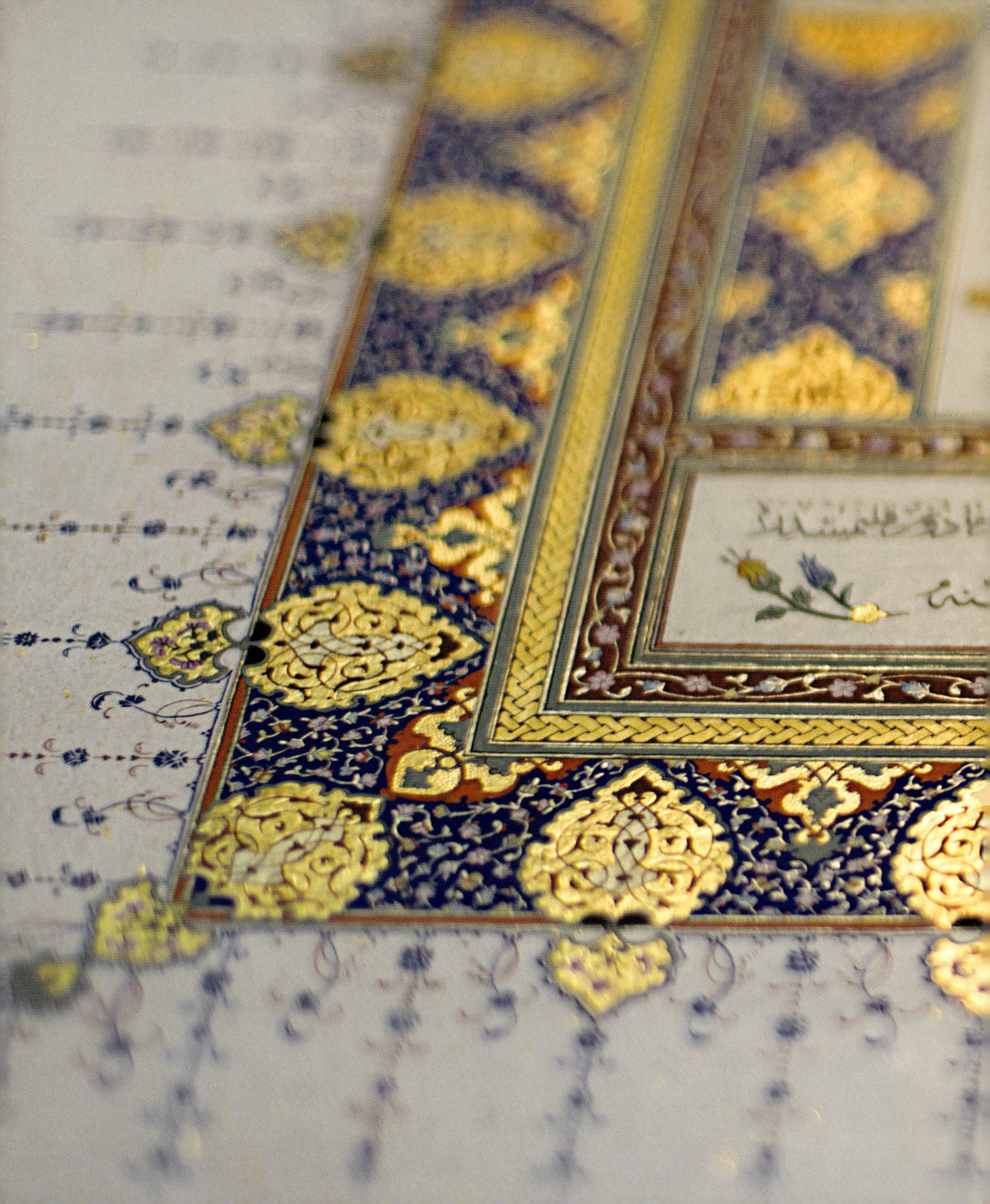

Part Two

Different Schools Developing in the Art of Illumination

DIFFERENT SCHOOLS OF ILLUMINATION ART

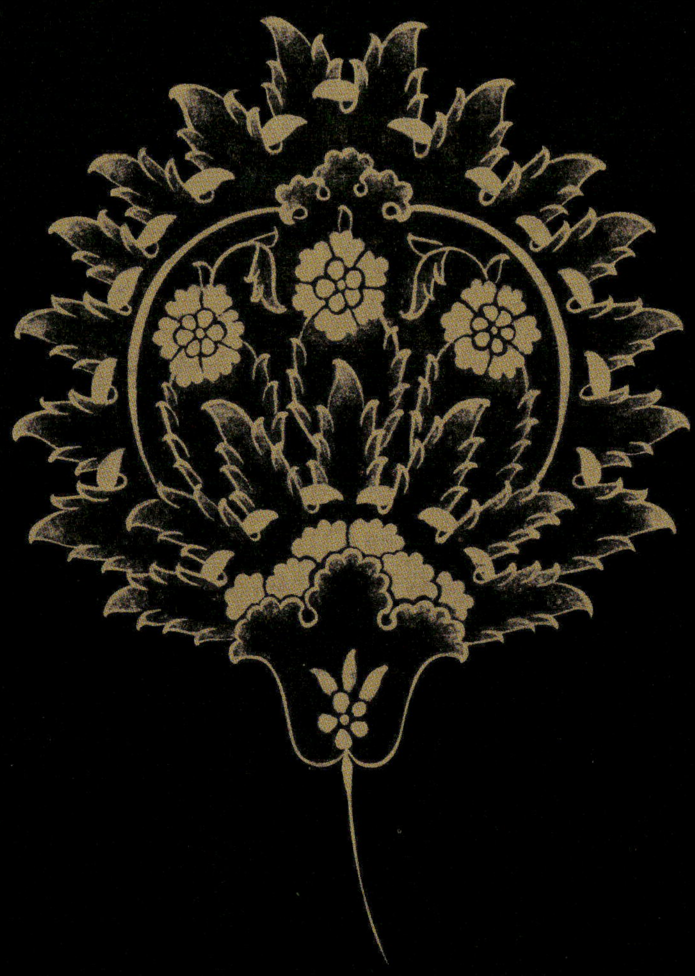

Figure 1 - *Halkar* Style

A. Halkar (Gilding) Style

This style makes light ornamentation with gold or gilt. It is applied in different styles like shadow gilding and combed gilding, and it is classified according to the painting style. Illumination made with single color or double color gold is contour gilding. Leaves, floral motifs (*khatai*), foliation with five cusps or points (*panch*), and rose buds (*gonca*) are used in the gilding designs. Although there is not much floral detail in this style, we've inherited refreshingly different design examples from the Ottomans.

In gilding (*halkar*) ornamentation, generally fluid gold designs are made from the middle of a piece to an extremity, and the gold is gathered at the extremities. Later, a thick contour is made around it.

If later, shadowing is made with a water color in the middle sections, where the gold is sparse, this technique is called *shikaf*.

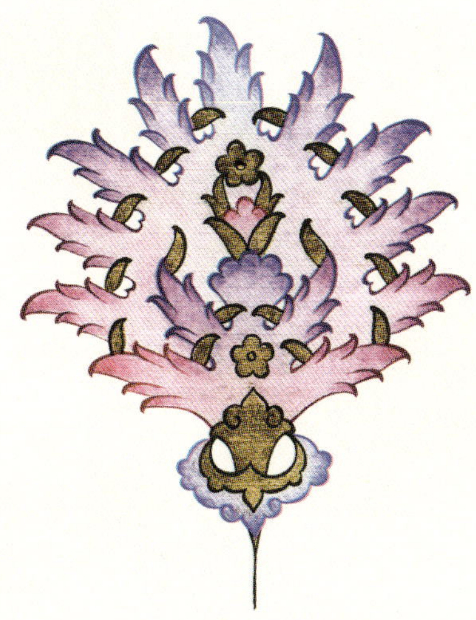

Figure 2a - *Shikaf*

Figure 2b - *Shikaf*

B. Sazyolu (Reed) Style

This style was introduced by Shah Kulu, a famous illumination artist during the reign of Sultan Suleyman the Magnificent. In the *Sazyolu* style, illumination works are made with black ink and a brush. In some places, the painting is made with watered down colors and gold or silver. What is striking about this style is that the main lines and the backs of leaves are adorned with a brush in distinctive contours and color is not usually used.

In the *Sazyolu* style, motifs tend to be more detailed than in the *Halkar* style and leaves are drawn more notched. In particular, these leaves—drawn in large sizes with their middle veins and main lines accentuated with thick contours—have rich details.

Among the main motifs of the *Sazyolu* are ornate and curly *khatai*-style flowers and buds; legendary animals like dragons, including the mythical bird *zumrudu anka*; wild animals like lions and tigers; various other animals like elephants, deer, turtles, rabbits, and butterflies; birds like pheasants and cranes; and human and angelic figures.[2]

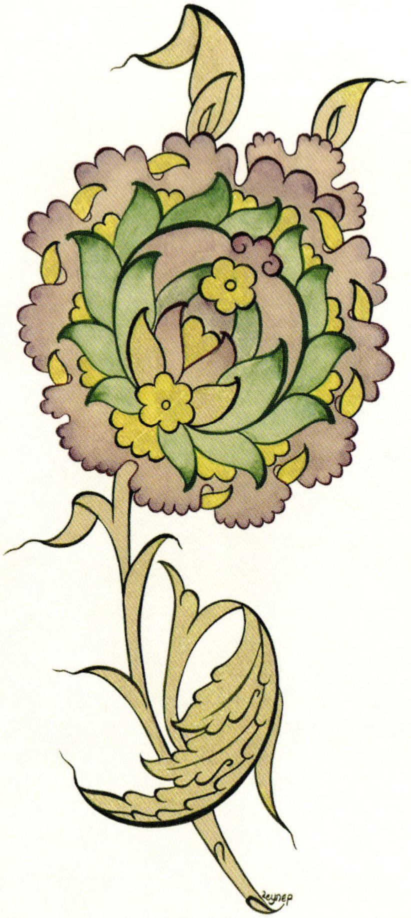

---

2 Özkeçeci and Özkeçeci, *Türk Sanatında Tezhip* (Illumination in Turkish Arts), p. 151

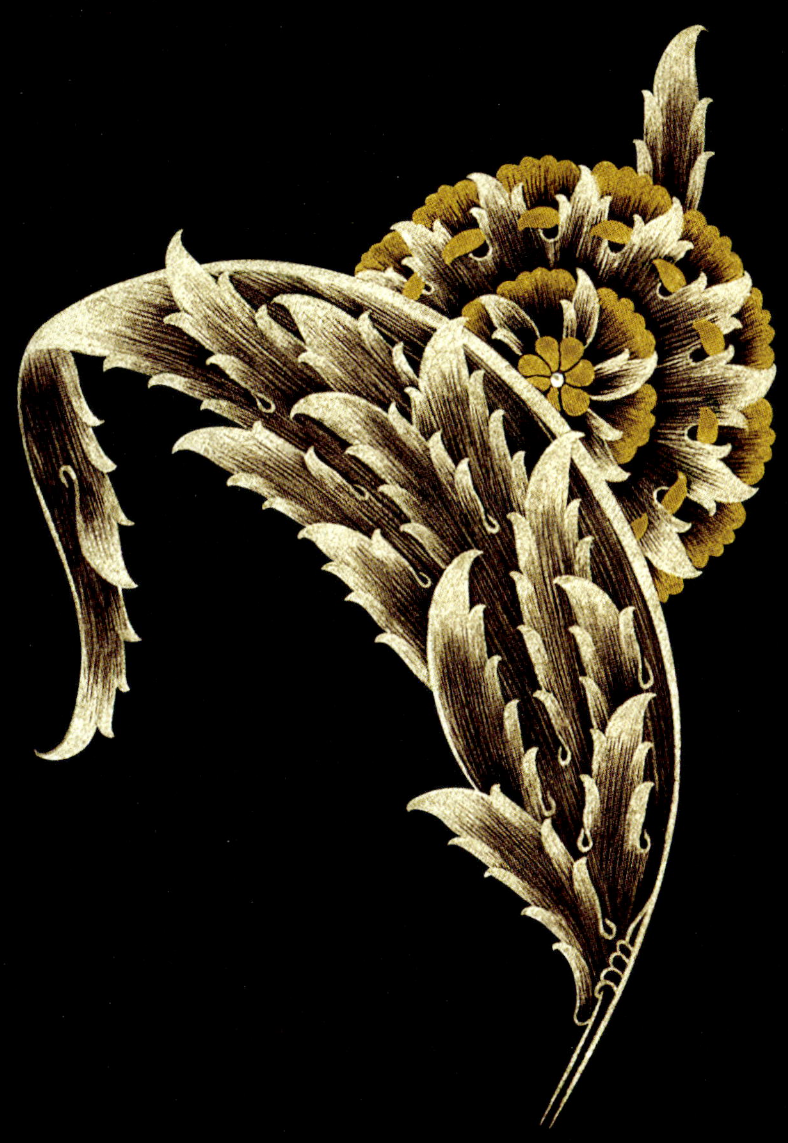

Figure 3 - *Sazyolu (Reed) Style*

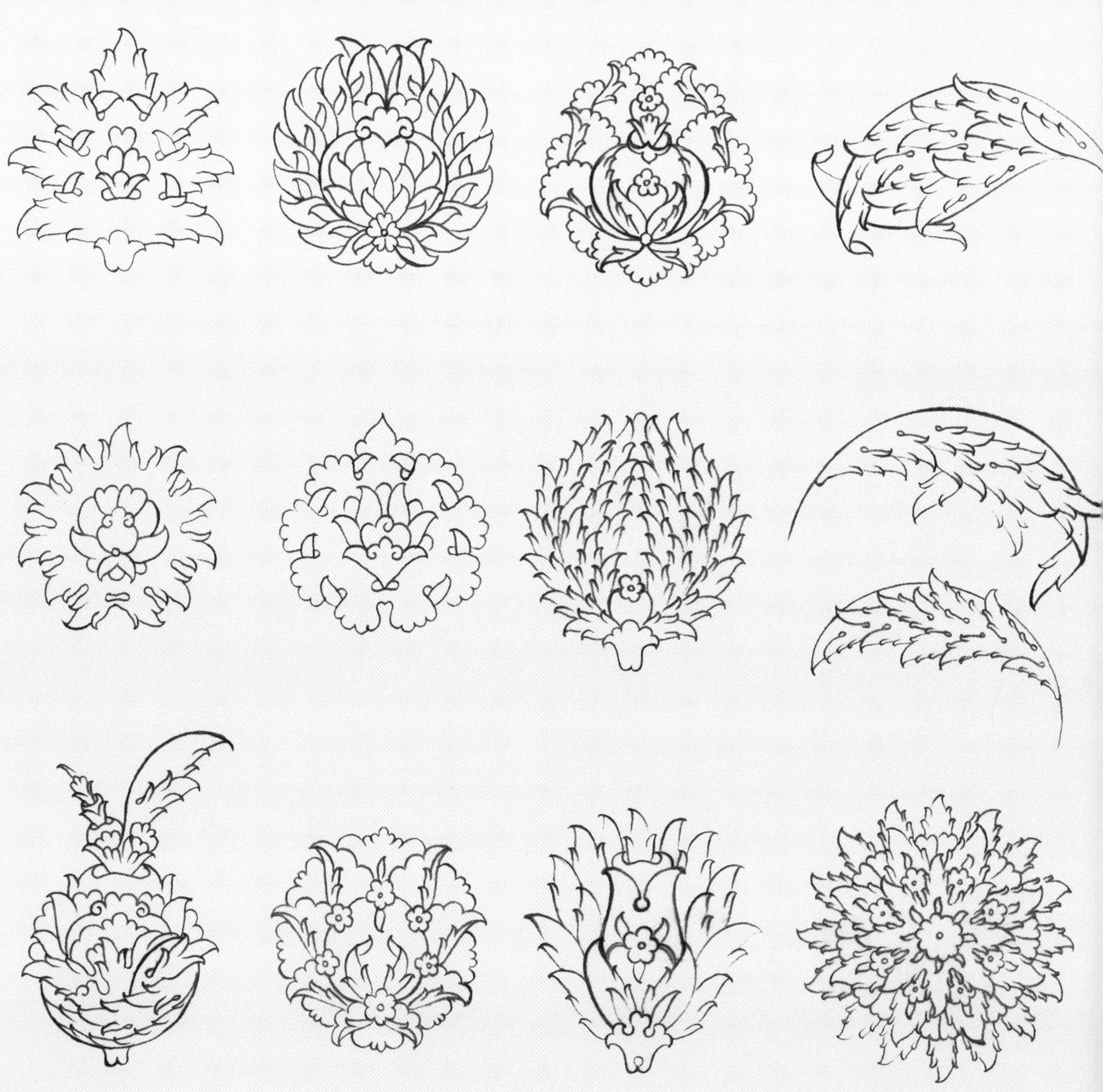

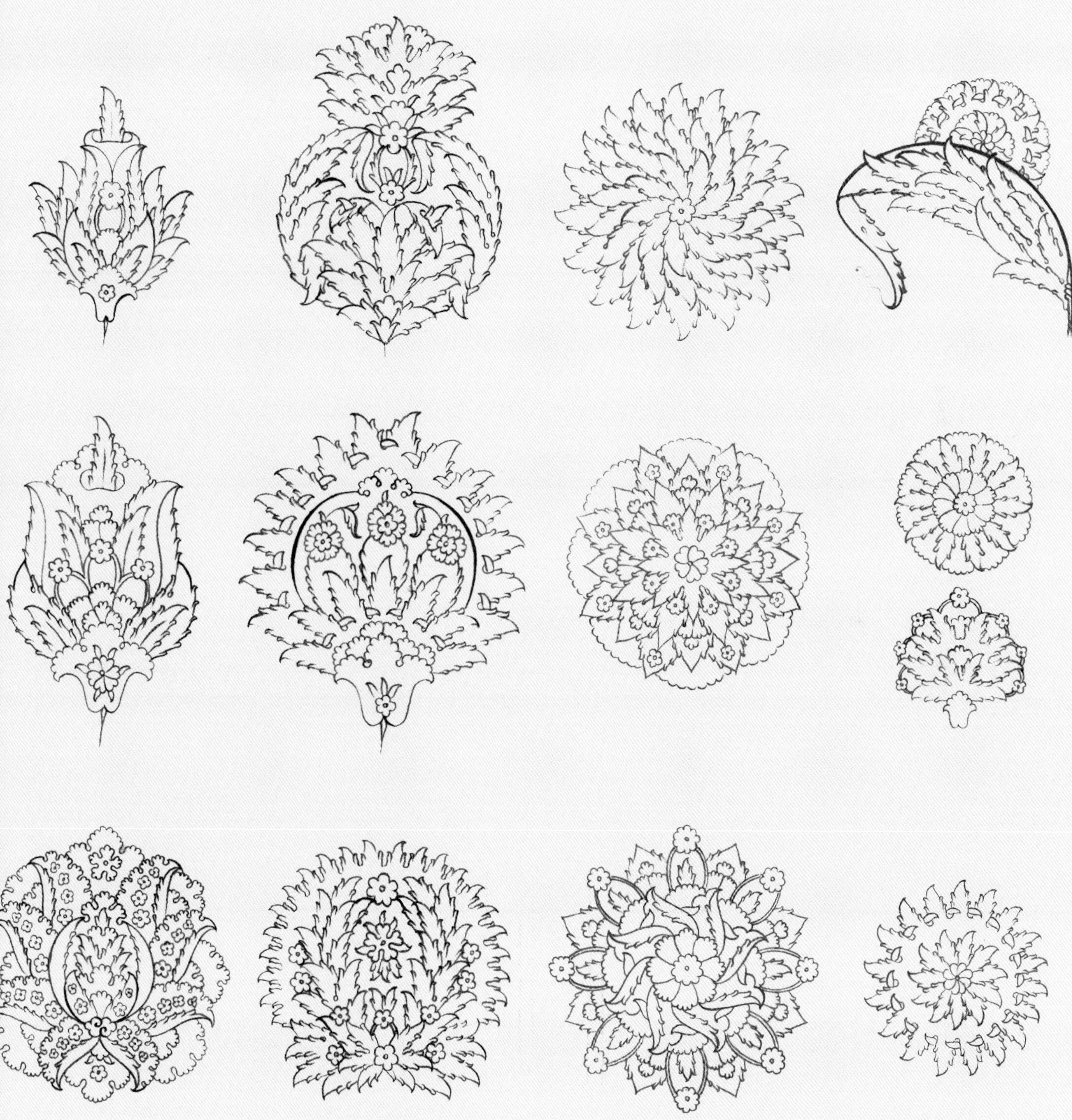

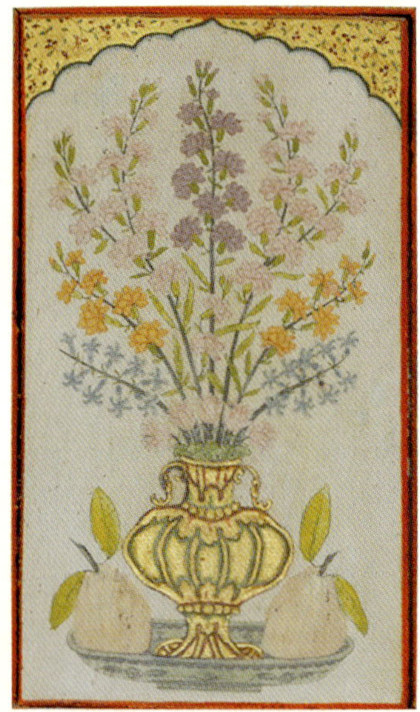

Detail from the *Fruit Room*

C. Turkish Rococo

This school was prominent from the late 18th century to the late 19th century. It appeared due to the influence of French Rococo art.

The most important motifs of the Rococo style are leaves with large and broad curls, flower bouquets in baskets, flowers in vases, rose garlands, ribbons and bows, light rays and zigzags, horns of plenty, C and S curves, and columns and curtains. The flower used most frequently in this period was the rose.[3]

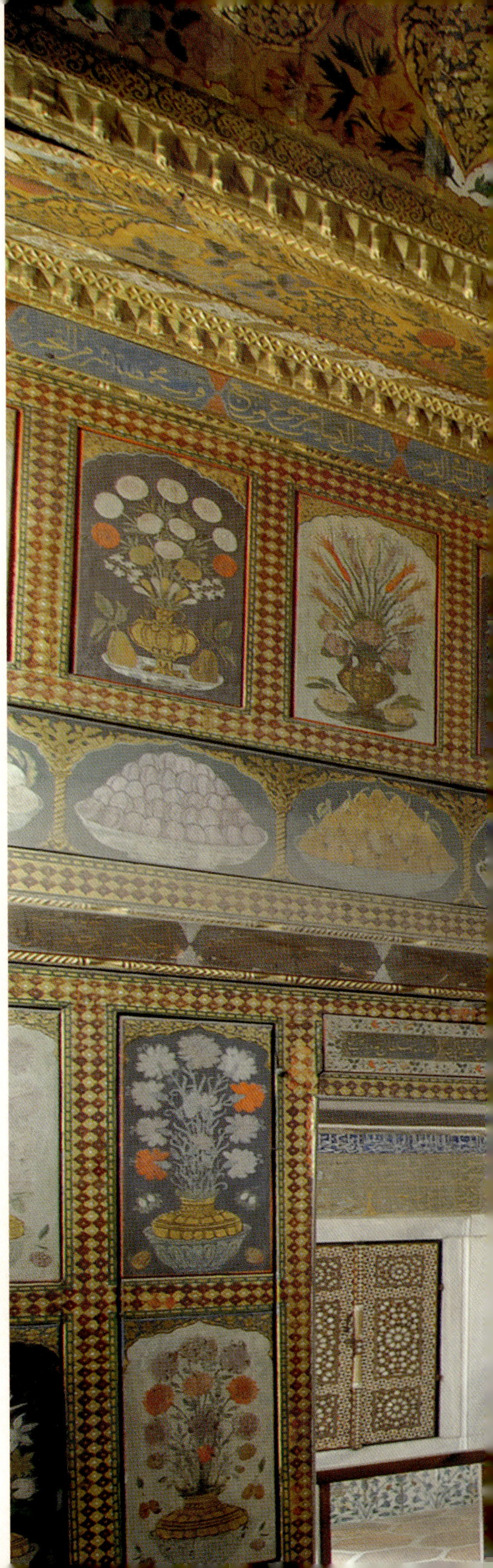

Turkish rococo paintings in the *Fruit Room, Topkapi Palace Museum*

3 For further illustrations see www.faruktaskale.com

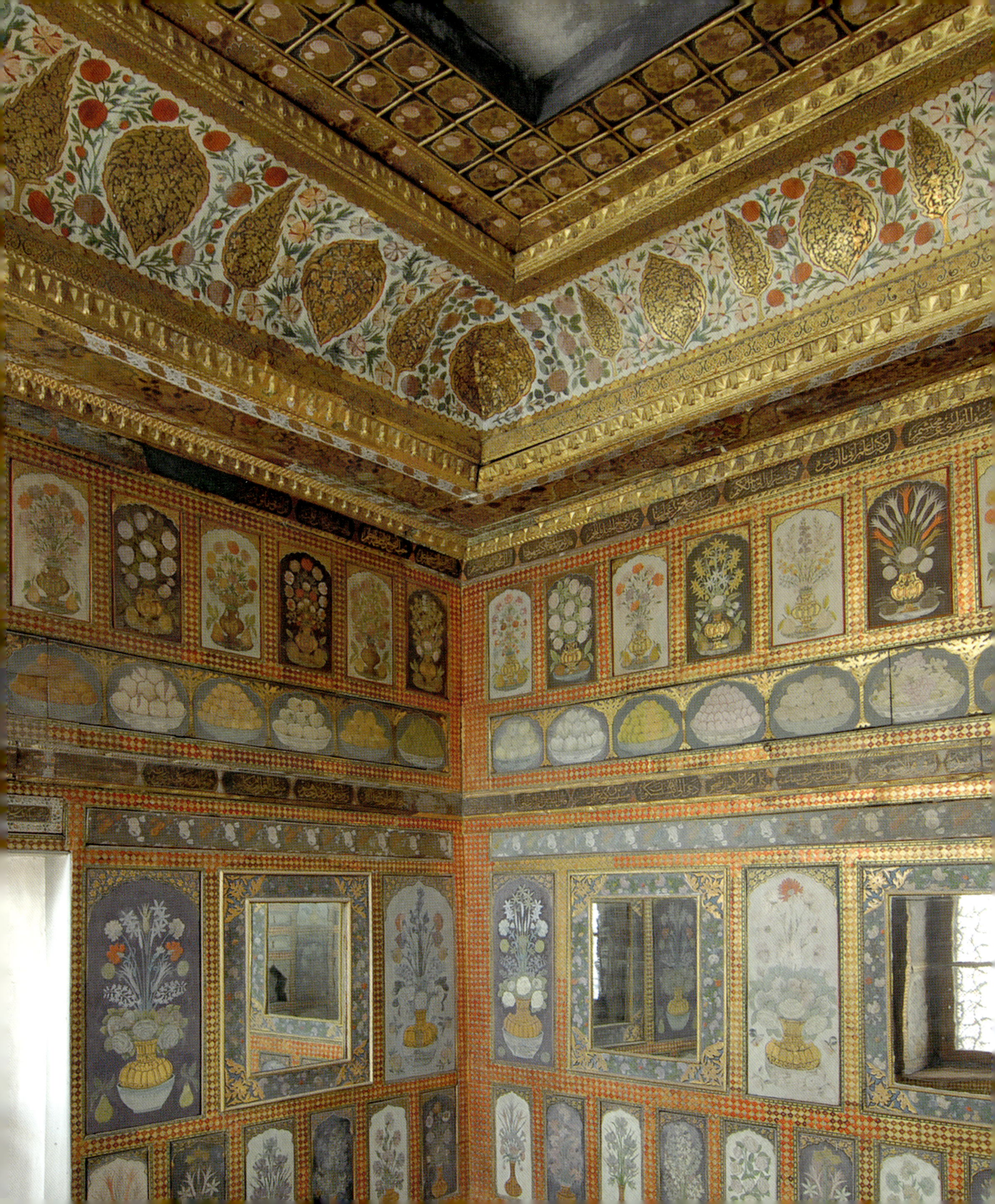

D. Classic Illumination

In classic illumination, motifs are small. It can be said that these motifs are drawn by reducing the details of flowers used in the gilding designs and by greatly diminishing them. Just as gold can be used in the background of classic illumination, the colors of navy blue, green, burgundy, and black are also preferred. Because the background is a dark color, light tones are used in the colors of flowers. Leaves are usually painted with gold.

In making classic illumination, first a composition is prepared in a way that is appropriate to the rules of the work the design is going to be applied to (Figure 5a). This design is put onto the foundation of the work. Gold is the first material to be spread onto to the foundation (Figure 5b). Later, these gold sections are polished and then the colored part is begun (Figure 5c). After applying the flower colors, ornamental lines are drawn around the gilding (Figure 5d). The remaining area in white is painted (Figure 5e). Finally, flower tones are made and, after making the needle-pointed *tigh* ornamentation, the design is completed (Figure 5f).

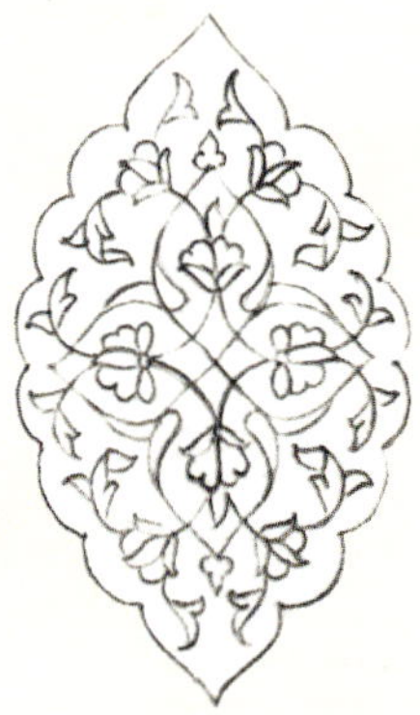

Figure 5a

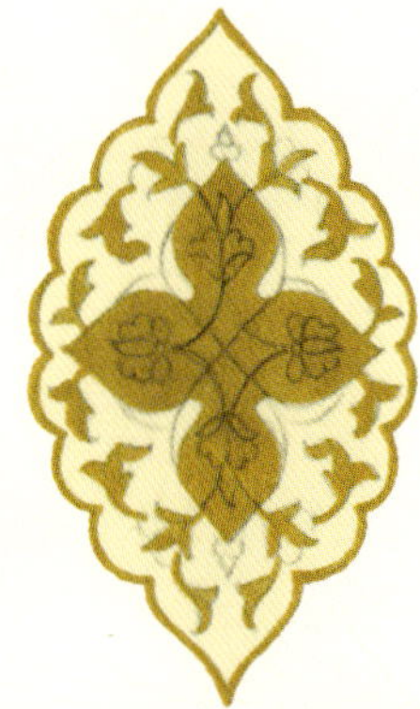

Figure 5b

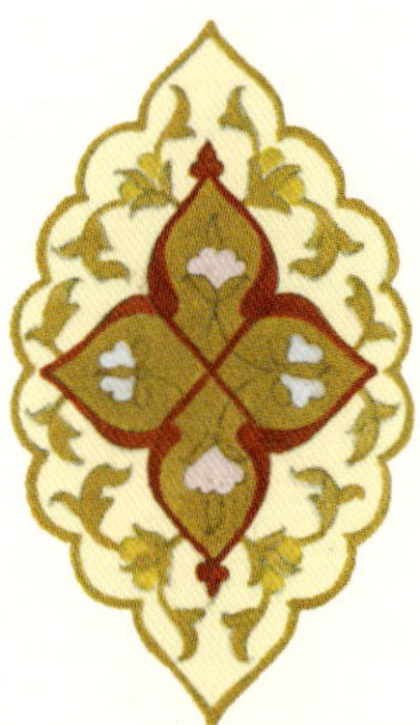

Figure 5c

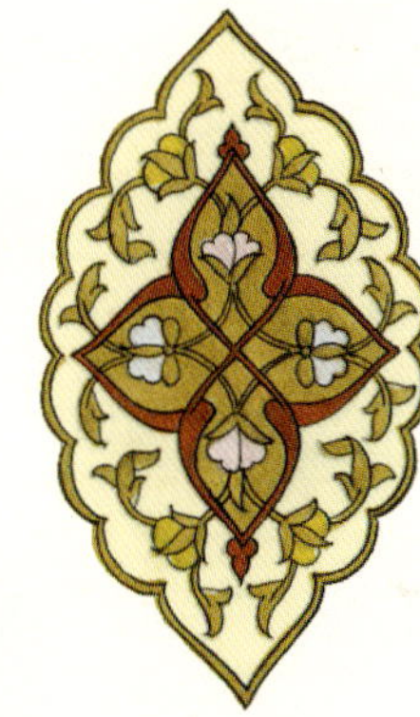

Figure 5d

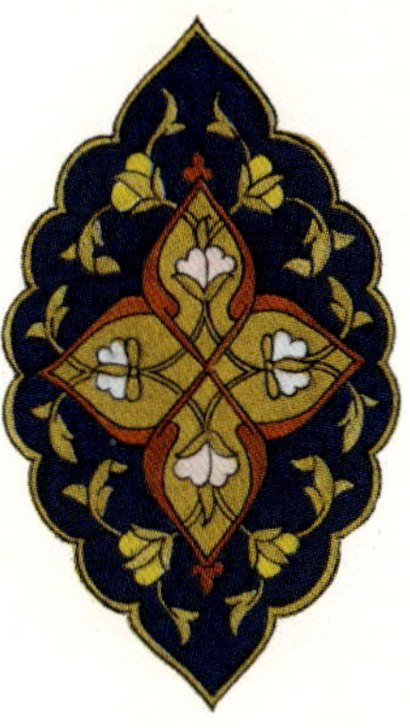

Figure 5e

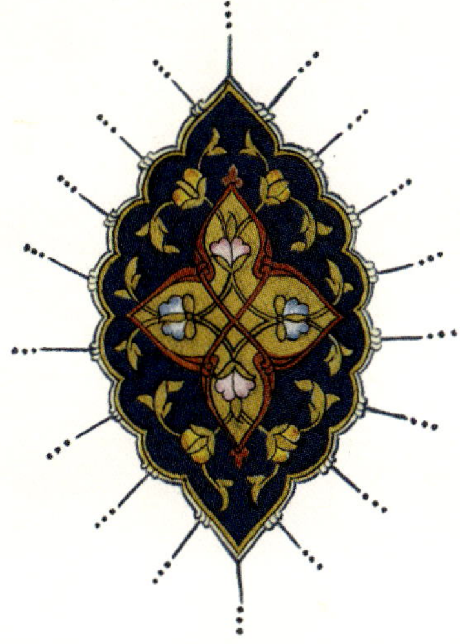

Figure 5f

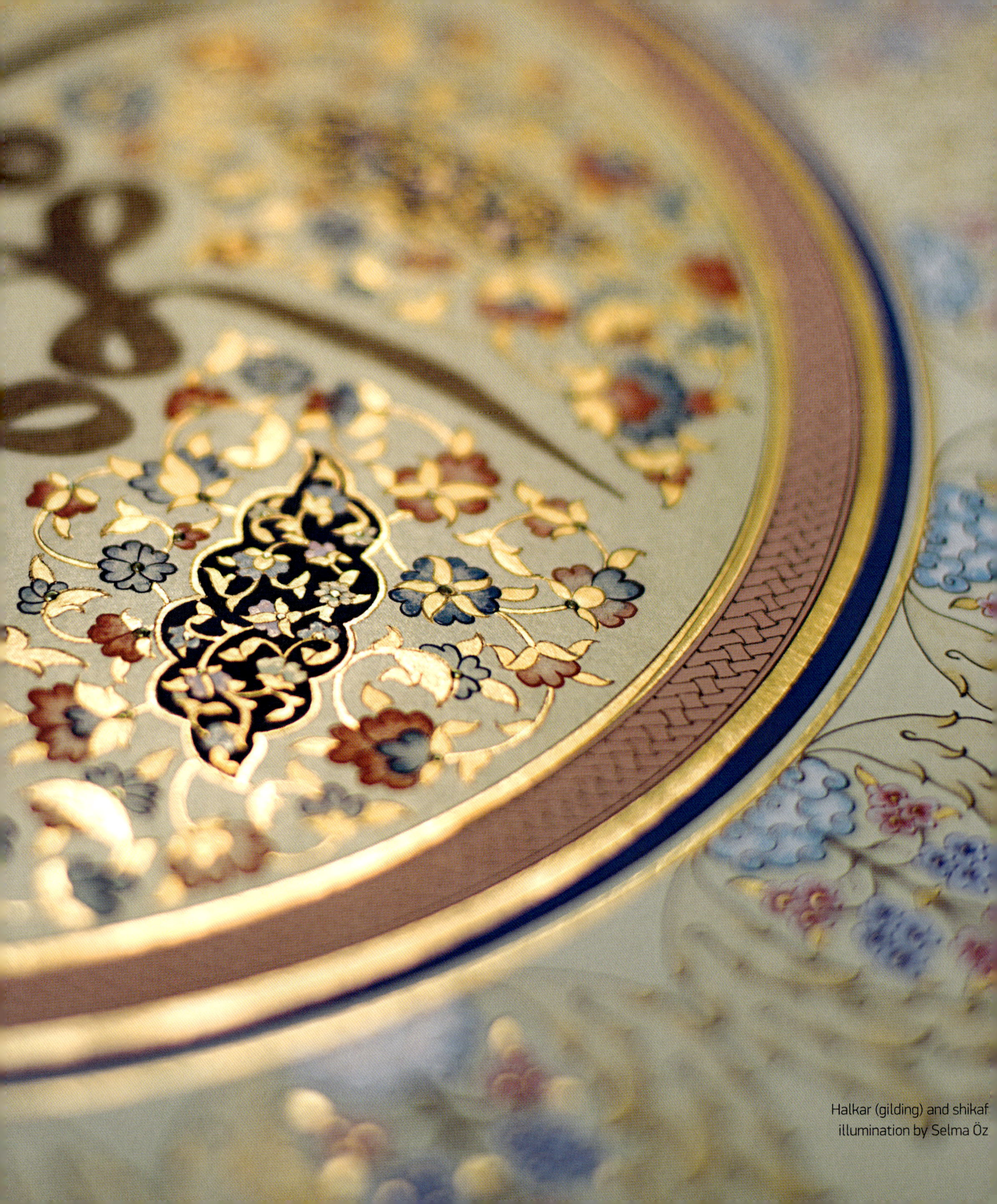

Halkar (gilding) and shikaf illumination by Selma Öz

Part Three

Motifs and Figures Used in Illumination

A. Leaves

They are the indispensable elements of nature and an indelible part of the *khatai* style. When we examine nature, we see that every tree has different leaves, curves, and stances. Stylized leaves made from recalling nature are the most important motifs that enrich the *khatai* style of ornamentation. While the composition design is being formed, leaves have a very important function in this style. We see their variety and detailed shapes in *halkar* and *Sazyolu* designs. Just as leaves can be drawn to stand alone, they can also be drawn in segments, serrated, or with ridges (Figure 6).

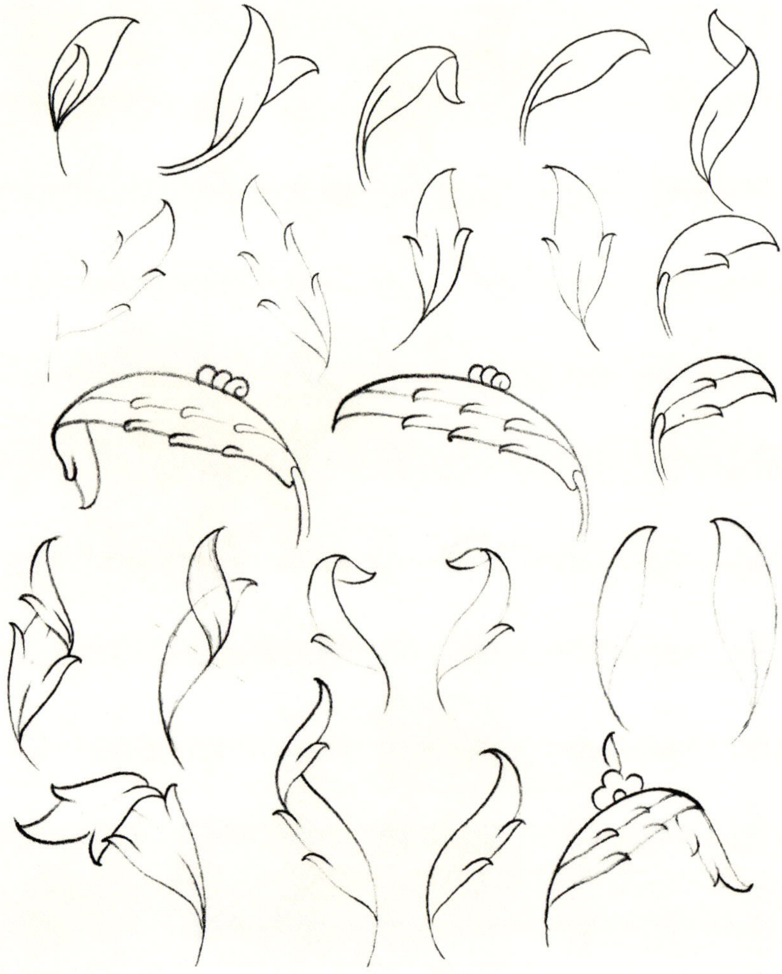

Figure 6 - Stylized leaf drawings

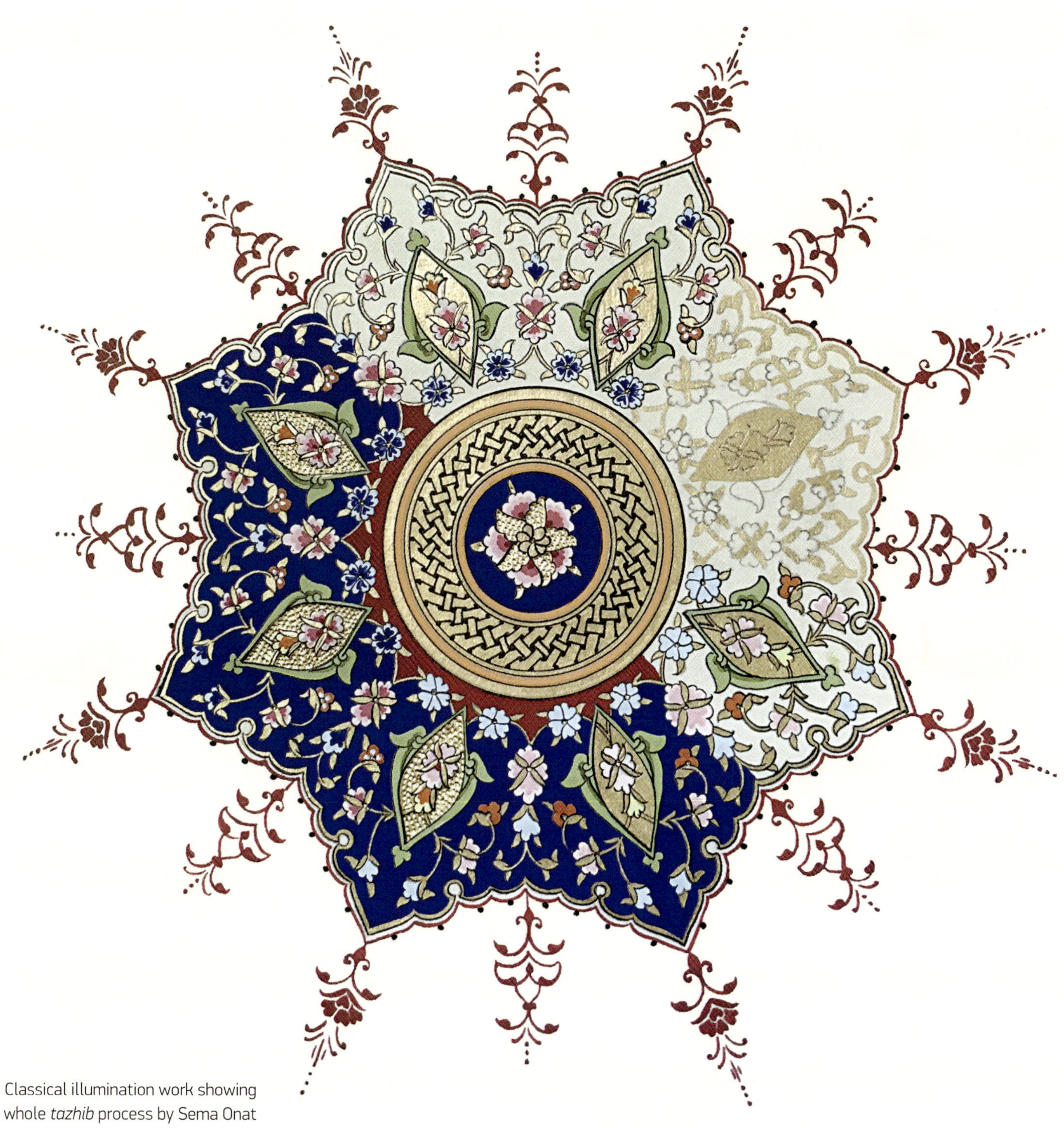

Classical illumination work showing
the whole *tazhib* process by Sema Onat

B. Stems

They provide connections between flowers. Branches have important and complementary duties in determining directions and in drawing the composition. When branches or stems do not come together, flowers and *khatai*s remain independent of one another and hang in the air. This is not compatible with the rules. Each flower has a beginning place and spreads together with branches in a shape compatible with the "S" rule (Figure 7).

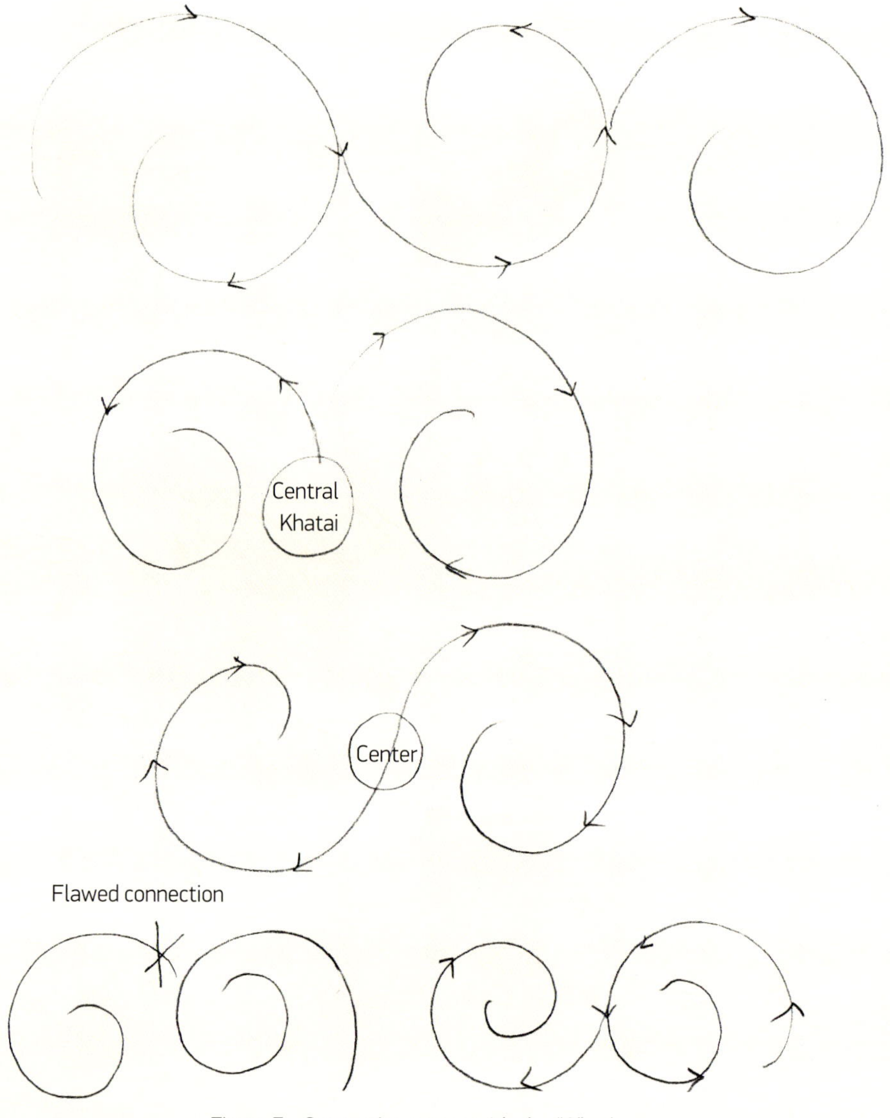

Figure 7 - Connecting stems with the "S" rule

C. Gonca (Bud)

Having a place in the *khatai* style together with the *khatai* flower and the *panch*, it is a style of ornamentation that takes on a more auxiliary motif role in the composition. The *gonca* flower resembles an unopened bud. It is used more for giving direction. In comparison to the other *khatai* group, *gonca* flowers have less detail and are smaller (Figure 8).

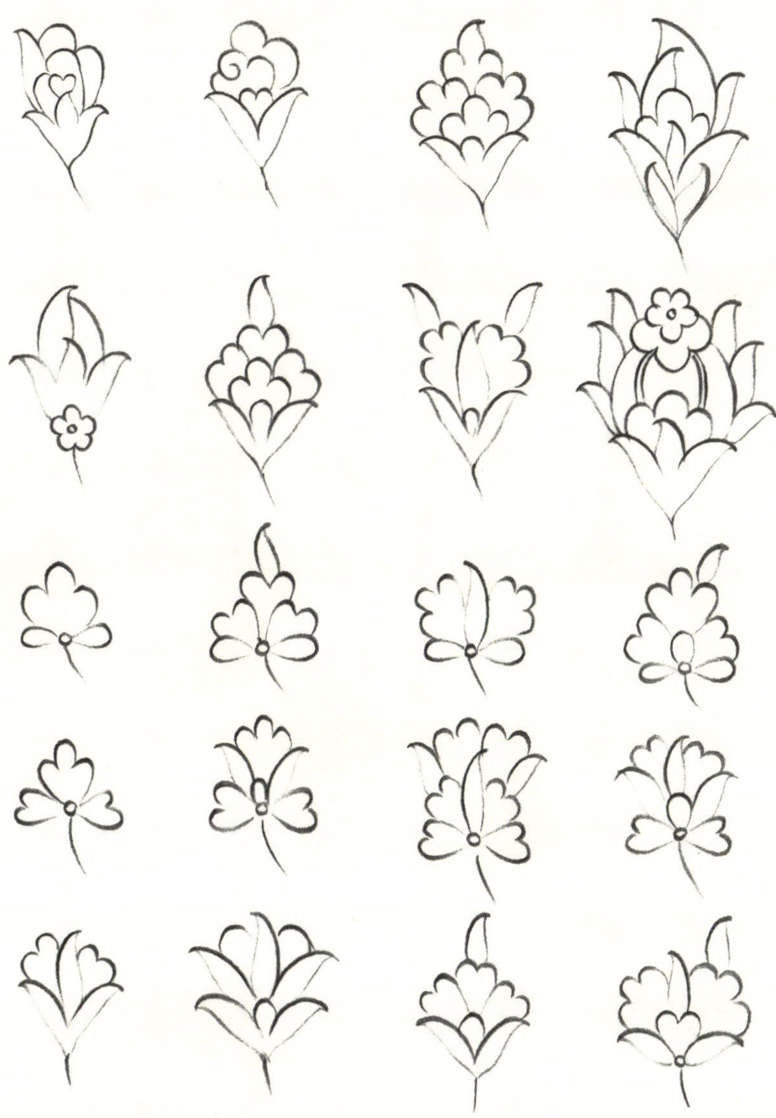

Figure 8 - Stylized buds used for giving direction in the design

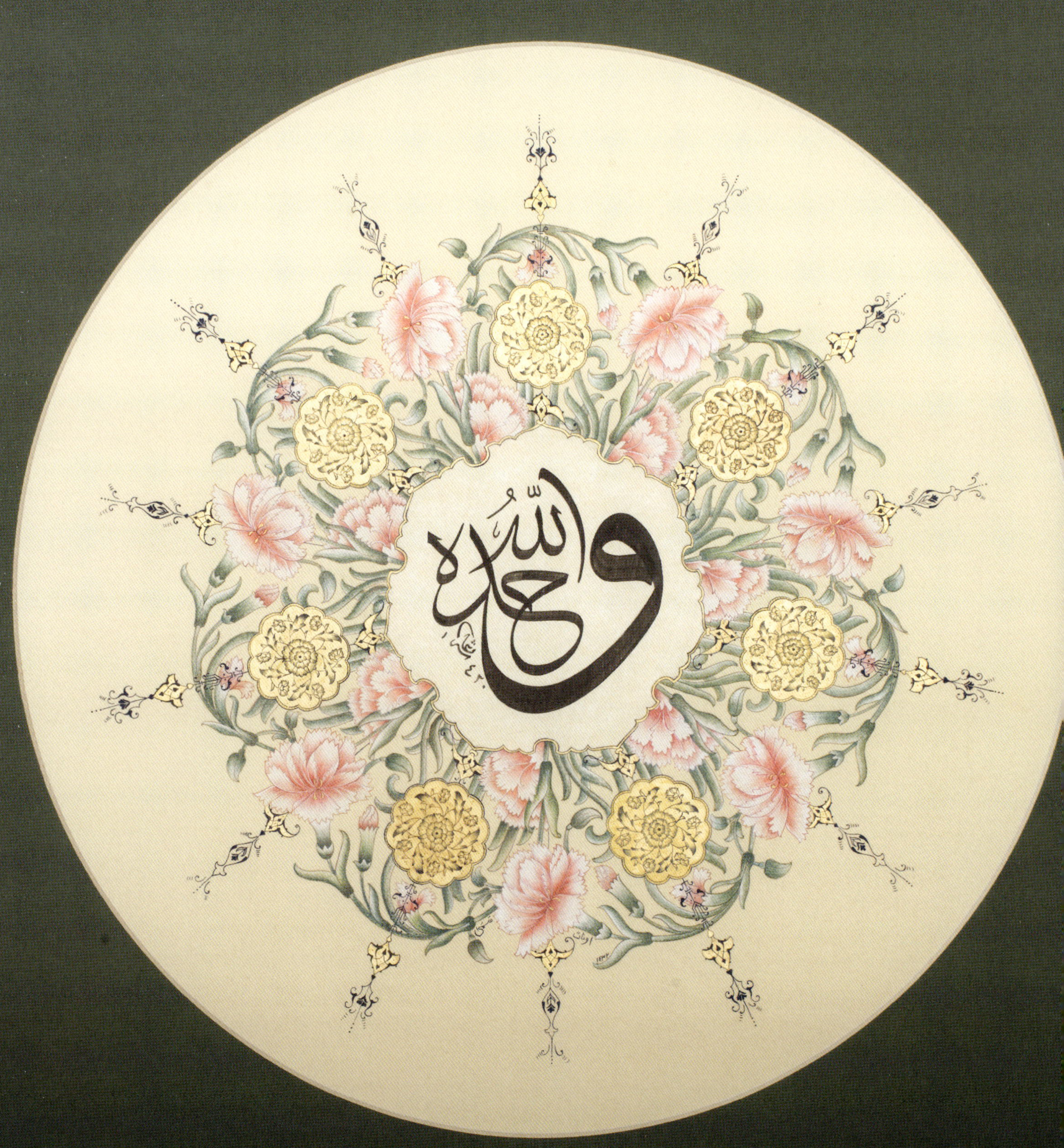

D. Khatai (Floral Motif)

It is one of the main motifs used in the ornamental arts. It is derived from the stylization of flowers found in nature. The original shape of *khatai* flowers is not fully known. Because it was constantly enriched by being given different interpretations by artists, there are many kinds of *khatai* motifs. *Khatai* flowers are generally symmetric, taking the vertical section of a segment of the flower as a basis. They are used to determine direction in a design. These are called directional *khatai*s (Figure 9).

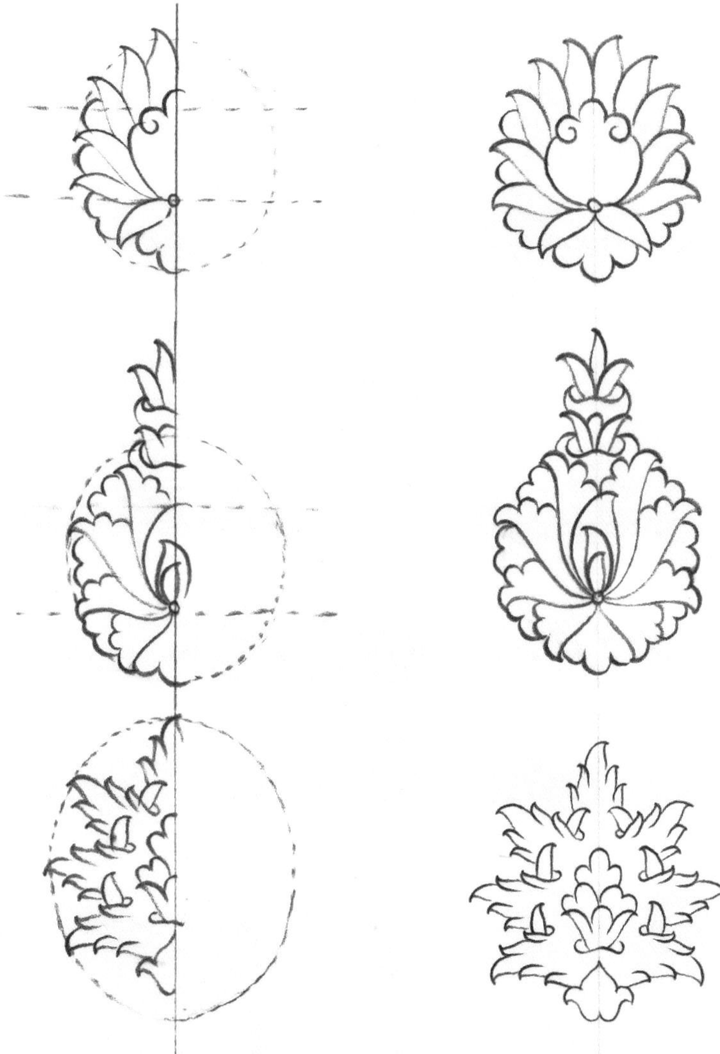

arnation illumination, ornate with
lded medallions by Sema Onat

Figure 9 - Khatai floral drawings

E. Panch (Foliation with Five Cusps or Points)

Another motif used in ornamental art is the *panch*. In Persian, the word *panch* means "five." *Panch* leaves are named according to their segments. A single layered *panch* is called "yabark," two-layered segments "dubark," three-layered segments "sabark," four-layered segments "jiharbark," five-layered segments "panchbark," six-layered segments "shashbark," and shapes made from intertwined leaves are called "sadbark" (Figure 10).

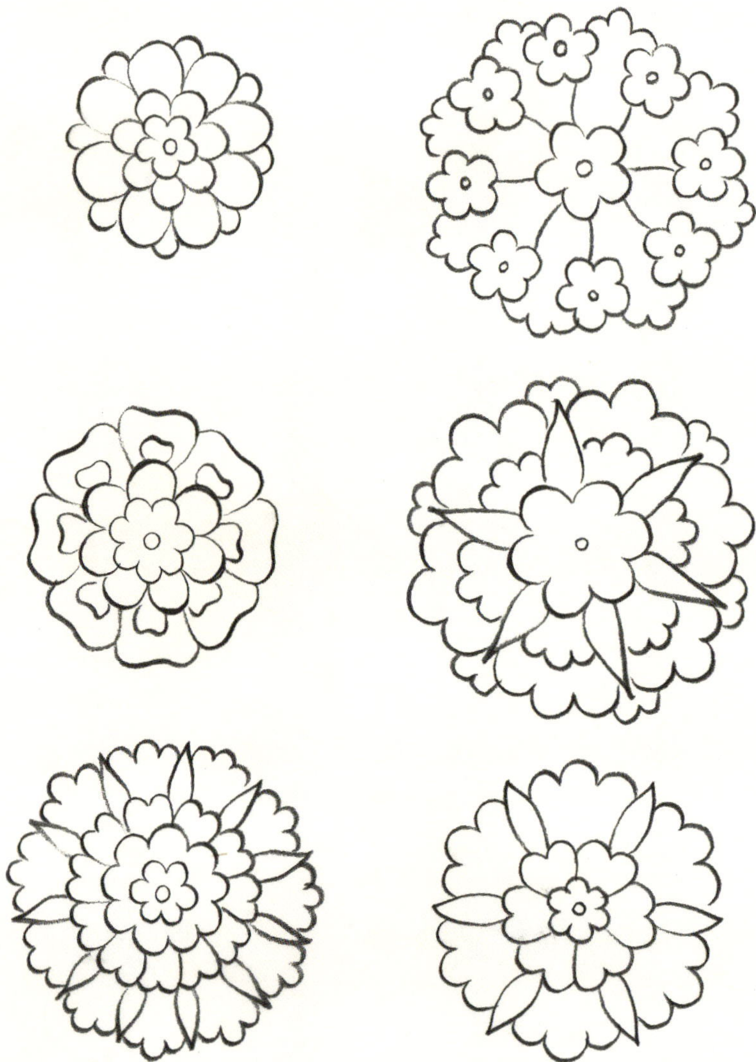

Figure 10 - Layered panch drawings

It is the aerial view of a flower in a circular form or a segment drawn width-wise. It is the stylized drawing of flowers appearing like daisies and chrysanthemums. Besides determining direction with *panch, khatai,* and *gonca* flowers, they can be used in the center and everyplace else for the beginning of a design. Because *panch* motifs are begun by appointing the center, they are often called central *khatai* flowers.

F. Spirals

These are patterns made on a basis of "S" spirals while forming a composition. The spirals are completed with leaves by placing *khatai*s and *panch*s on the design and stems. The most important thing with spirals is that the branches turn in a fully round shape. The spaces between the spirals must be proportional (Figure 11).

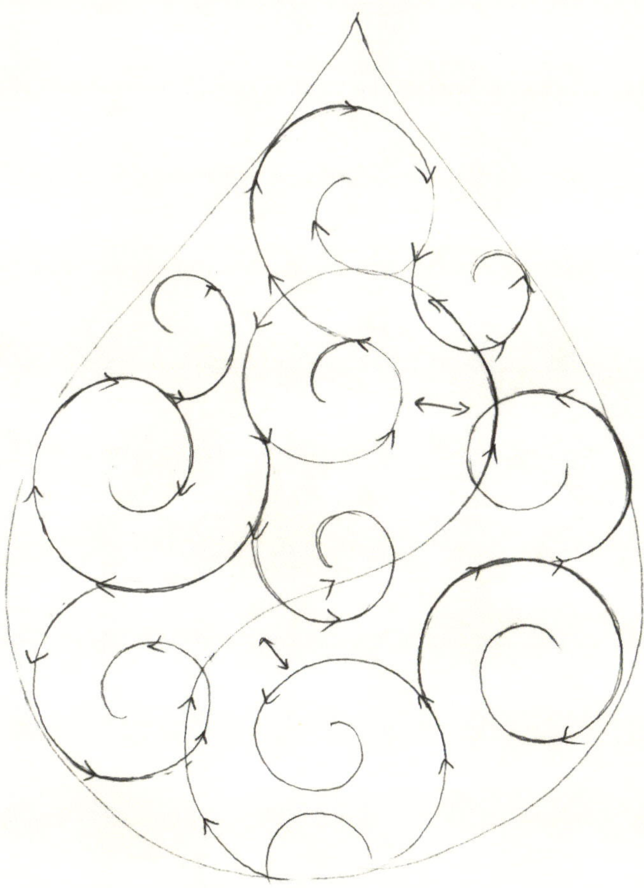

Figure 11 - Forming a design with "S" spirals

G. Bulut (Cloud) Motifs

The cloud motif has a distinct place and importance among other motifs in the ornamental arts. As obvious from its name, the cloud motif is drawn in a stylized way by imagining the position and movements of clouds in the sky. There are many kinds of clouds seen in the art of illumination. Due to the constant changes in shape of clouds in nature, different forms of the cloud motif appeared (Figure 12).

The names of clouds differ according to the shapes they are drawn in:

Free Clouds: These are drawn independent in a composition.

Aggregate Clouds: While they are drawn as heavy, aggregate clouds in certain places within the movement of free clouds, they can also be put at the beginning of a motif in a design. Compositions beginning with a cloud motif are usually comprised of aggregate

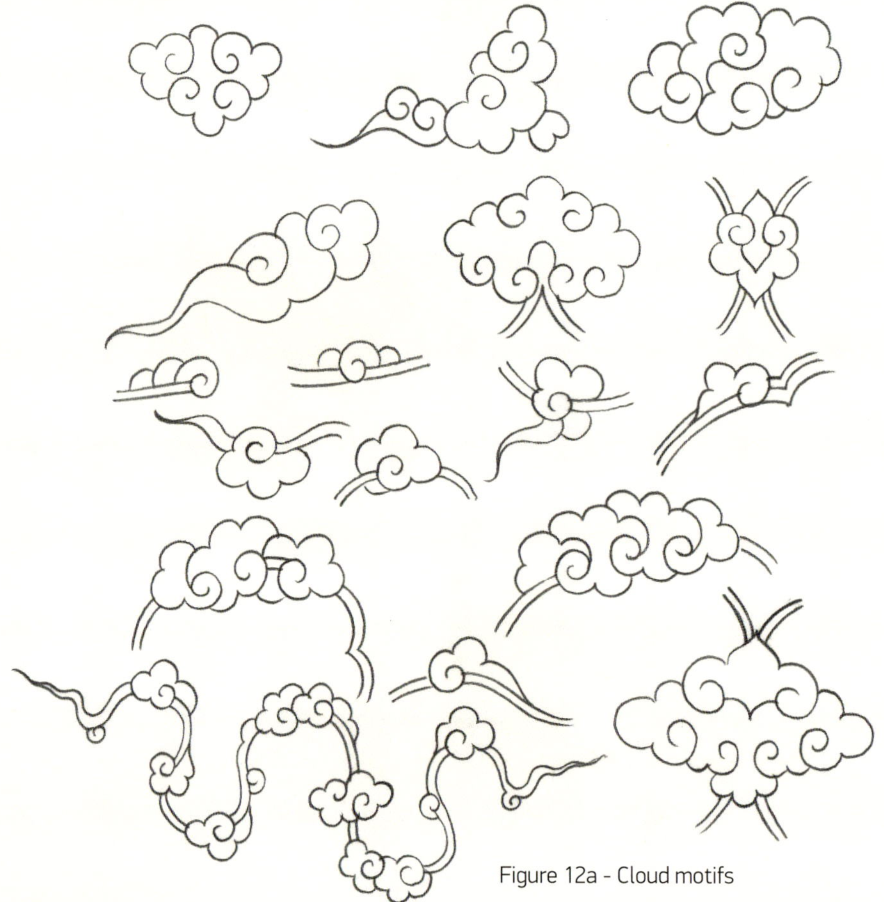

Figure 12a - Cloud motifs

clouds. In a design separated into sections, aggregate clouds are drawn in merging places, thus giving the design a harmonious and complementary state. In order to give motion to the cloud, sharp extensions are drawn on the edges.

Clouds According to the Position in the Composition:

Point Clouds: They are drawn like aggregate clouds. They are applied to the points of departure of branches in the motifs.

Separation Clouds: They are used to create diversity on the background in the design stage, just like in pictures.

Crest Clouds: They indicate the end of the designs. They are used in the circumscription of the composition.

Small Clouds: They are used to give detail to the inside of motifs in large designs or plant forms.

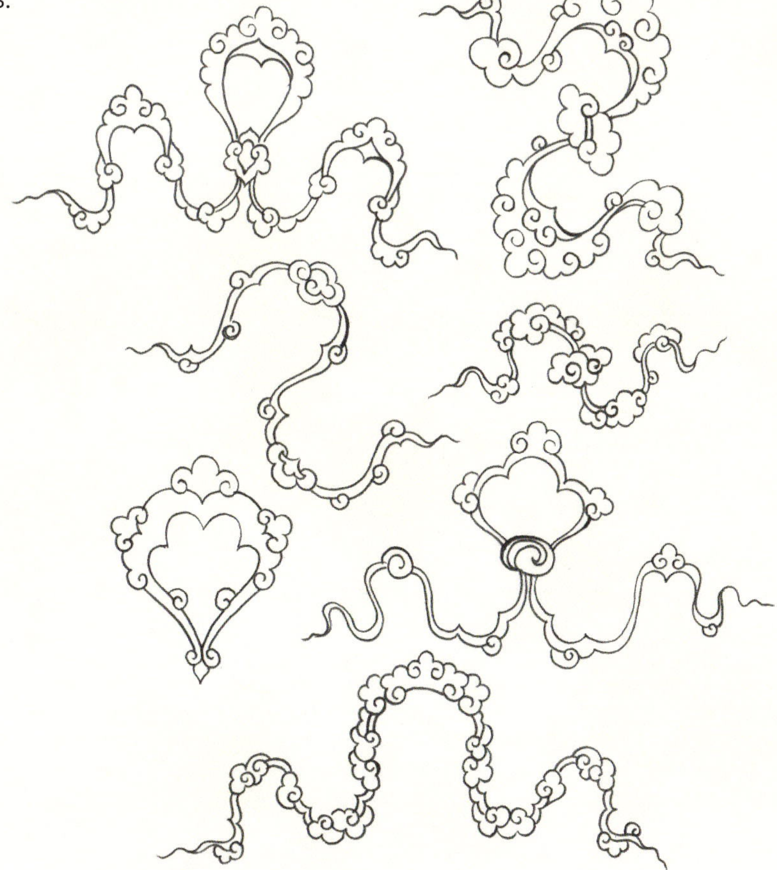

Figure 12b - Various cloud motif compositions

H. Rumi

Coming originally from Central Asia and further developed by the Anatolian Seljuks, *Rumi* is an ornamental motif that came about by stylization of the wings, legs, and trunks of animals. Beginning with a very plain state, the *Rumi* motif has undergone serious changes and developments and there are many *Rumi* varieties. It is placed on spiral branches in a form resembling an almond half. For the continuation of the composition of *Rumi*s placed on spirals, wing branches are made. This comprises the most varied designs in periods when the *Rumi* form was used (Figure 13).

Rumi motifs are separated into the following divisions:

1. Plain Rumi
2. Small Rumi
3. Segmented Rumi
4. Twisted Rumi
5. Middle Tie Motif
6. Crests

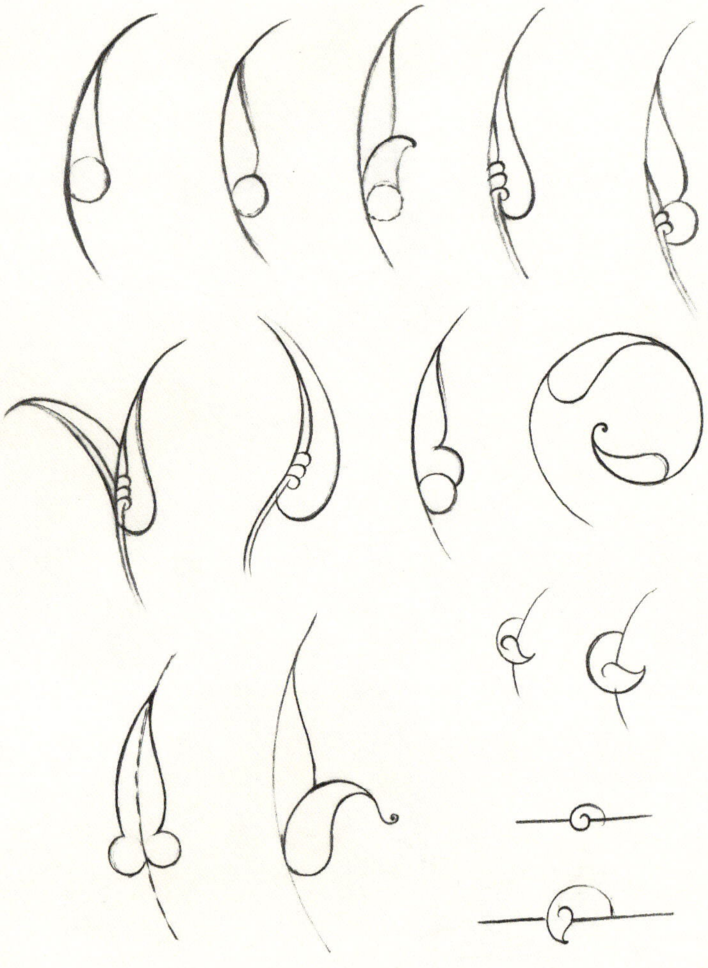

Figure 13 - Rumi motifs

Plain Rumi: As its name indicates, its forms are plain, simple, and without detail. While making the sections in the design, plain Rumis are used to separate the background. When the closed forms comprising Rumi designs are painted different colors, beautiful designs appear (Figure 14).

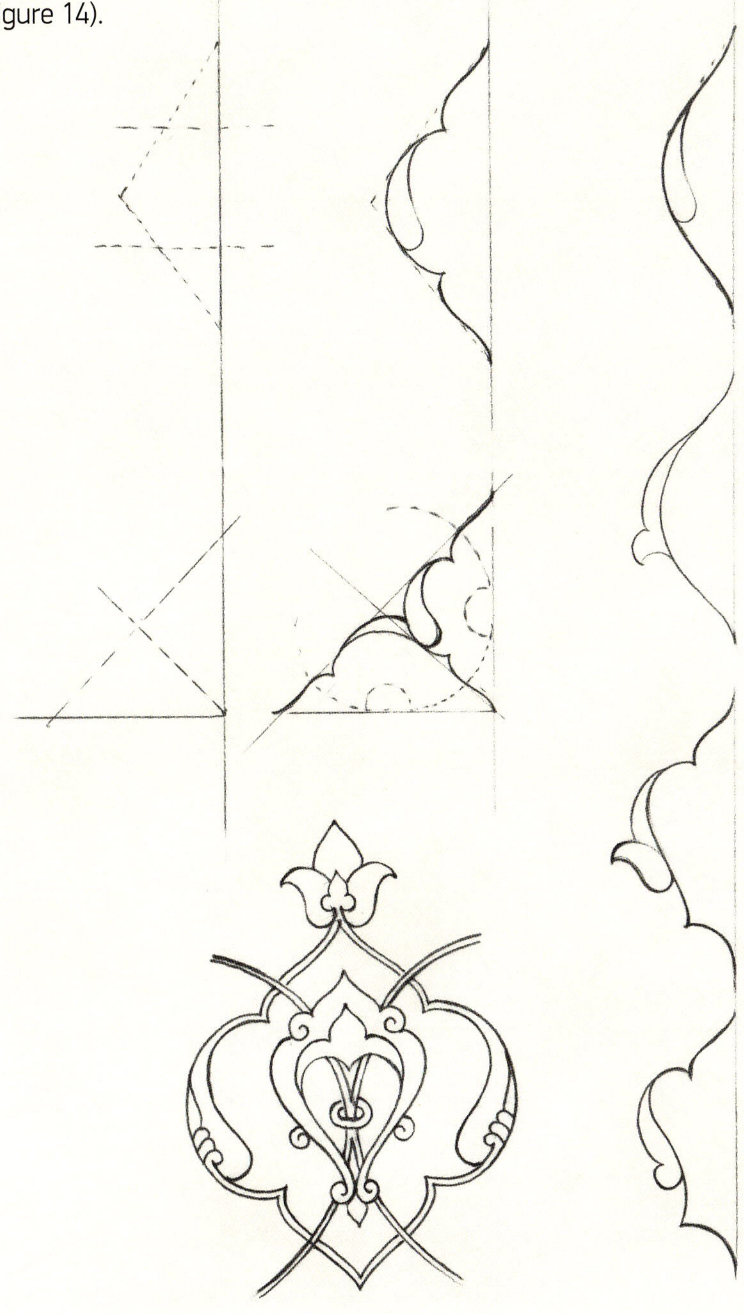

Figure 14 - Drawing a plain Rumi design

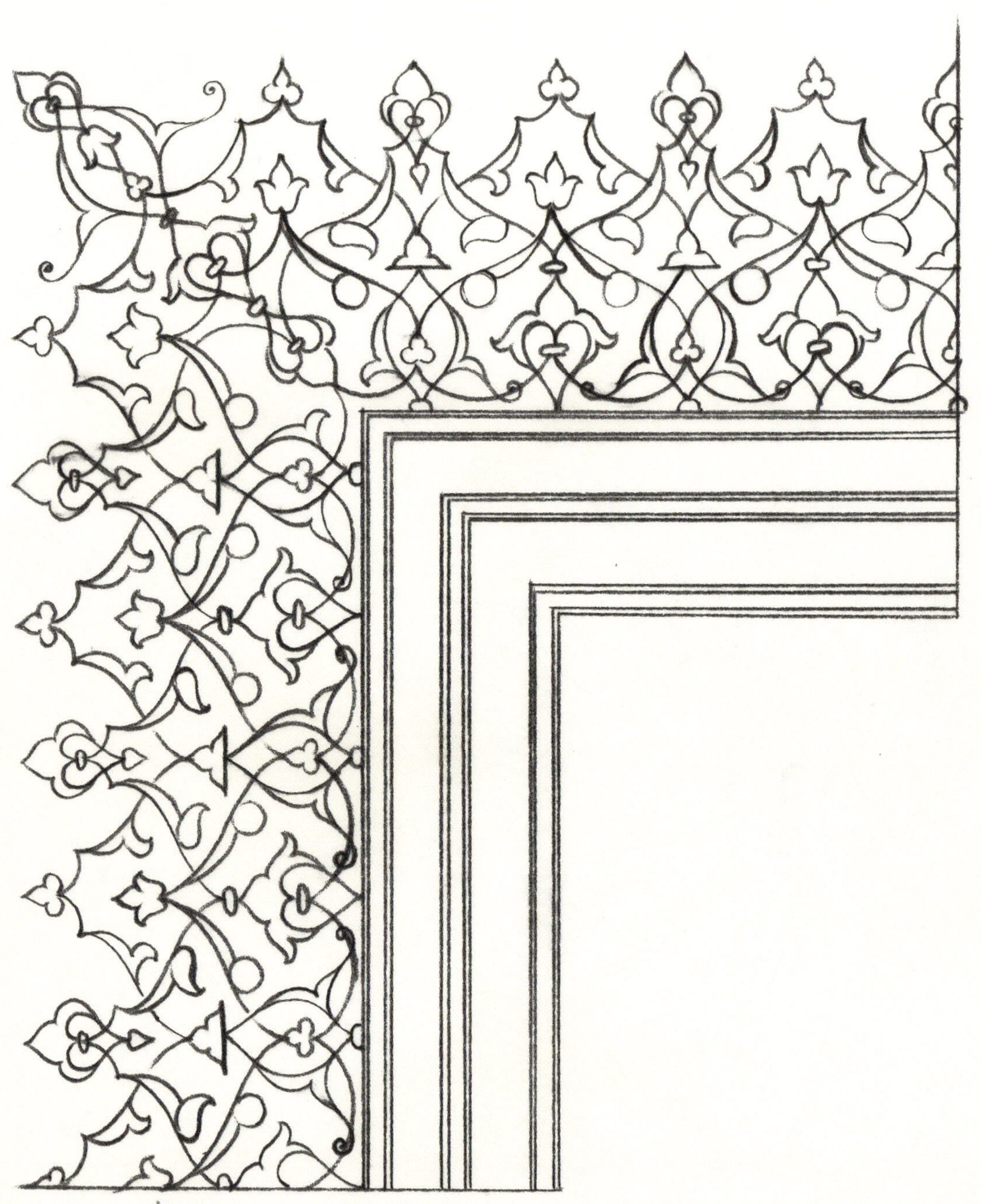

Figure 15 - Plain Rumi design

Illuminated plain Rumi design enci
with tigh work by Sema

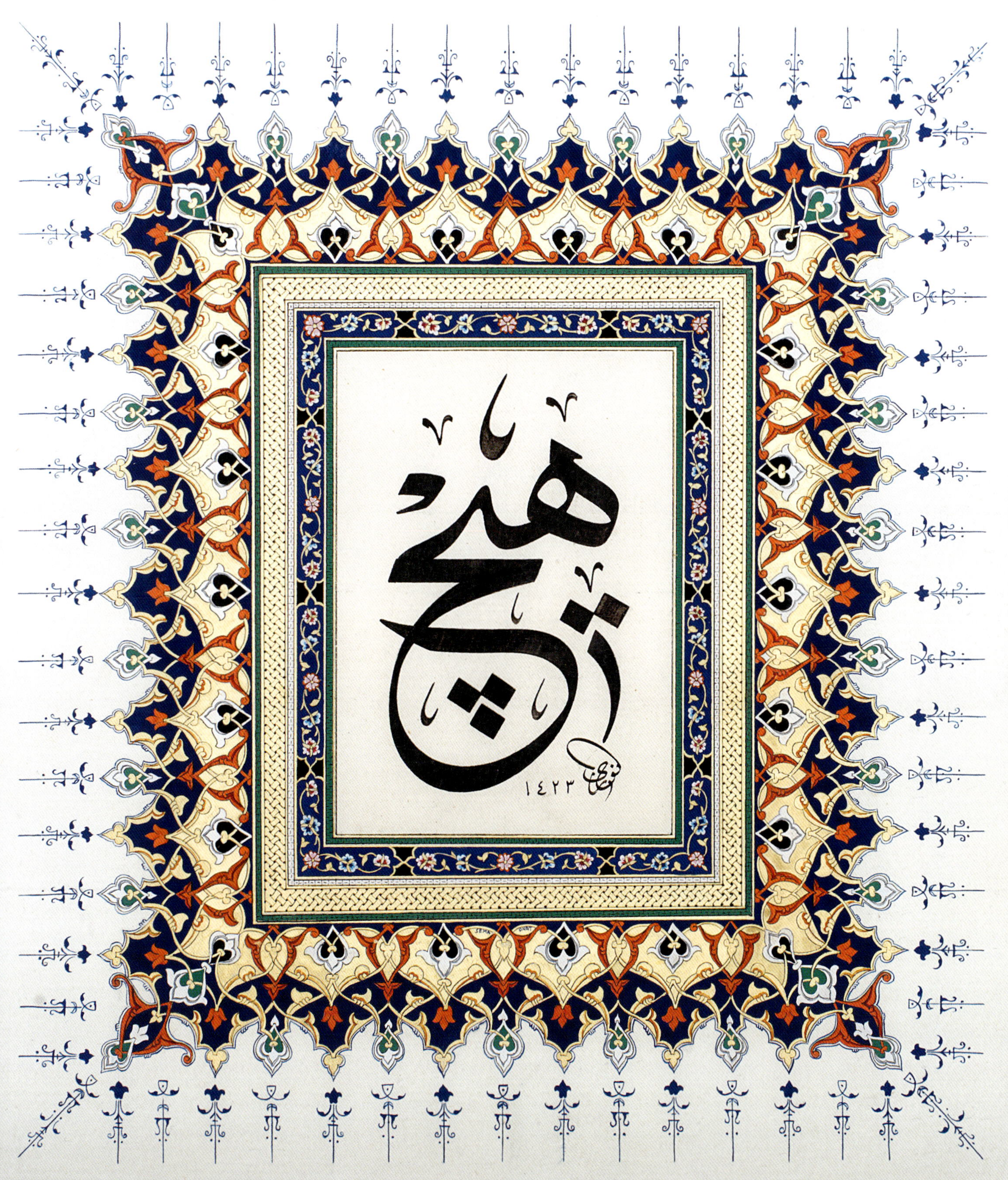
١٤٢٣

Small Rumi: This is the drawing of large Rumis in the design concept and filling in their inner spaces with tiny and varied Rumi motifs. Rumis to be put into the larger form are spread and drawn in a balanced way in conformity with the rules (Figure 16).

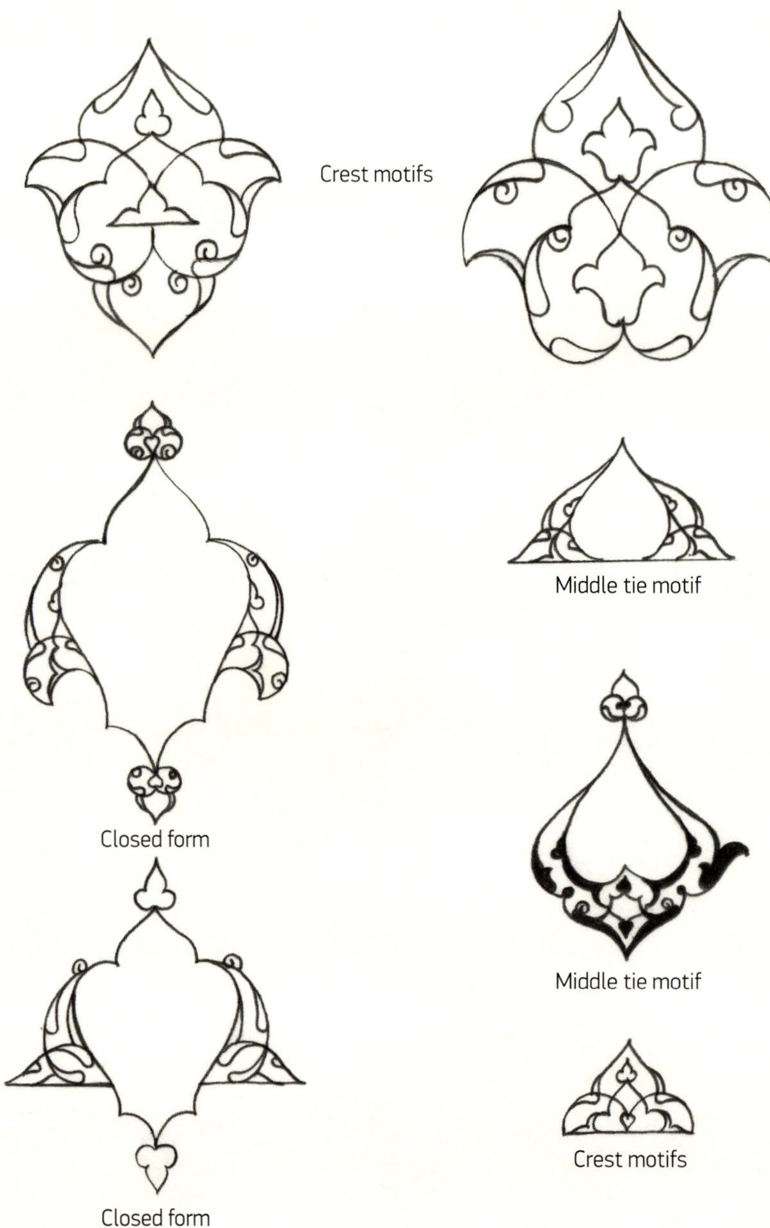

Figure 16 - Crest and middle tie motifs

Detail from an illumination work with cre[s]
and middle tie motifs by Sema O[r]

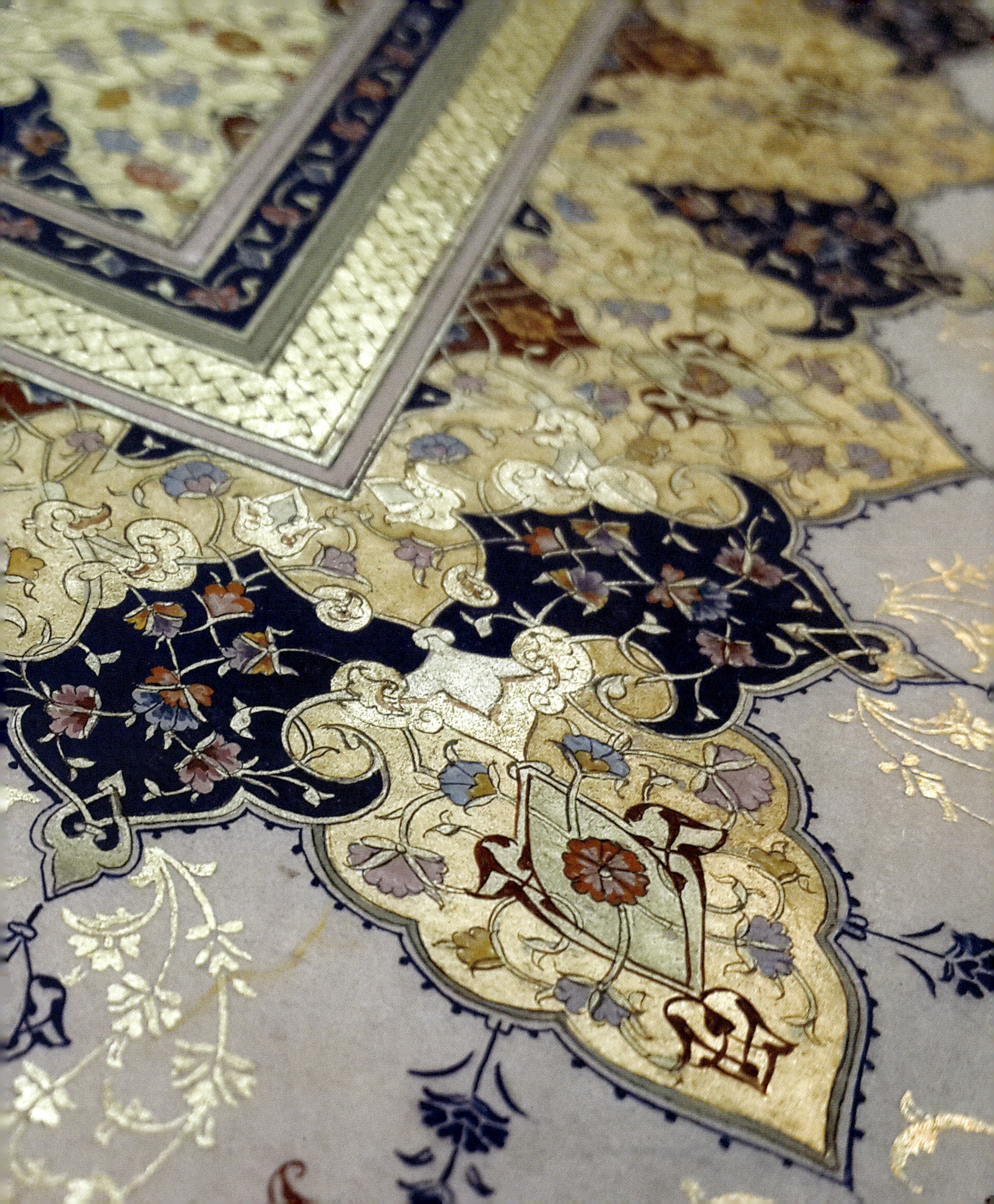

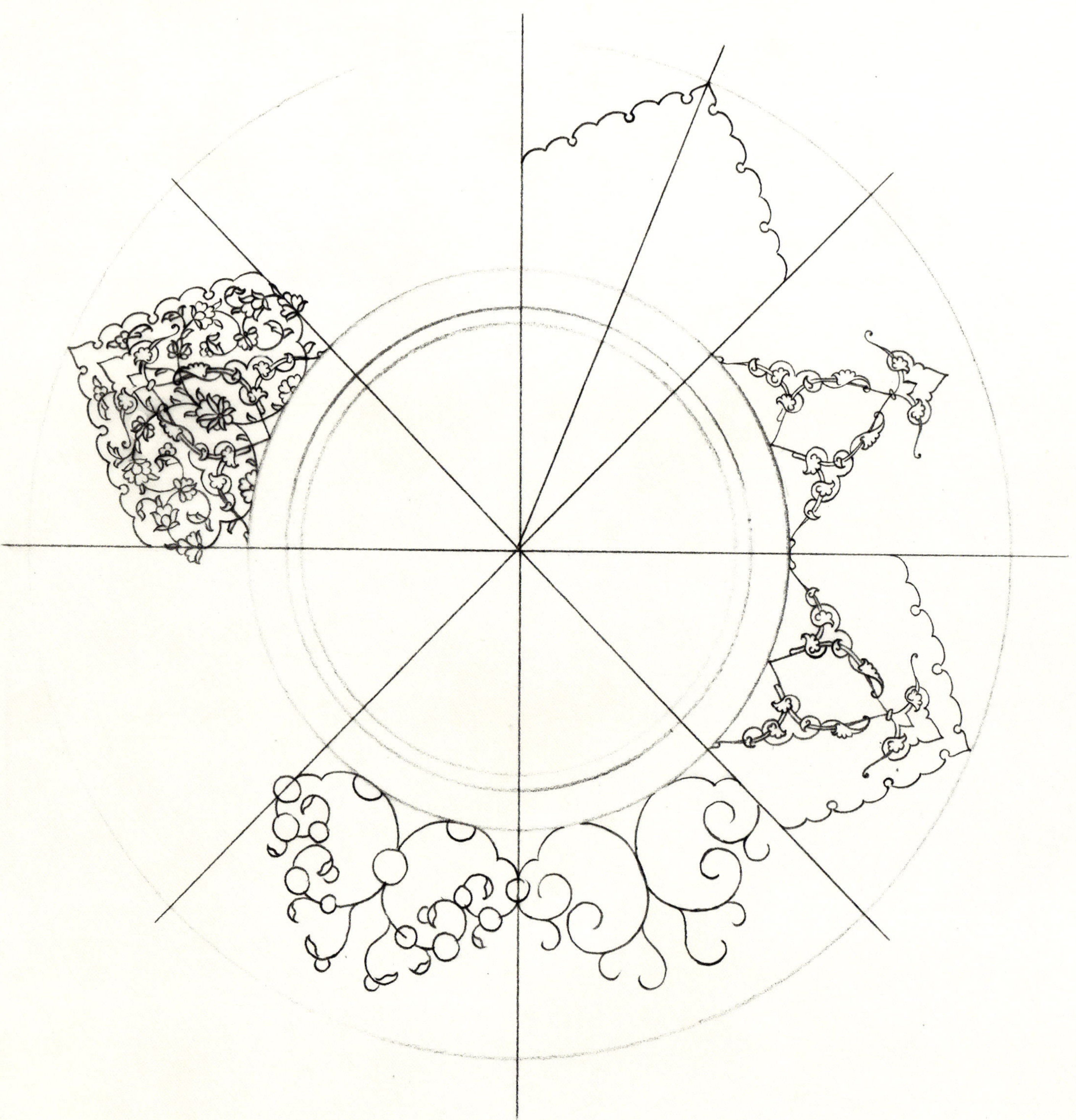

Figure 17 - One-eighth repeating Rumi-Khatai design in circular form

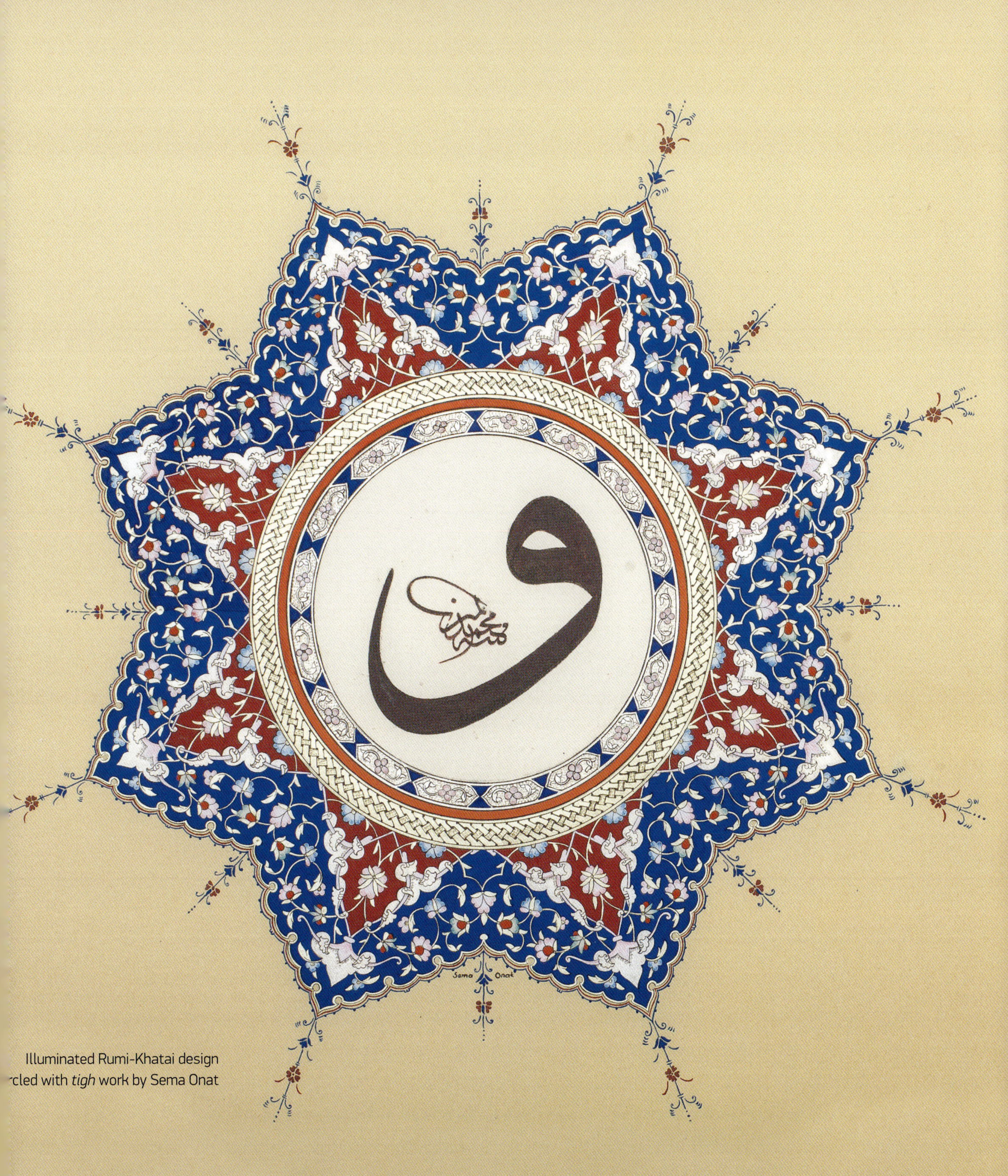

Illuminated Rumi-Khatai design
rcled with *tigh* work by Sema Onat

Segmented Rumi: With the detailing of Rumi motif outer forms, more refined and elegant designs appear. There are very beautiful examples of segmented Rumis which take different forms according to the places where they are used in the design concept (Figure 18).

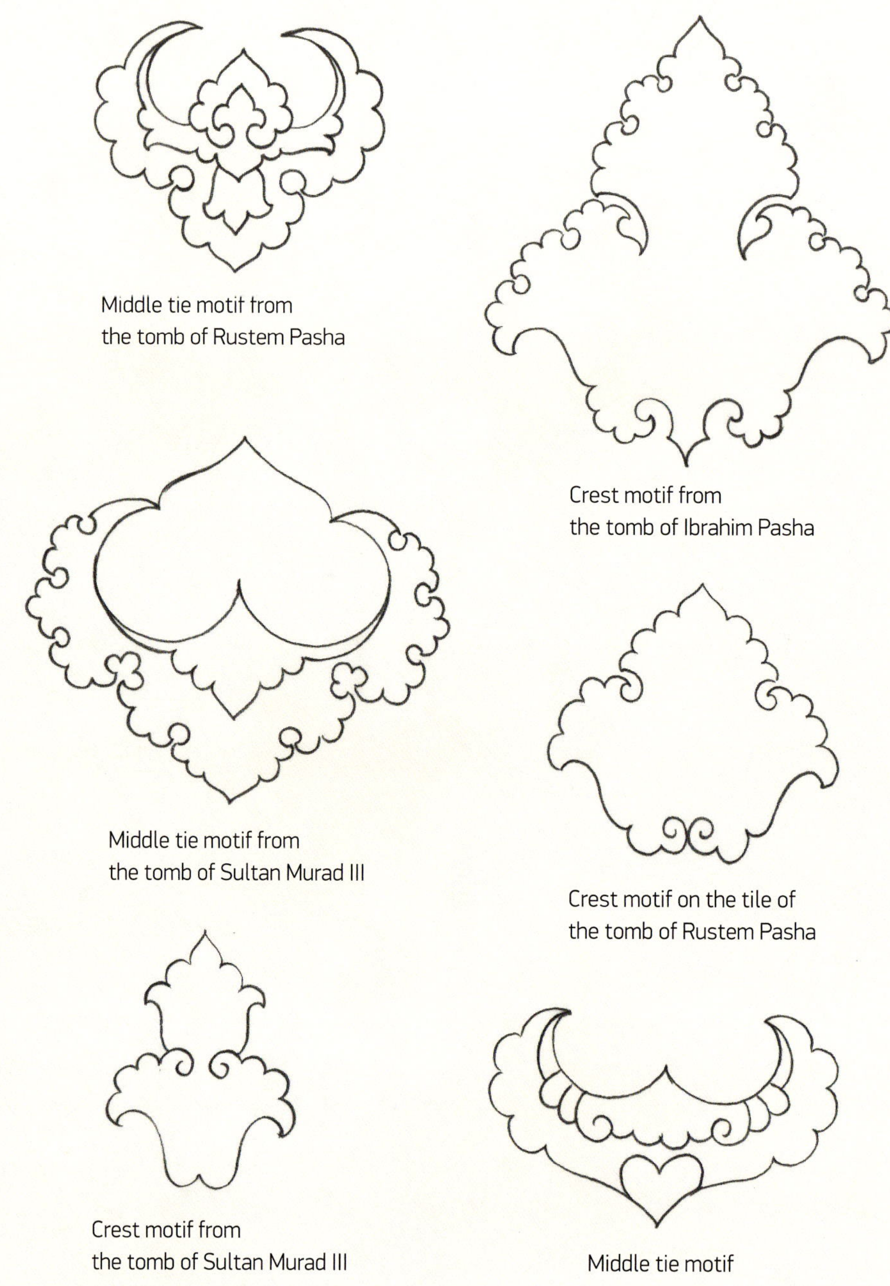

Figure 18 - Crests and middle tie motifs used in segmented Rumis

Twisted Rumi: Very rich varieties have been formed with the tiny twists made from the main Rumi form. All Rumis are used in places compatible with their own form in the design to be used (Figure 19).

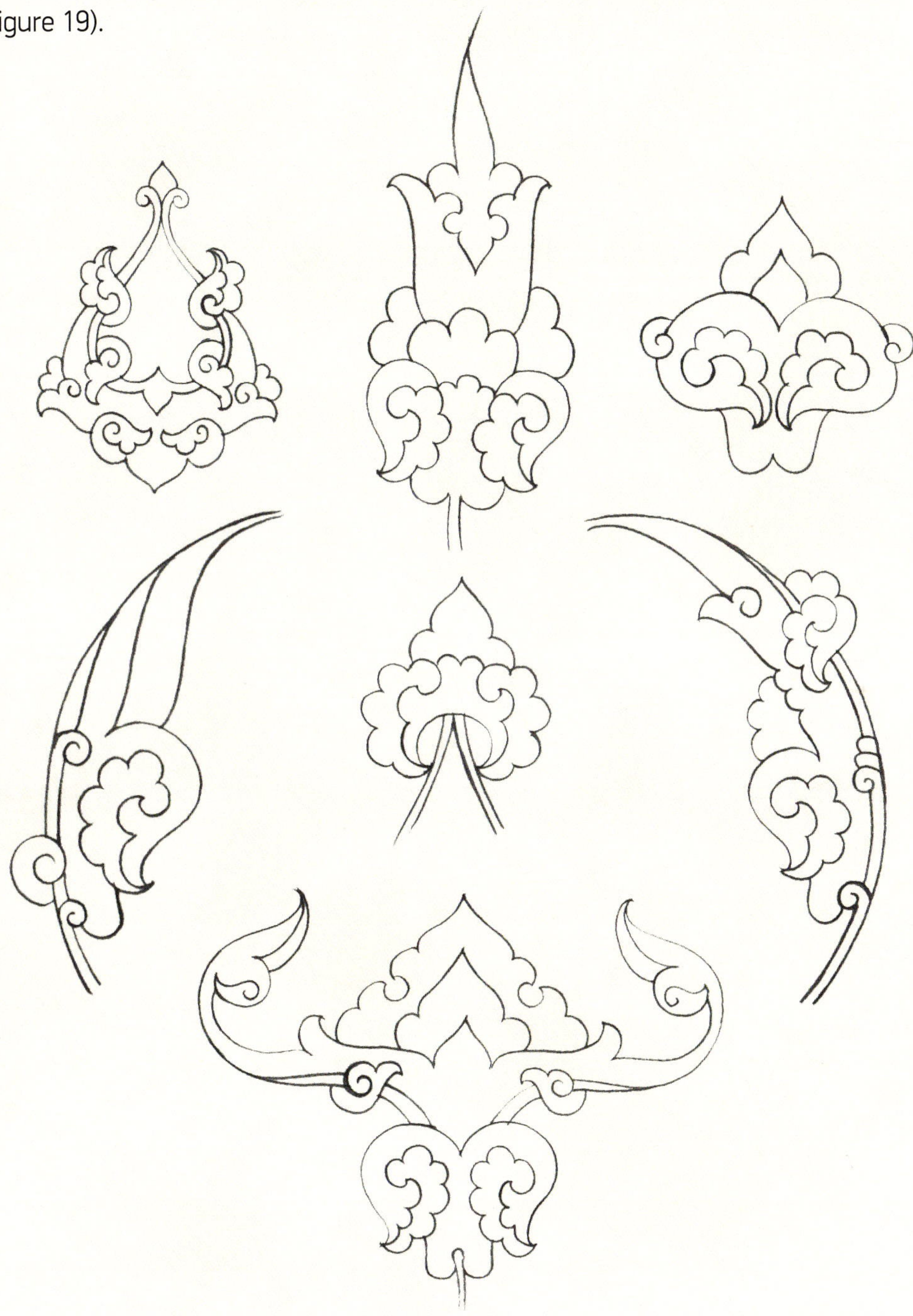

Figure 19 - Twisted Rumi motifs

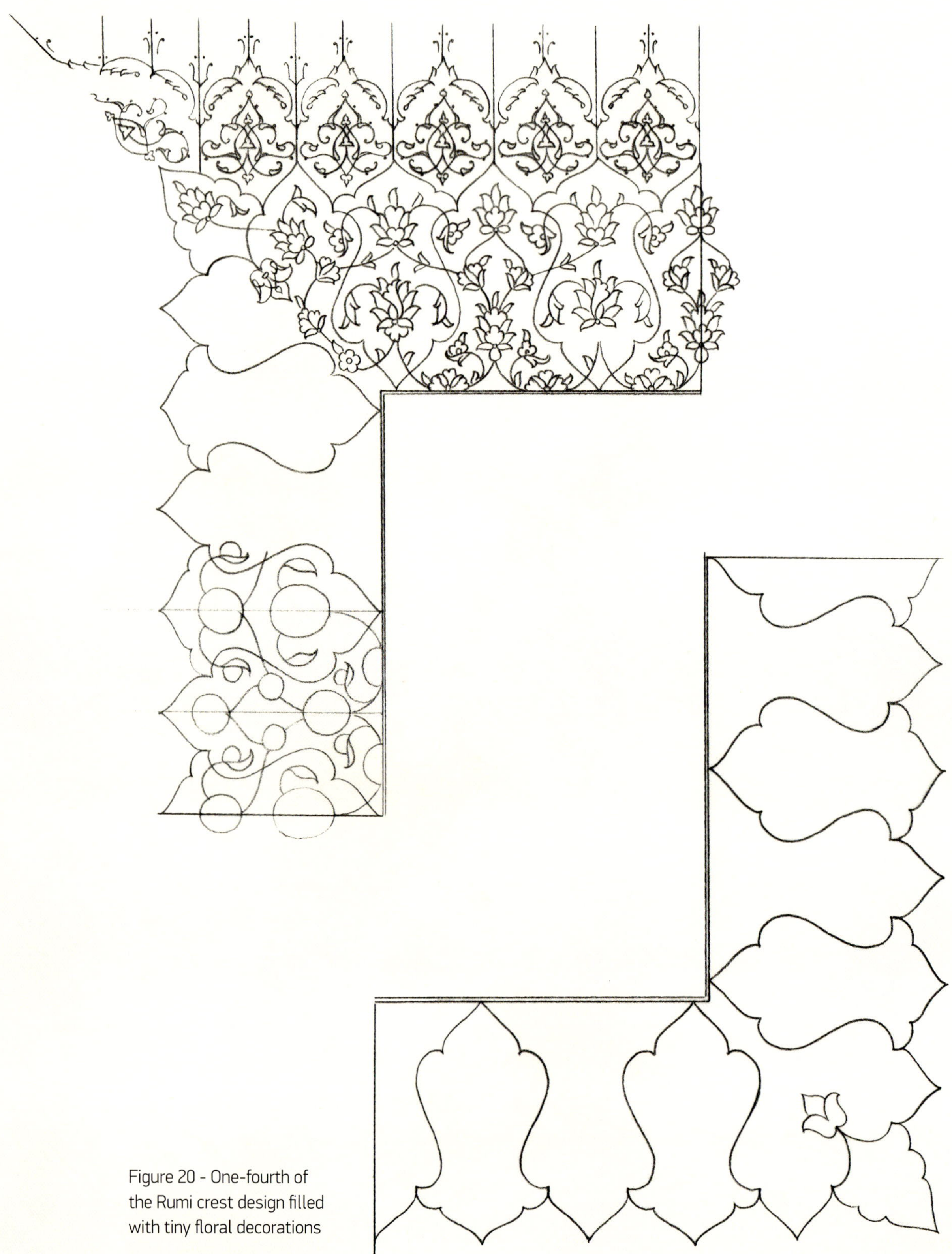

Figure 20 - One-fourth of the Rumi crest design filled with tiny floral decorations

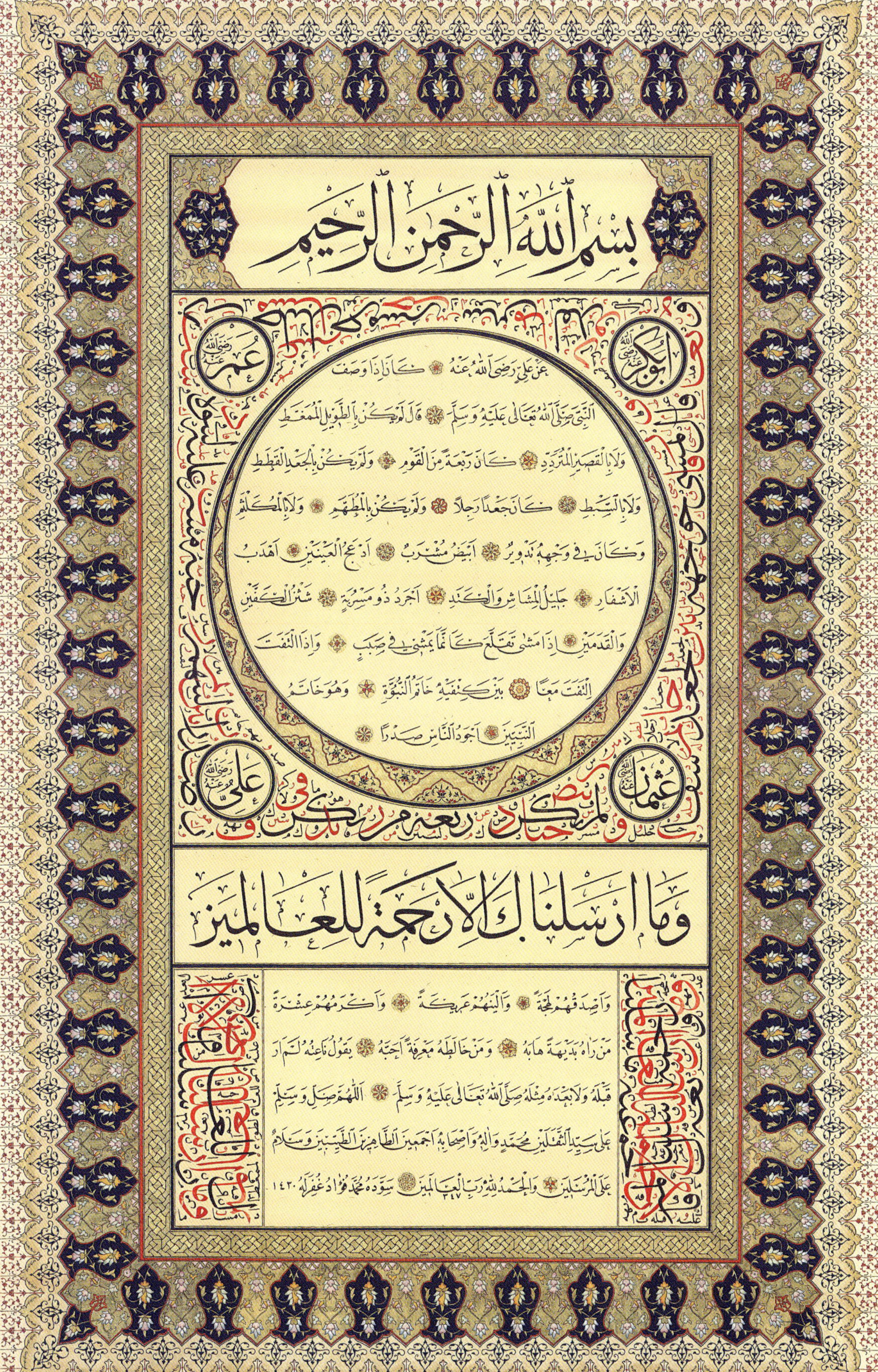

uminated Hilya
ith Rumi crests
by Sema Onat

Middle Tie Motif: Rumi is used as an indispensable tie in compositions. It is also called as an *ağraf* or *bağlaç* in Turkish. In most designs, it serves as a beginning or root.

Crest Motif: It is the second indispensable motif in the Rumi composition. They are complementary elements in the Rumi designs formed (Figure 21).

Just as Rumis are used in many varied places in the design, they are also used in borders and chains. Examples of these have been given. Beautiful designs appear when Rumi compositions are enriched with *khatai* and cloud designs.

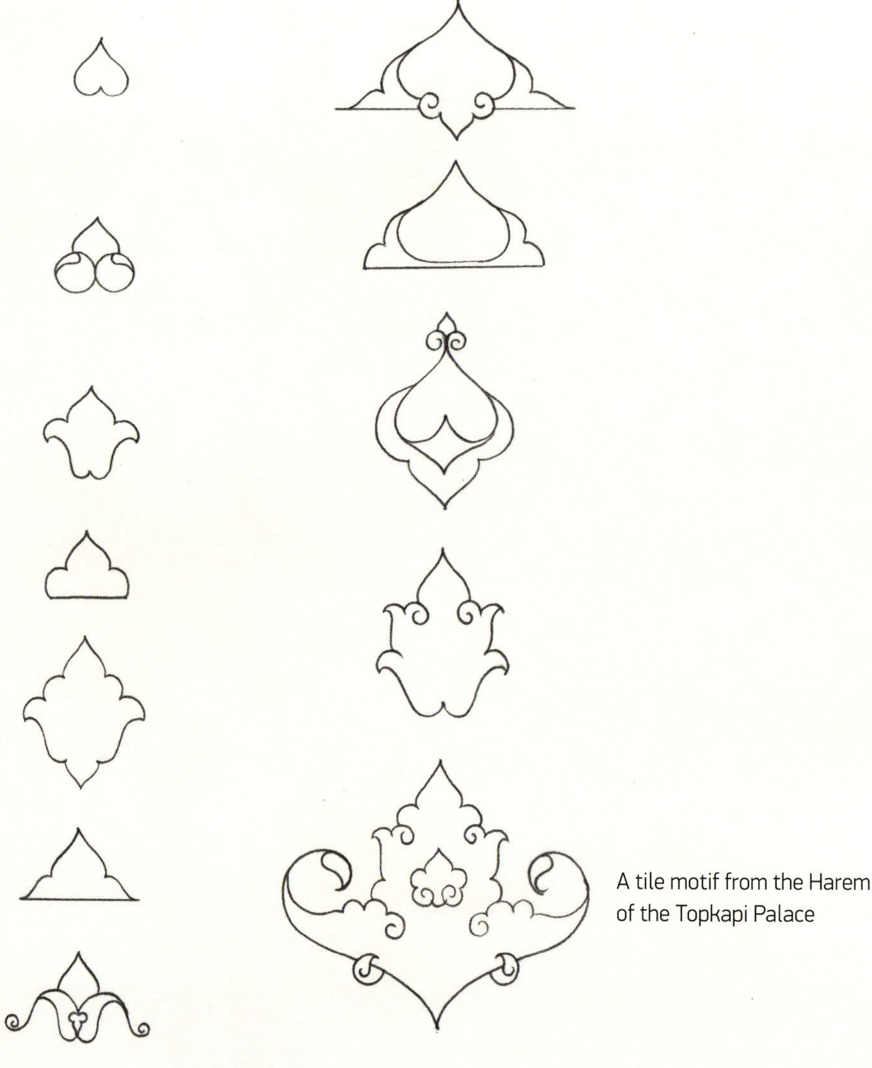

A tile motif from the Harem of the Topkapi Palace

Figure 21 - Various crests and middle tie motifs used in Rumi designs

I. Geometric Motifs

Holding an important place in Turkish ornamentation art, geometric motif examples are found especially in the Seljuk Era. Motifs resulting from combinations of geometric forms like the square, rectangle, triangle, circle, polygon, star, and diamond shape were used to represent infinity (Figures 22-23).

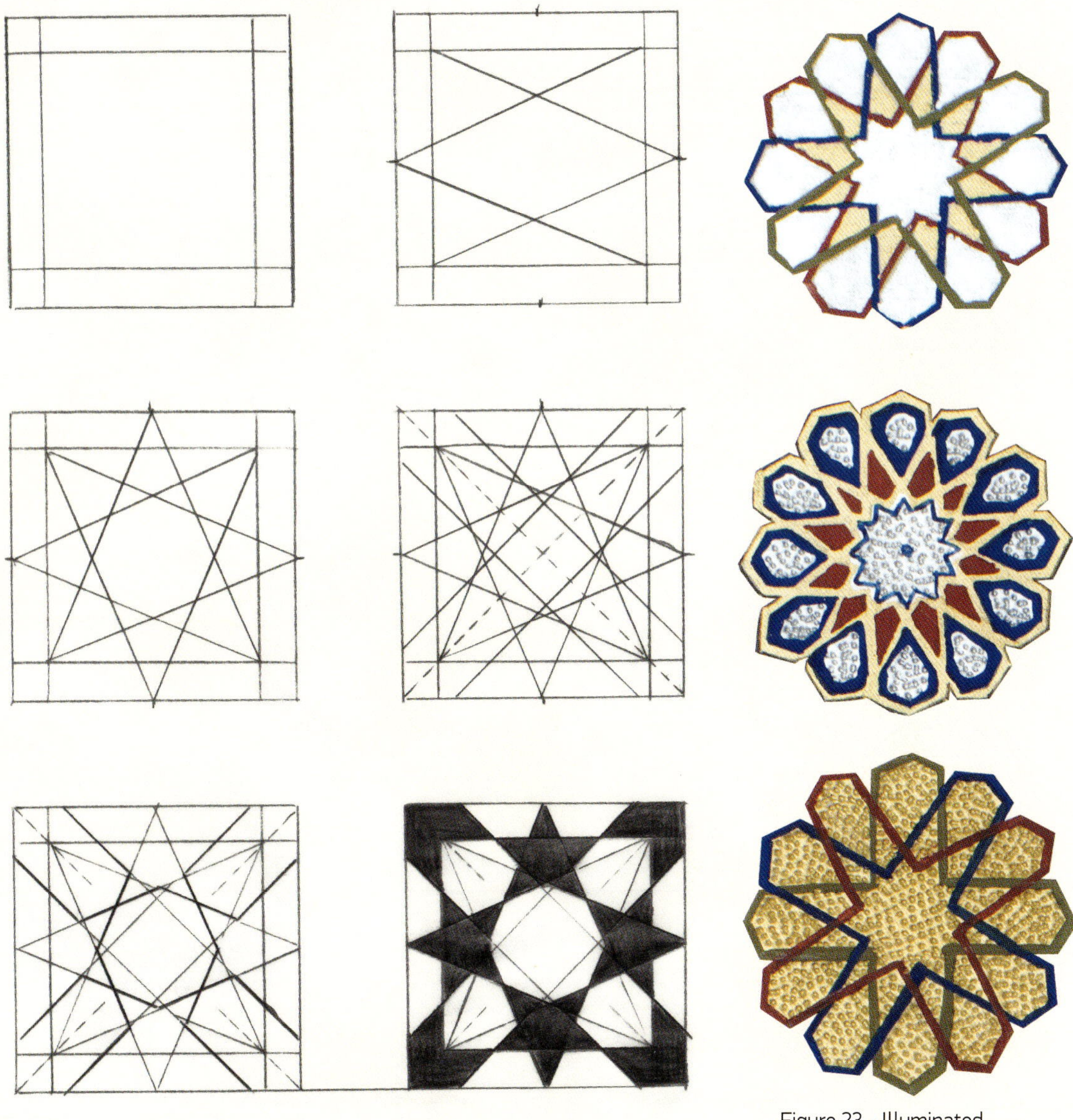

Figure 22 - Geometric motifs by A. Akar and C. Keskiner

Figure 23 - Illuminated geometric motifs by Sema Onat

J. Munhani (Curved) Motifs

This is a kind of design that was used very frequently between the 11th and 15th centuries in ornamentation of handwritten manuscripts. As conjoined forms and with original coloring, these gradient colored curve motifs (*munhanis*) comprised a unique style in the art of illumination. They were used mostly during the Seljuk period (Figure 24).

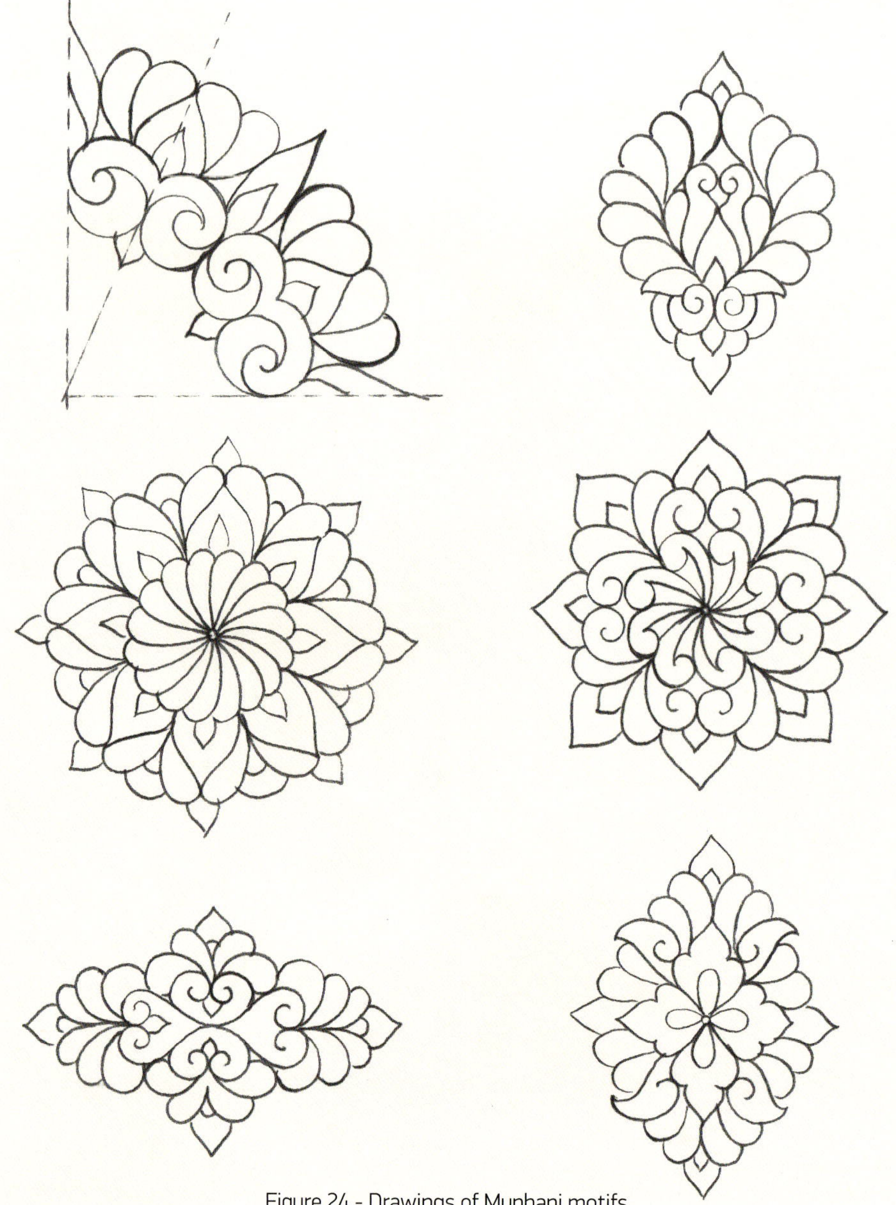

Figure 24 - Drawings of Munhani motifs

K. Shukufa (Naturalist Flower) Style Motifs

Painted with a natural appearance, naturalist flowers were first seen in Ottoman art in the 17th century and later on. They are seen in Baroque and Rococo styles which developed with foreign influence.[7]

This style includes the most beautiful examples of modern illumination work. It appeared by means of the stylization of different kinds of flowers found in nature, in particular, the rose, tulip, carnation, violet, and iris. Making strokes with a very fine brush, the tone is made by giving each layer a distinct lightness and darkness. The strokes of the brush are so fine that a naturalist drawing emerges with the flower appearing to be animate (Figures 25, 26).

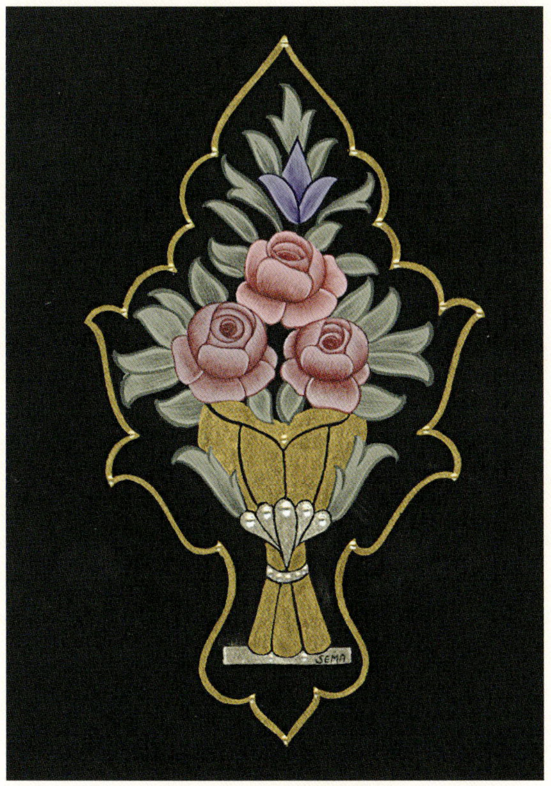

Figure 25 - Shukufa style flower by Sema Onat

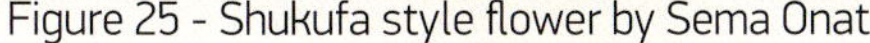

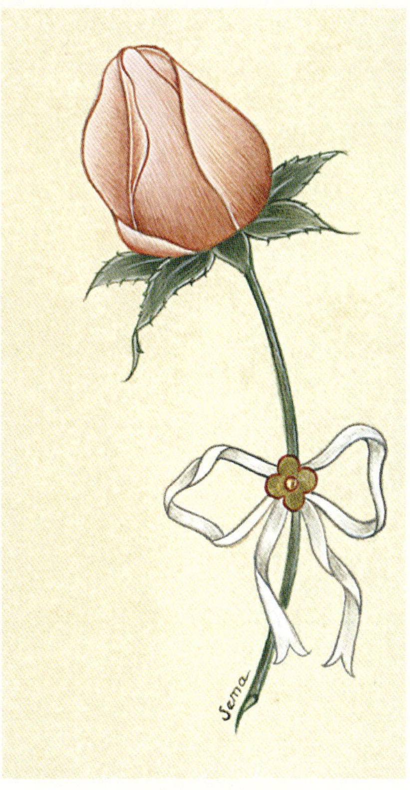

Figure 26 – Shukufa by Sema Onat

7 Özkeçeci and Özkeçeci, *Türk Sanatında Tezhip* (Illumination in Turkish Arts), p. 76

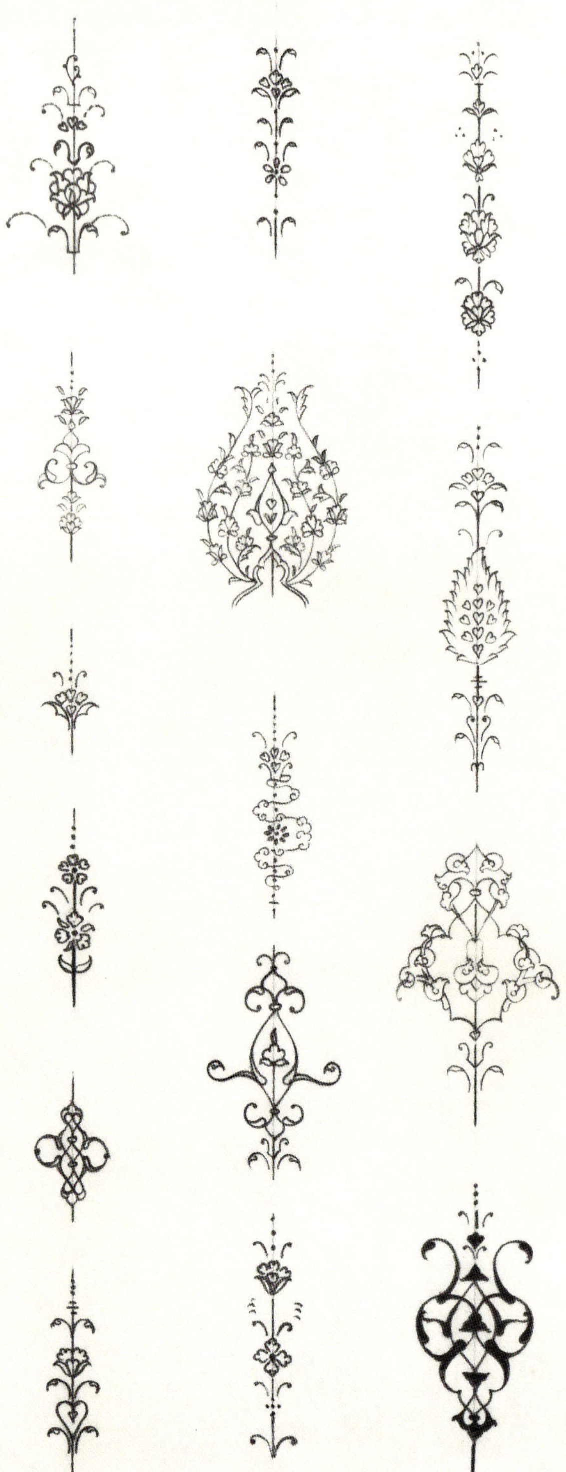

Figure 27 – Tigh motifs

L. Zarafshan (Scattering Gold)

This is another technique among ornamentation applied at the edges of the writing. *Zarafshan* is made on a dark surface without crushing the gold leaf. First a paste used in gluing paper is rubbed on the surface. Immediately after this, gold leaf is put into a sieve and, being broken down with the aid of a brush, it is sifted onto the surface. In the next step, when the surface is close to drying, it is covered with sketch paper and with the help of a stamp, the sifted gold is crushed under the sketch paper which allows it to thoroughly stick to the surface. *Zarafshan* is an easy and beautiful style of ornamentation.

M. Tigh (Needle-pointed) Motif

With an important place in illumination, *tigh* work is the most external section that completes the design. It is the section that begins where the illumination ends and is a fine, sharp line that extends outward (Figure 27).

N. Karamemi

In the middle of the 16th century when a return to nature began, it was one of the favorite motifs in Ottoman ornamentation arts. Flowers like roses, tulips, carnations, hyacinths, irises, Japanese quinces, and violets are given a stylized tree form. Flowers of this stylized form used in *Karamemi* are sometimes pictured in blossom and sometimes as buds, just as in nature (Figure 28).

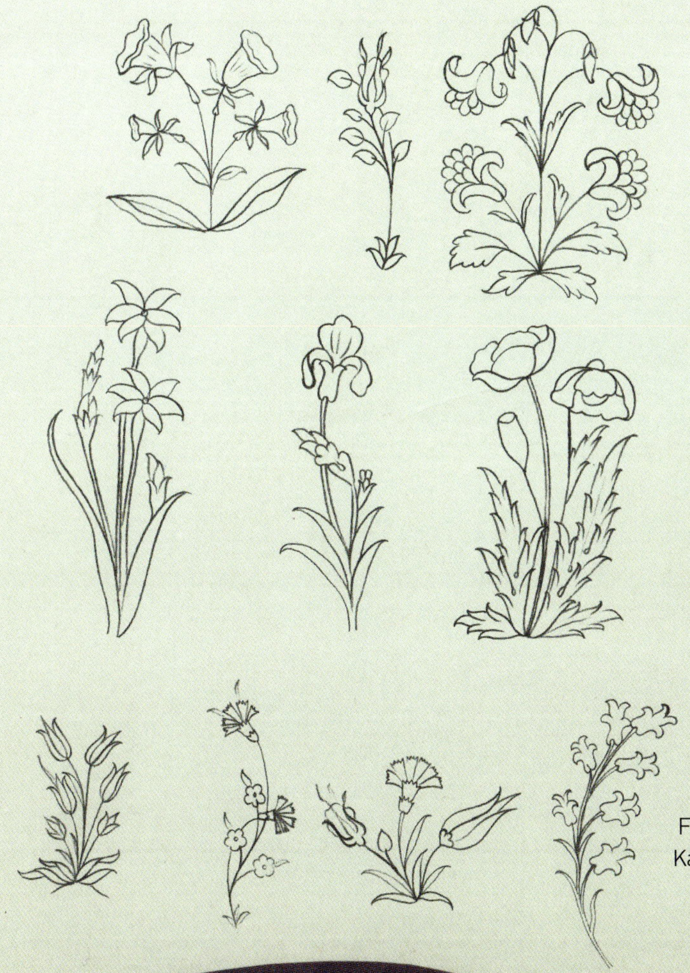

Figure 28 - Semi-naturalist Karamemi flower designs

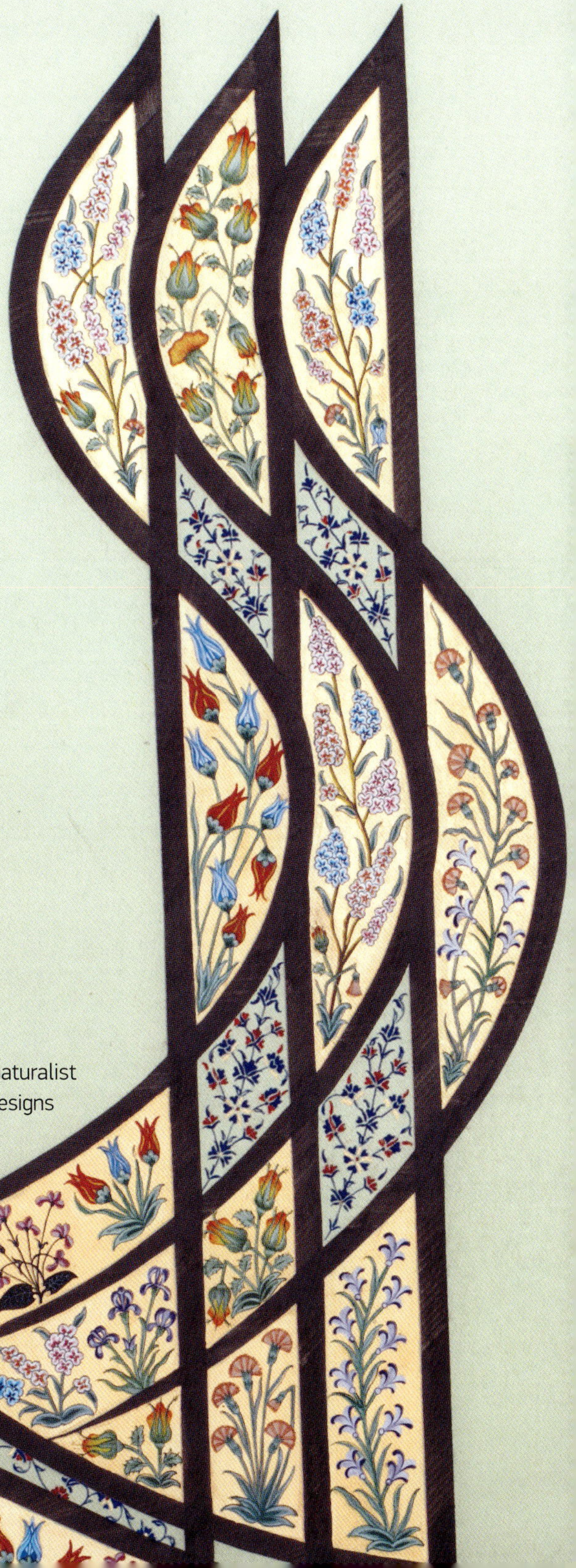

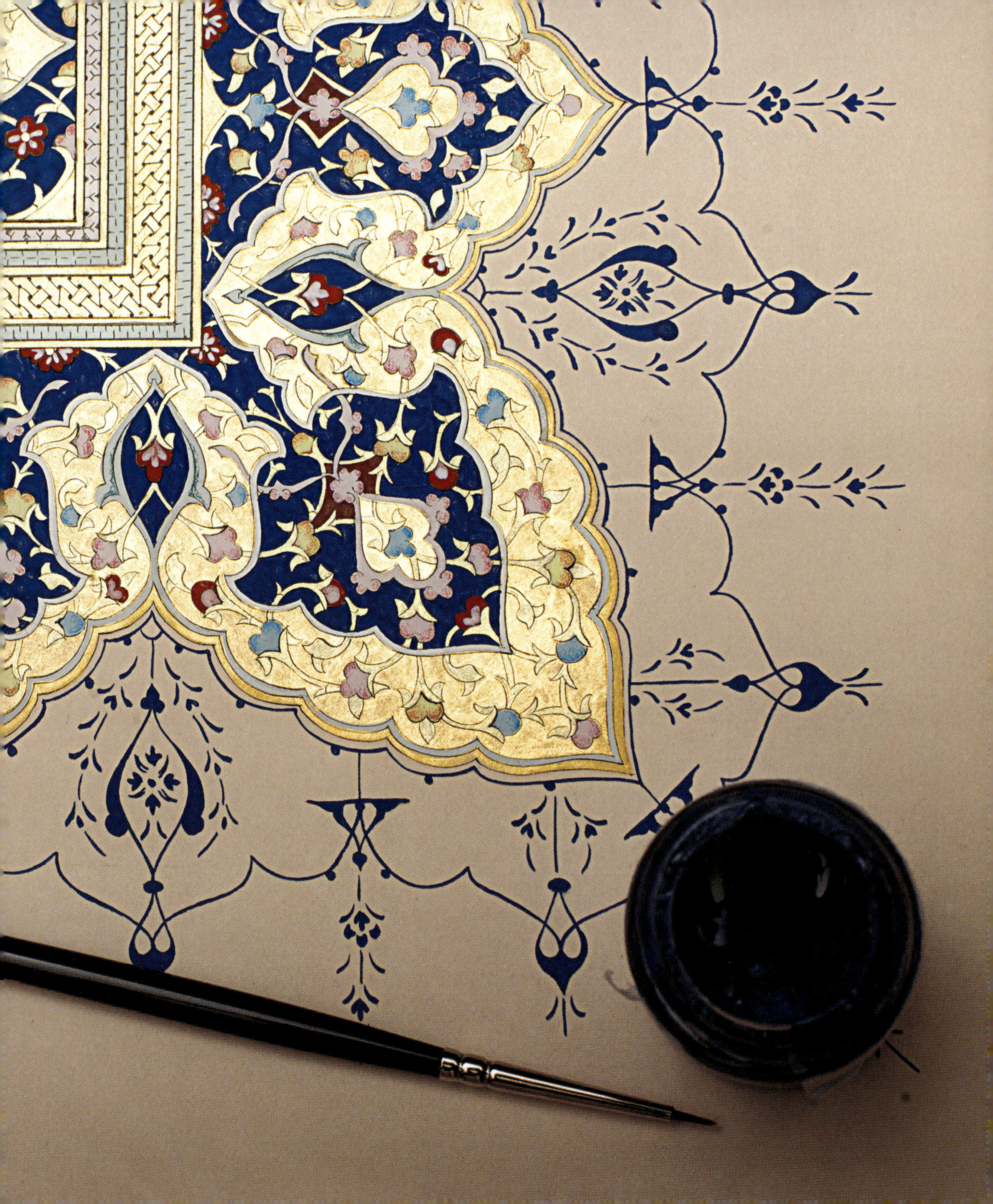

Part Four

Materials Used in Illumination

MATERIALS NEEDED FOR ILLUMINATION

Arts that have come down to us from the past show variation because of the variety and different quality of materials used in their execution. As in all cases, using the best materials in illumination raises the quality of workmanship.

Paper: In early ages, man used stone, wood, bronze, and ivory surfaces in place of paper. With the invention of paper, man's writing became easier, and this situation contributed greatly to the development of education. Now fabricated products are used in place of the hand-made paper used in the past. The usage of hand-made paper in artistic drawings increases the period of preservation of the work. The raw paper to be used for the work needs to be engrained first. There are many helpful elements for coloring the paper. The most natural of these are tea water, coffee, onionskin, henna, dark cabbage, walnut shells, and similar products. By using these products, alternative colors can be made on surfaces where illumination will be applied.

After the coloring is done, the surface has to be treated. For this task, what we call "*nishasta ahar*" (starch finish) is made. The starchy paste is cooked, cooled and put aside. Then, after straining it through a piece of silk, a creamy consistency is obtained. This mixture is spread on the paper with the help of a porous sponge or brush. After the paper has dried completely, in order to eliminate the wrinkles on the surface, the paper is pressed with the help of sketch paper. After this, in order to understand whether or not the paper has been fully treated, it is necessary to test the paper. A piece of gold is rubbed onto the edge of the paper. If the paper absorbs the gold, the treatment has been insufficient. In this situation, the starchy paste has to be applied anew. If too much paste was used, the surface will not accept the gold and paint, and will throw them off.

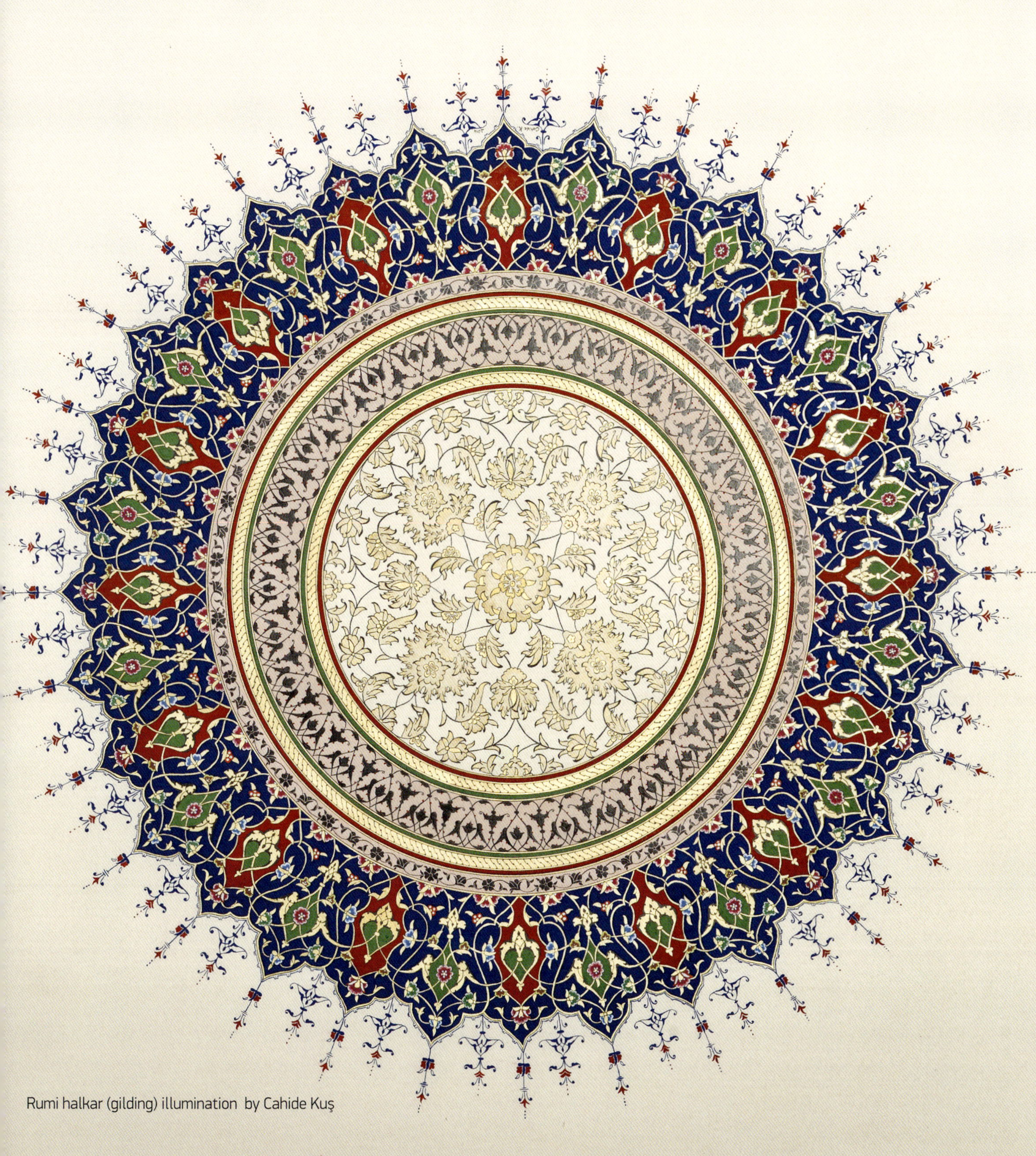

Rumi halkar (gilding) illumination by Cahide Kuş

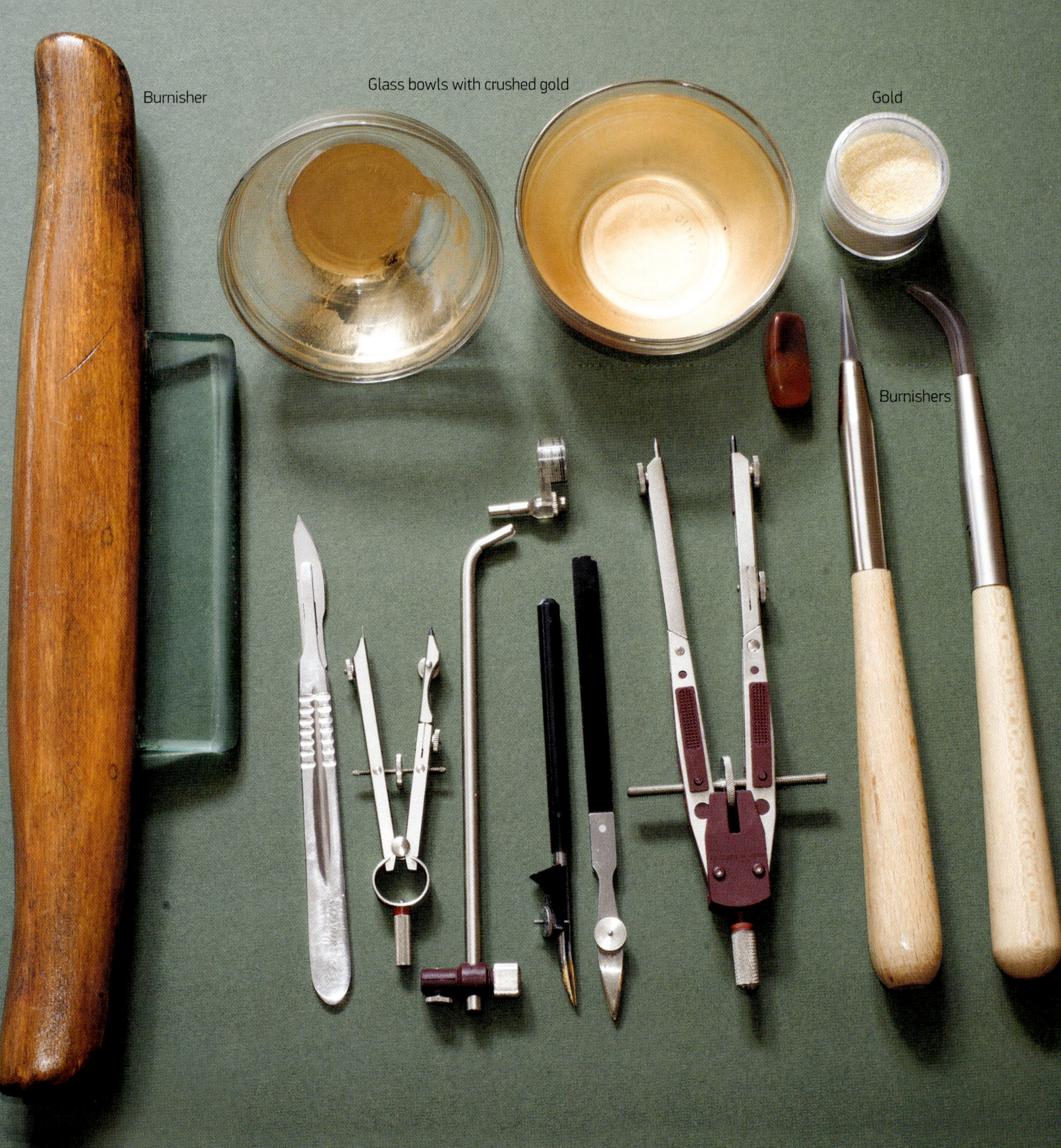
Burnisher
Glass bowls with crushed gold
Gold
Burnishers

Burnisher (*Muhra*): Used to make the surface of hand-made paper smooth, this tool has different shapes. The polishing surface of the tool used on broad surfaces is larger. There are handles on both sides of the instrument to make polishing easier. The glossing surface of the tool is either cornelian or glass. On glossed or unglossed paper, it is used by putting sketch paper on the surface. The purpose of using sketch paper is to prevent the burnisher from making scratches on the paper. In the polishing of gold applied during ornamentation, burnishers with fine edges are used. In order to use this fine edge easily, the burnisher is designed in the shape of a pen. The rubbing part of the fine edged burnisher is made from cornelian, jade, and agate stones. In order for the gold to be made to shine better, it is recommended that the burnisher be rubbed on hair or oily skin before using it.

Gold: The usage of gold is very important in the art of illumination. Gold leaf becomes ready for use by being crushed in the hands of the craftsman. Until the end of the 19th century gold leaf was produced in the Ottoman capital of Istanbul in the districts of Bayazid and Suleymaniye in places called gold leaf *han*s and markets. Very superior in regard to purity and carats, Ottoman gold leaf was unable to compete with cheap fabricated gold leaf coming from Europe and this craft disappeared in time.[4]

Crushing Gold: Two kinds of gold are used in the art of illumination. Just as gold leaf can be applied directly, it can also be used in crushed form. The direct application of gold leaf is called "transfer gold." This kind of layering gold leaf over a surface is usually preferred for broad surfaces. However, unlike crushed gold, transfer gold can separate from the surface.

4 Özkeçeci and Özkeçeci, *Türk Sanatında Tezhip* (Illumination in Turkish Arts), p. 179.

In illumination, in order for gold to be permanent on the surface, specks of gold are applied with a brush. For this, first the pieces of gold leaf have to be crushed and thinned. This traditional way of crushing the gold is still done by hand and is a highly regarded form of gilding. Before beginning this process, a large, round, smooth porcelain or glass bowl is obtained. After dropping three-four drops of what we call Arab gum in the middle of the bowl and adding powdered gelatin with the edge of a teaspoon, we mix these two materials by making circular crushing movements in one direction with our index finger. In order for the mixture not to dry, we occasionally add a few drops of water. Continuing this process, we take gold leaf with the same finger, add it to the bowl and with the same circular motion, we begin the process of crushing the gold. All the pieces of gold leaf are put into the bowl one-by-one and the gold crushing process continues. Using our index and middle fingers, we continue crushing the gold until there is no gold residual. To be sure the gold has been crushed well, we see if our finger makes a squeaky noise when we rub it on the gold and check to see that the mixture is not gritty. This result is achieved after a process of crushing gold for about three hours.

The gold that has been smeared on the bowl as a result of the crushing process is gathered in the middle of the bowl with the help of water. This watery mixture is strained through a silk handkerchief and poured into a small bowl. The mixture is left to stand for about six hours. After six hours the gold will have fallen to the bottom. The water remaining on top is emptied with one motion. The small amount of water that remains in the gold on the bottom is evaporated by putting heat under the bowl and the gold is completely dried. This long and tiring gold crushing process is proof that the art of illumination is fully an effort done by hand and an eye-straining art from beginning to end.

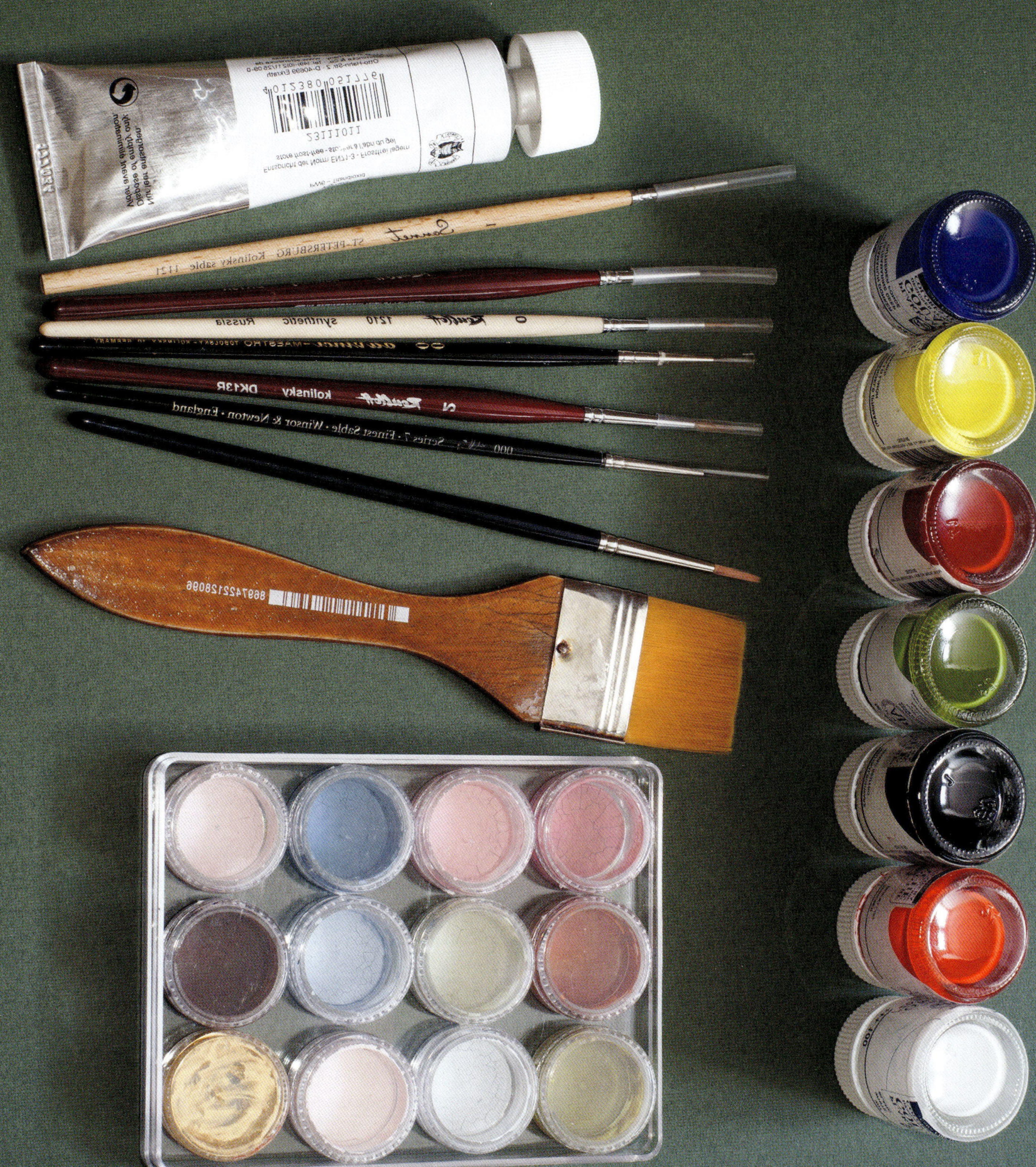
ST-PETERSBURG Kolinsky sable 1121
synthetic Russia
kolinsky DK13R
Series 7 · Finest Sable · Winsor & Newton · England

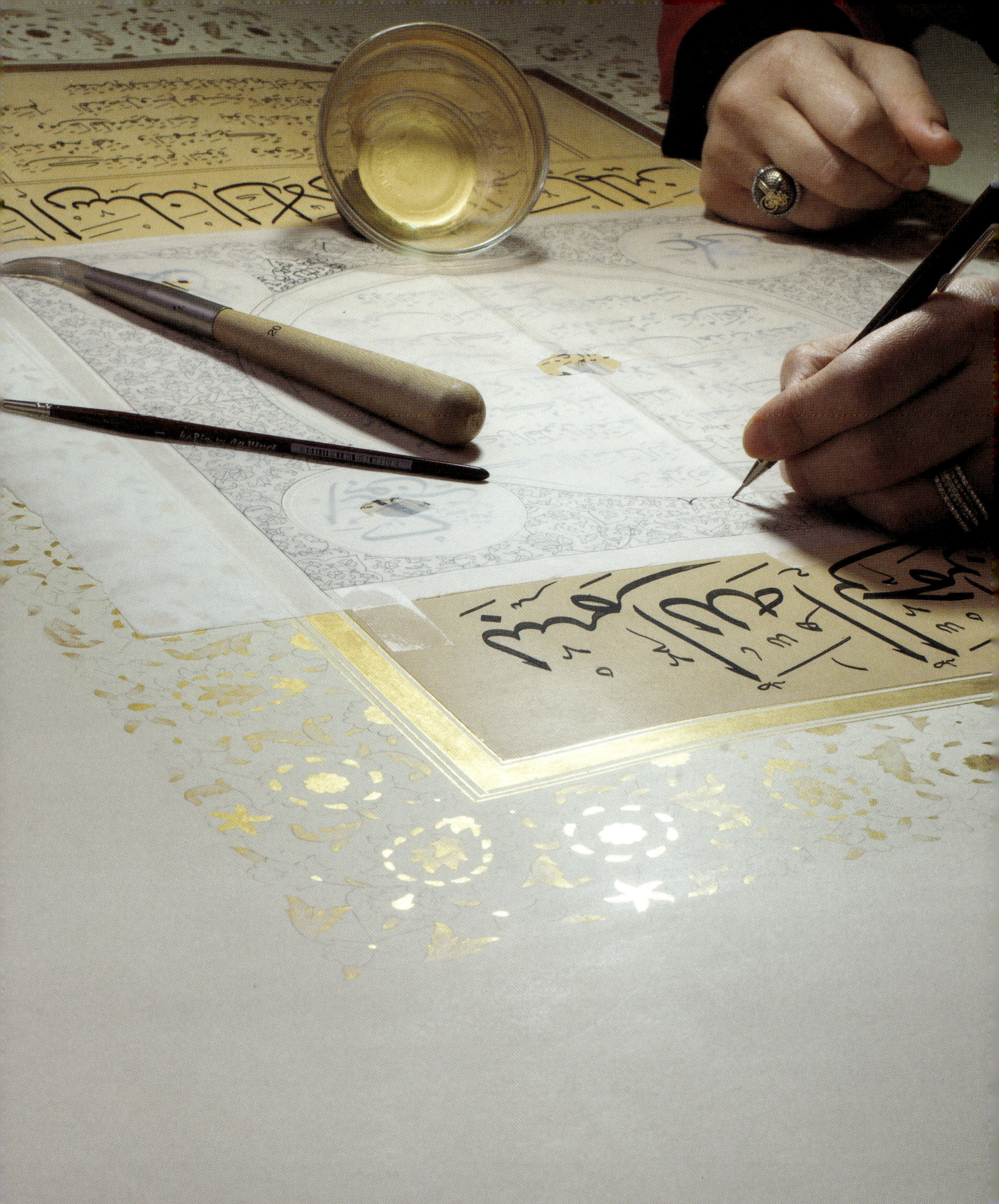

Gold Application: The crushed gold is applied to the surface with the help of gelatin water. It is understood at this time whether or not the gold has been crushed well or not. If the gold that is stirred with a brush is gritty, then this means the gold was not well crushed. If while applying the gold, it is smooth, like the consistency of paint, and if it shines well when it is polished with the burnisher after being applied, then this means it was well crushed. While ornamenting a work in illumination, the first thing to be done is the application of the gold and its polishing, regardless of which ornamentation style is used.

Paint: Besides gold, the colors red, yellow, green, and white are also used in illumination. Formerly, when the colors were being prepared, root or earth paints were made. After making the paint into a fine powered state, it is crushed with Arab gum and used. After gold, navy blue is the color most used in illumination. Its complementary colors are orange (containing red lead) and lemon mildew green. White, black, flower-toned pink, lilac, blue, and yellow are auxiliary colors.

Paperboard (*Muraqqa*): *Muraqqa* is the handmade paperboard used for executing the art of illumination. Due to the difficulty of making it by hand, today, ready-made passe-partout is used.

Muraqqa is made by gluing together three or four pieces of paper according to certain methods. In the first stage the paper's dimensions are prepared. The main paper dimension is determined and cut according to the size of the work. The second paper is cut two cm larger than the rectangle of the main paper. Depending on the thickness of the paper, three or four pieces of paper are prepared. After the papers are prepared, it is time for pasting. A paste is prepared for this. Starch, water, alum, and gelatin are used to make the paste. It is cooked with about three glasses of water, three heaping tablespoons of starch, a piece of alum the size of a chickpea, and two sheets of gelatin. After the paste has cooled, it is drained through a cloth. The base used for pasting the papers must be unfinished wood. For the pasting task, the front and back of the main paper with the smallest dimensions are wetted with the aid of a thick sponge. The purpose of this step is to enable the paper to relax itself.

The wet paper is spread on the wood. The prepared paste is taken in hand and the surface of the paper is spread liberally with paste, first sideways and then lengthwise. Then, the second paper is wetted and it is pasted in an opposite way to the water directions on the paper. This step is done with all the papers in turn. It is very important here to arrange the papers contrary to the water directions. What we call the water direction here is the webbing of the paper. The purpose of placing the paper opposite to these is to prevent the paper from wrinkling. Because the paper on top with the largest size is the one where the design will be applied, this paper can be carefully chosen. Remaining on top, this paper is also spread with paste. In order for the paper not to separate from the wood base and become wrinkled during the drying stage, strips two fingers wide are cut and prepared. Using these strips like a band, they are placed on the four corners of the *muraqqa.* After it dries, sketch paper is placed on it and, pressing it with a stamp, it is made smooth. Finally, using a ruler, the paperboard is cut with a curved knife in the dimensions of the paper on the bottom and the excess is removed.

Brush: In order to make illumination well, the brush is the most important tool and it should be chosen carefully. Just like a brush made from the hair of sables, synthetic brushes can also be used. While fine haired sable brushes can be used while making contours, brushes with more hair can be preferred for broad areas.

The calligraphy of Rumi's couplets ornamented with illumination above is glued to the *muraqqa*—hand-made paperboard.

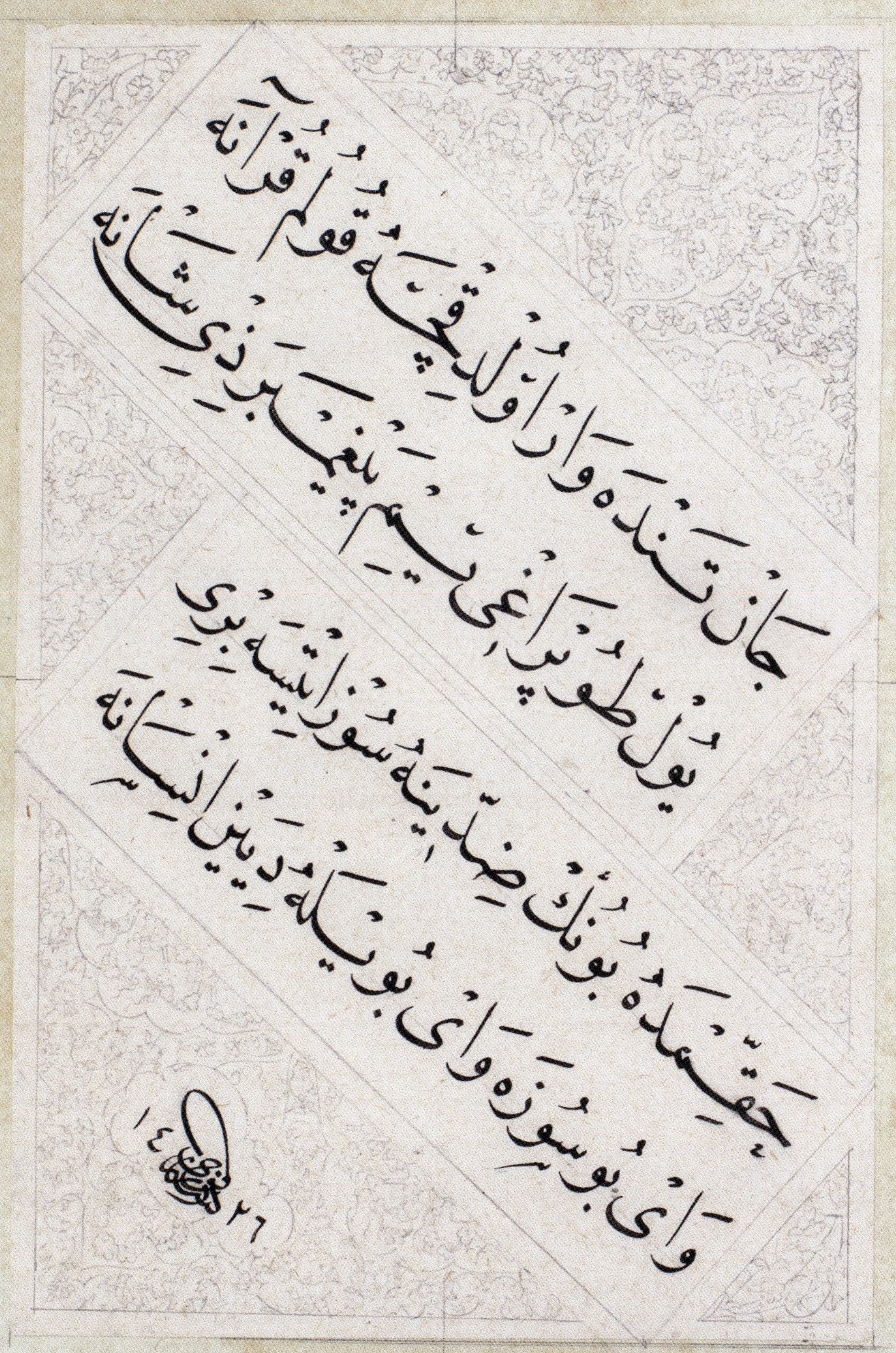
جان تنده وار اولدقجه قولم قرآنه
يول طوتارغيم پيغمبر ذيشانه
حقمده بونك ضدينه سوز اتسه بري
واي بو سوزه واي بويله دين انسانه
٢٦
١٤٠٢

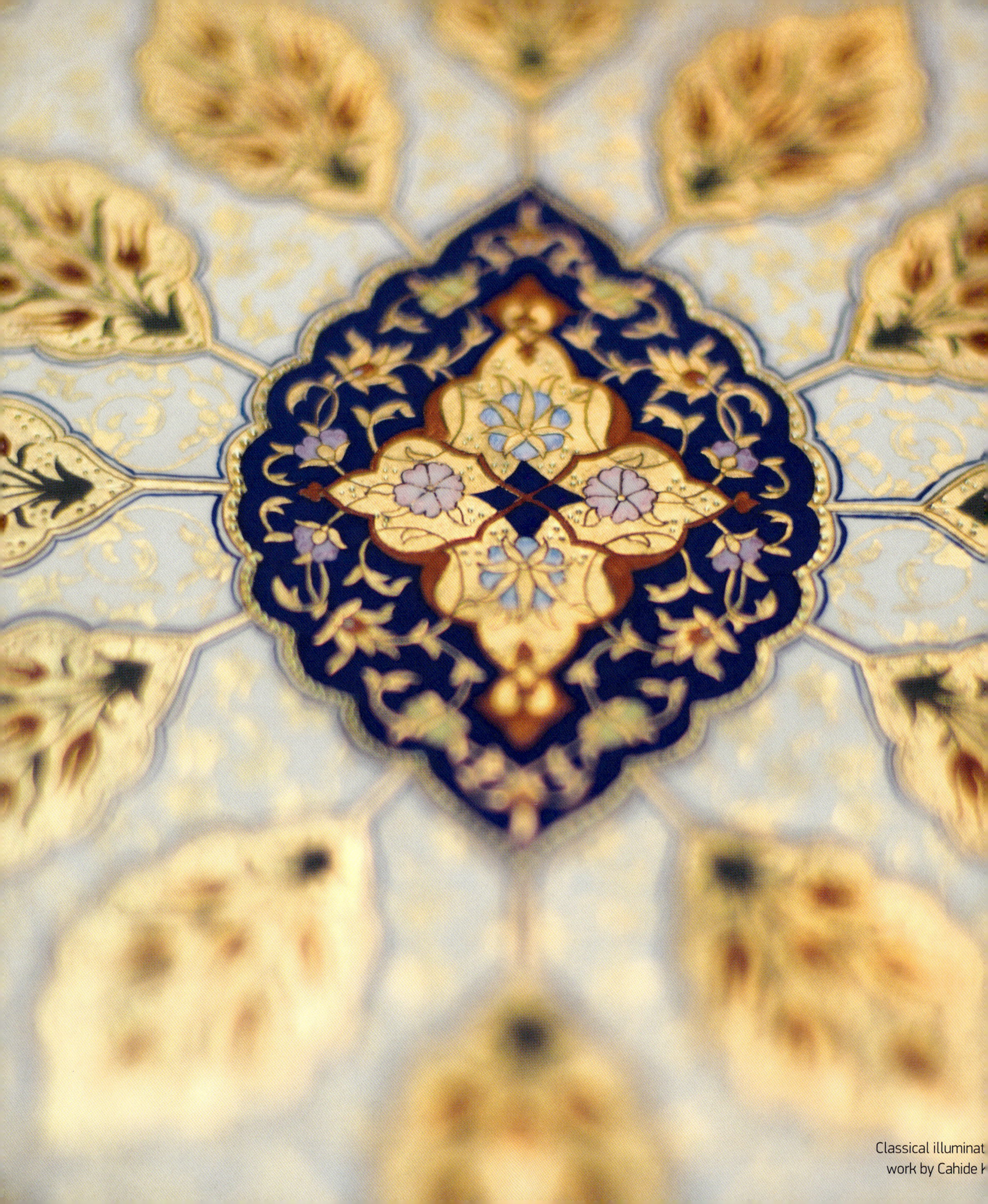

Classical illuminat
work by Cahide K

Part Five

Making Illumination

MAKING ILLUMINATION

In addition to the art of illumination being explained in various sources like books and electronic means, it is absolutely necessary to take lessons face-to-face from a good teacher in order to learn this art. The reason for this is the necessity of the teacher's examining and evaluating the drawings made and to experience the general spiritual atmosphere of the surroundings.

In this section, the way to execute the art of illumination will be explained, stage by stage. Let's not forget that in order to draw a design that appears unified, a long and patient effort is needed.

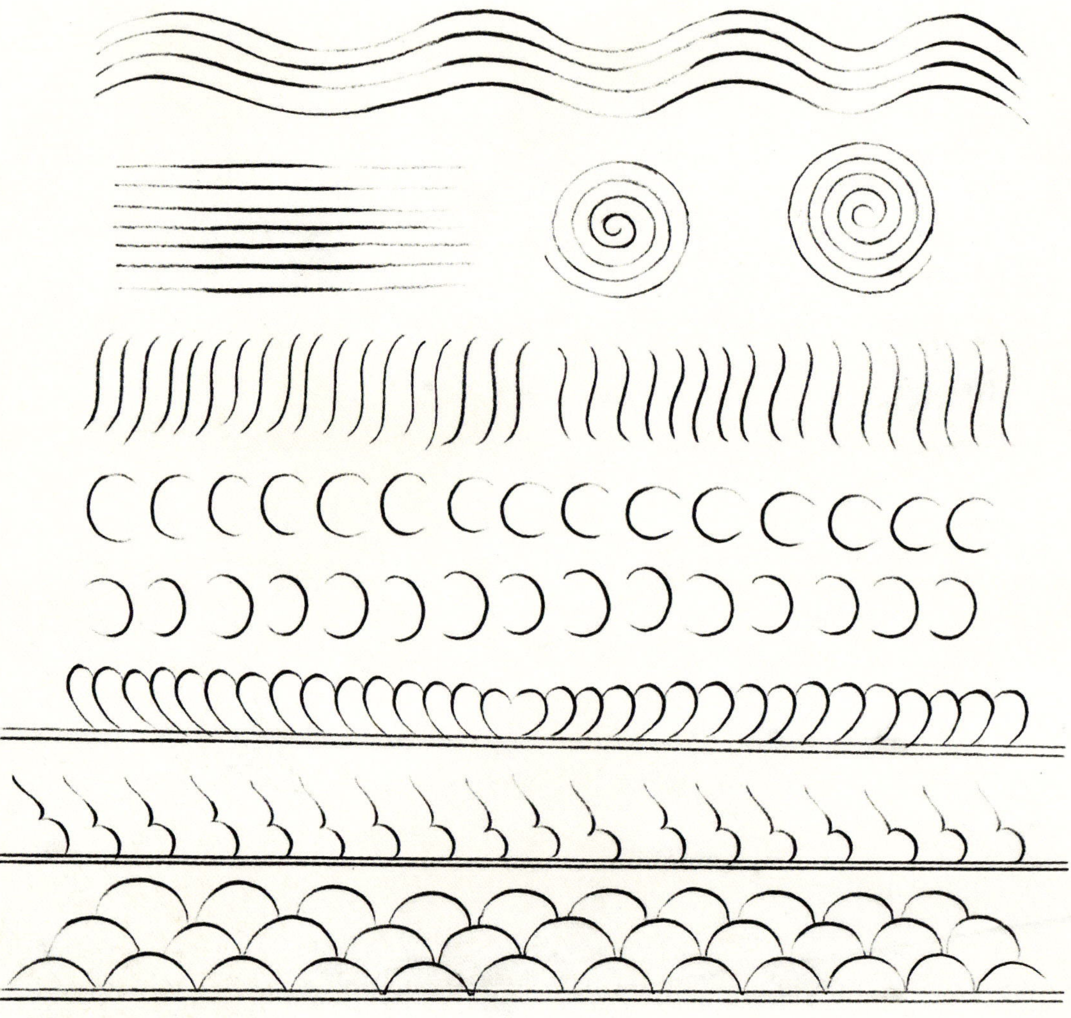

Figure 29 - Free style drawings

A. Drawing Efforts

First Step: In the first stage of illumination, the hand meets the pencil and, in order for the ability to control the pencil to increase, free-style drawings are made. While making the drawings, they are made with one motion without raising the hand and interrupted lines are not used (Figure 29).

Second Step (Leaf Drawings): When we examine leaves in nature, we see that there are many kinds of leaves. In the illumination lesson after we have passed the first stage, our hand is able to control the pencil more easily.

In the second stage of drawing leaves, the main lines of leaves are formed in vertical, horizontal, round, and spiral shapes. Branches drawn in these shapes are turned towards a leaf with a line that brings them together. This line is imagined as a widened upper lip and drawn like that (Figure 30).

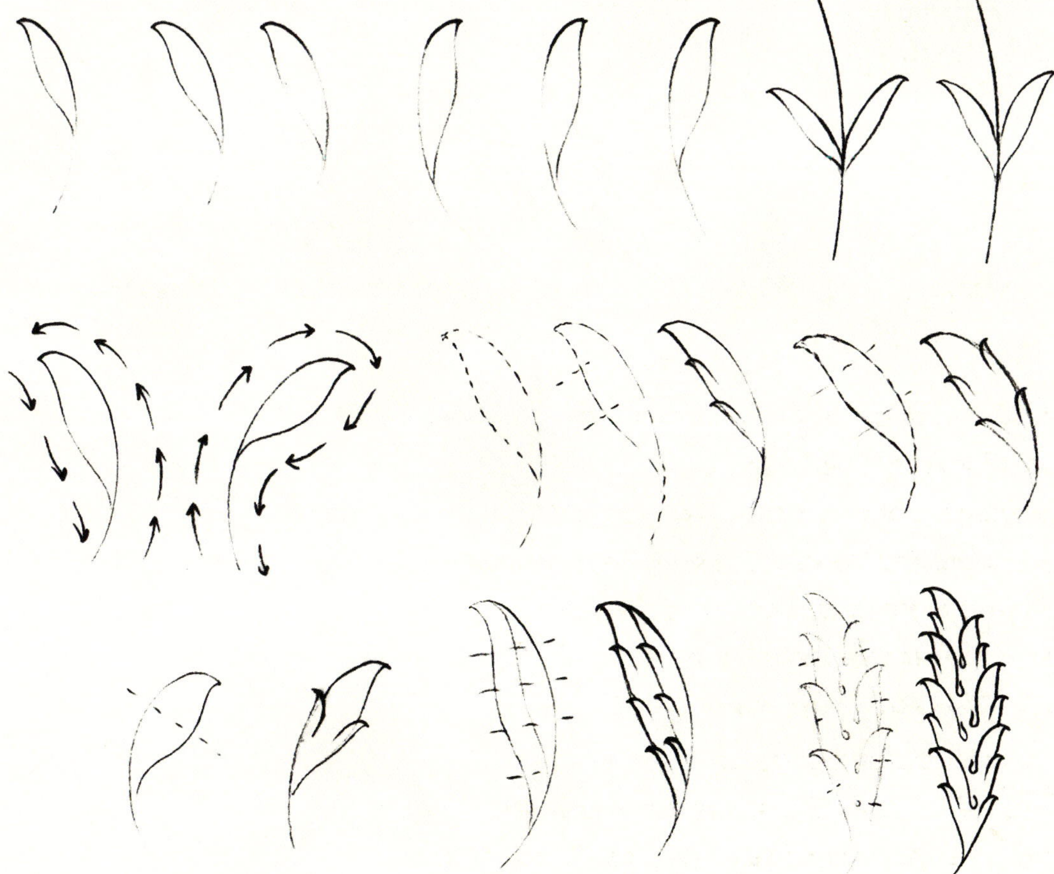

Figure 30 - Leaf drawings

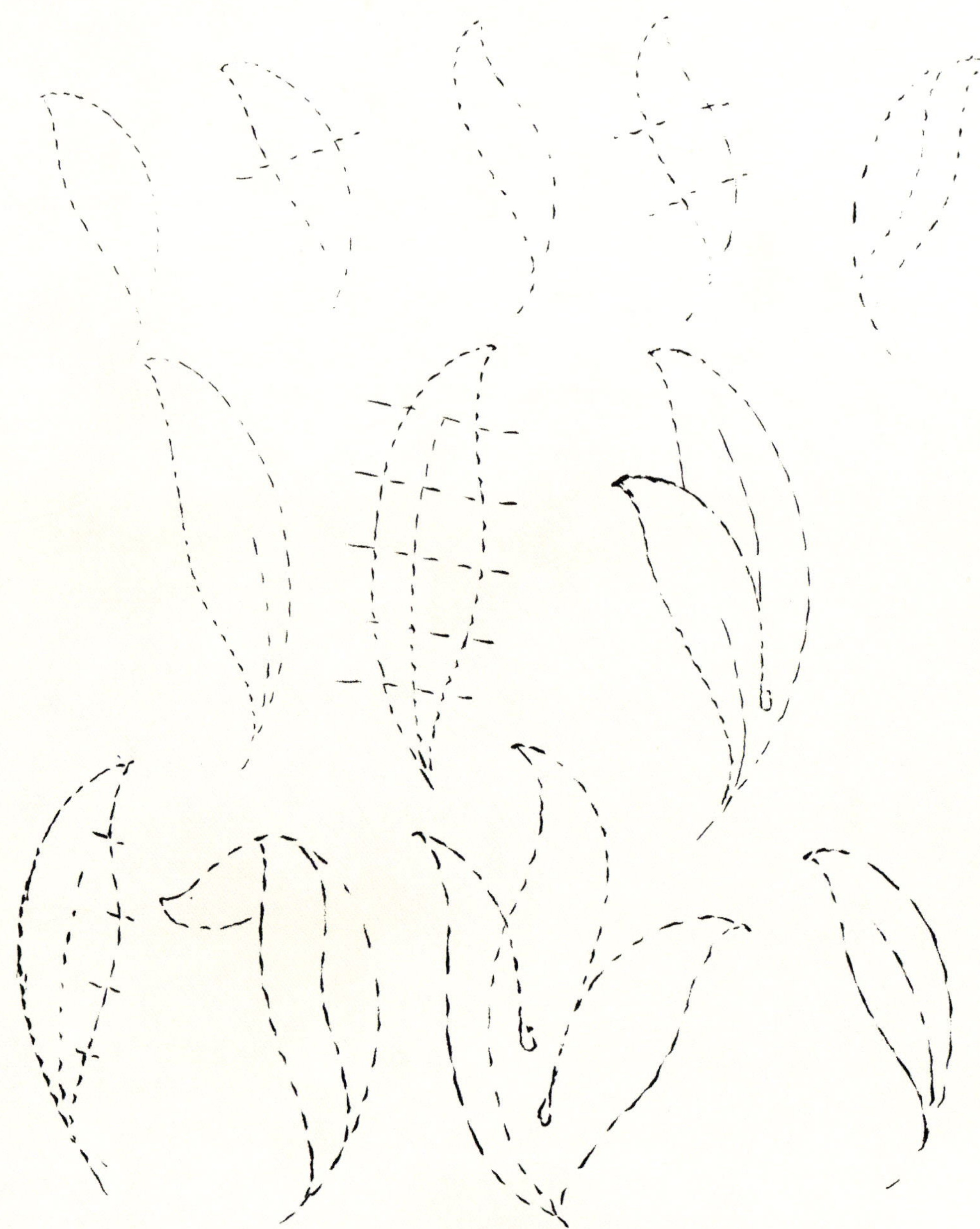

Figure 31a - Drawing well-proportioned leaves

Proportion is important while drawing leaves. When the width of the leaf is divided into three parts from the upper and lower curved lines, the top and bottom parts should be of the same proportion. A great variety of leaf motifs are used in illumination. Just as very plain leaves are used, serrated or very serrated leaves are also used (Figure 31).

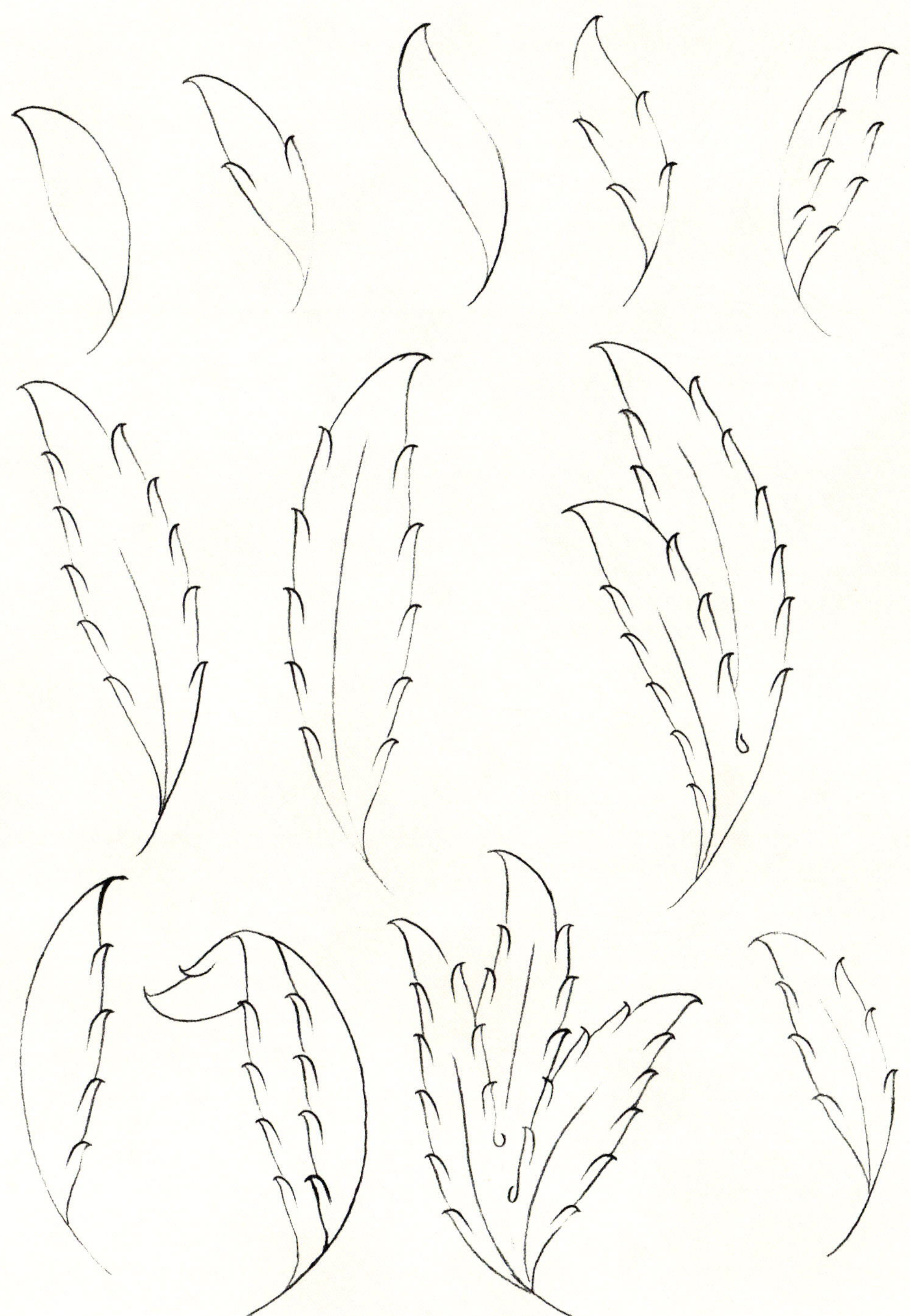

Figure 31b - Serrated leaves

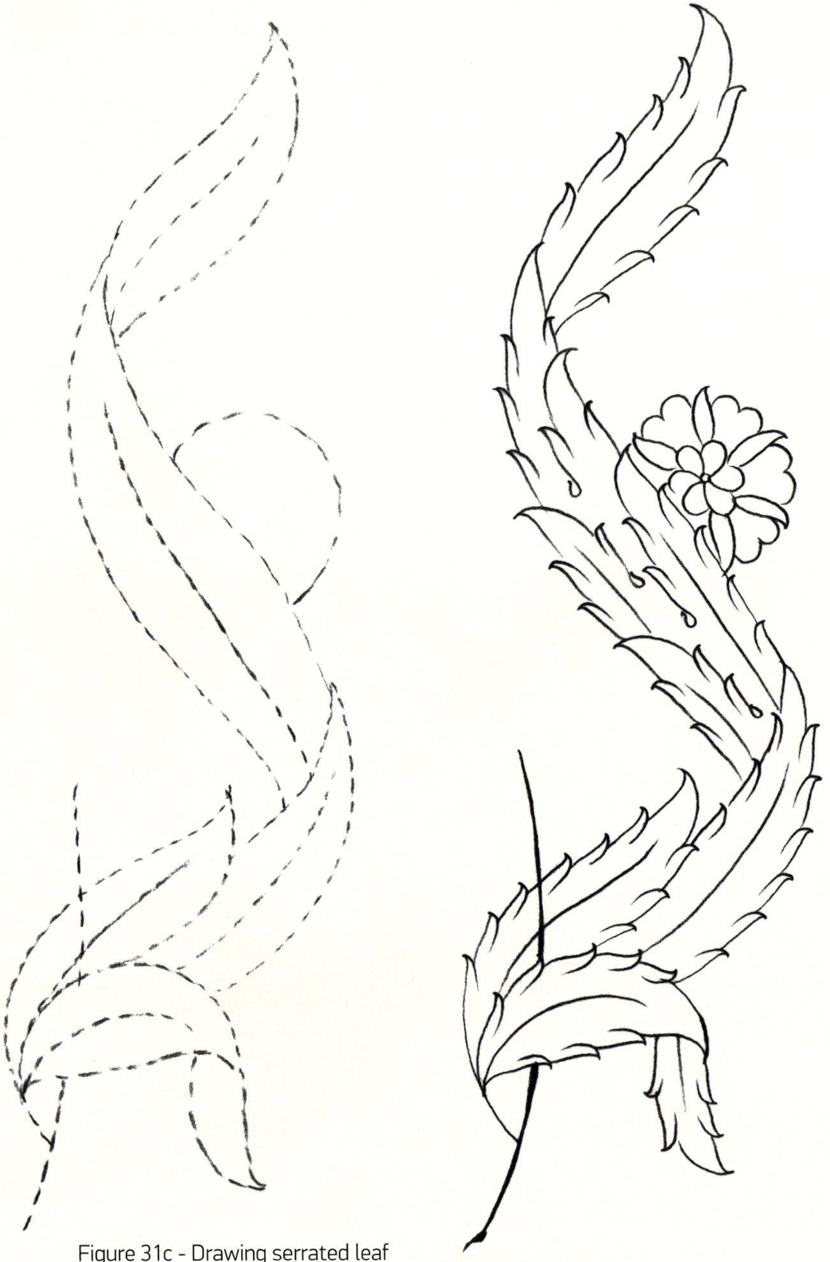

Figure 31c - Drawing serrated leaf

After the hand begins to grow accustomed to drawing simple leaves, other serrated leaves are also drawn. Drawn as a whole, a leaf is serrated from within. These serrations express the serration and notches on the edge of real leaves. In the drawing of serrated leaves, the first thing we do is take the leaf shape as a base and detail the serrations on it. Leaf drawing is a stage in the learning of the art of illumination that requires patience and a lot of hard work.

Shikaf and baroque style illumination by Selma Öz

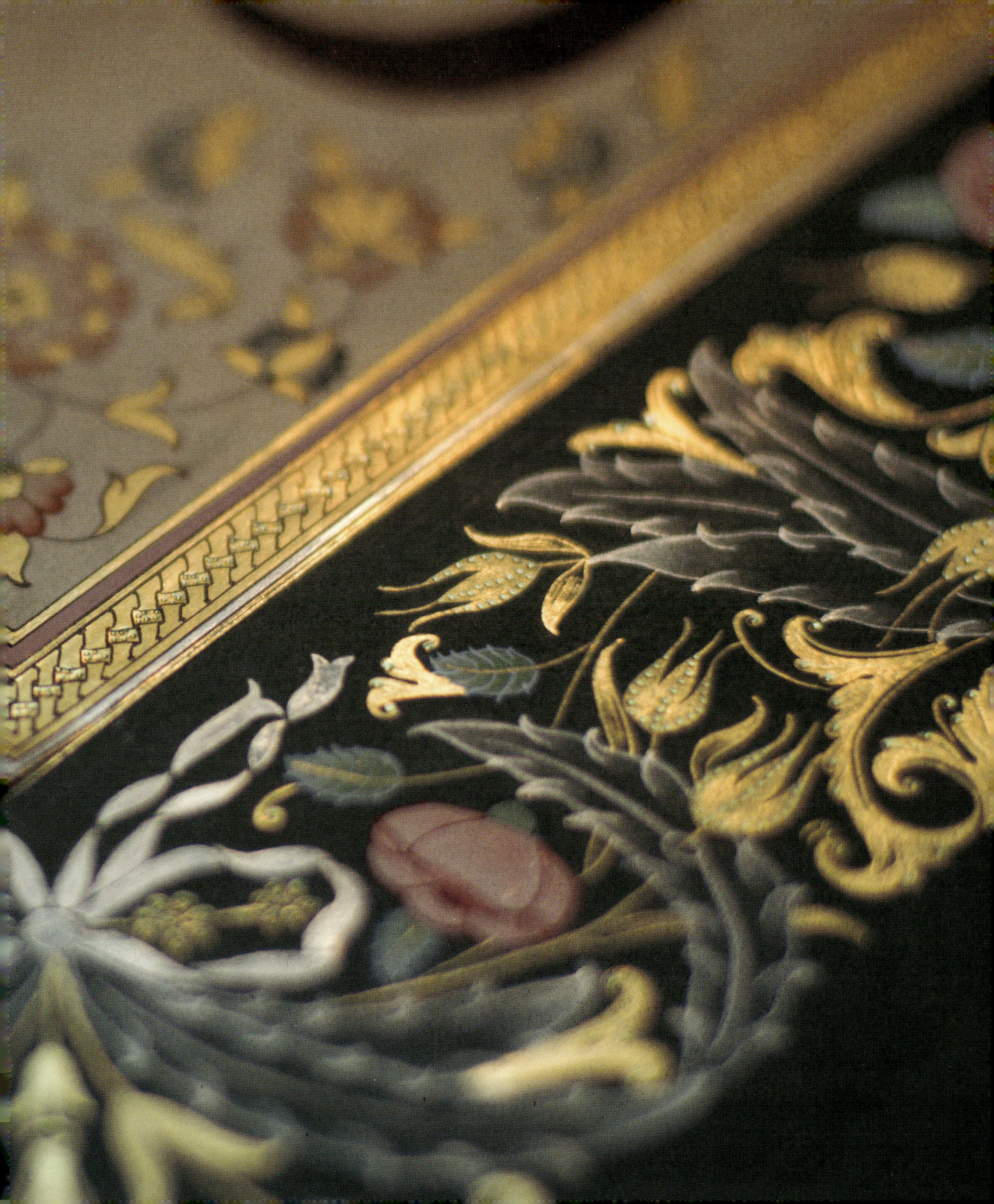

Nuance is also an important detail in the *khatai* floral motifs and leaves used in the art of illumination. Nuance is the width formed on the outer edges of the leaves and flowers. It provides balance. While making a line in one motion without raising the hand, nuance must be given naturally. Drawing nuance continues at the same time as drawing the leaf. If the illumination student has gained the ability to draw leaves well, she will progress more quickly in later stages (Figure 32).

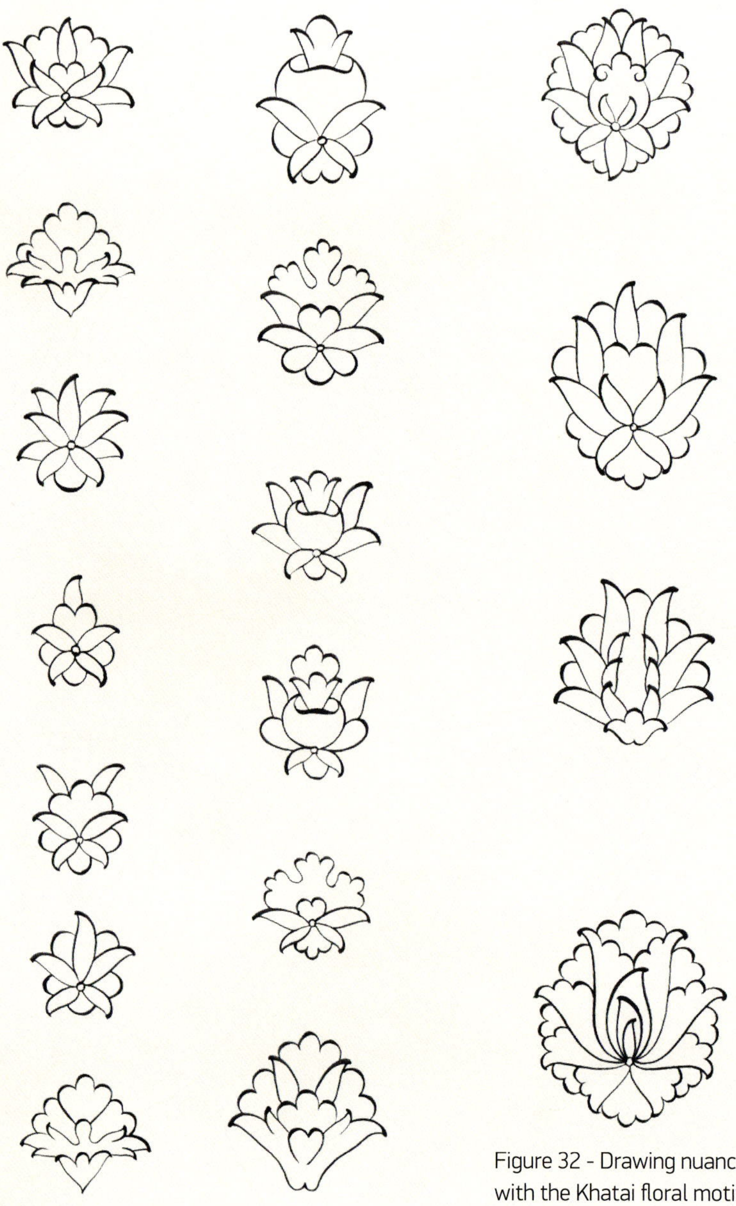

Figure 32 - Drawing nuance with the Khatai floral motifs

Third Step (Khatai Drawings): Lessons on drawing flowers begin with the buds. It is to be noted that buds are used in narrow spaces between designs. They are usually drawn taking symmetry vertical straight line as an axis. Buds include the leaves on the branch and flowers that complete them from above. There are many different models (Figure 33).

After the buds, *khatai* lessons continue with directional floral motifs. First a model drawing is prepared for these. Due to the model, drawing the floral motif becomes easier. Oval and vertical straight lines are drawn for this. This oval is divided into three parts across its width. While the upper and lower parts are arranged to be equally proportional, the body

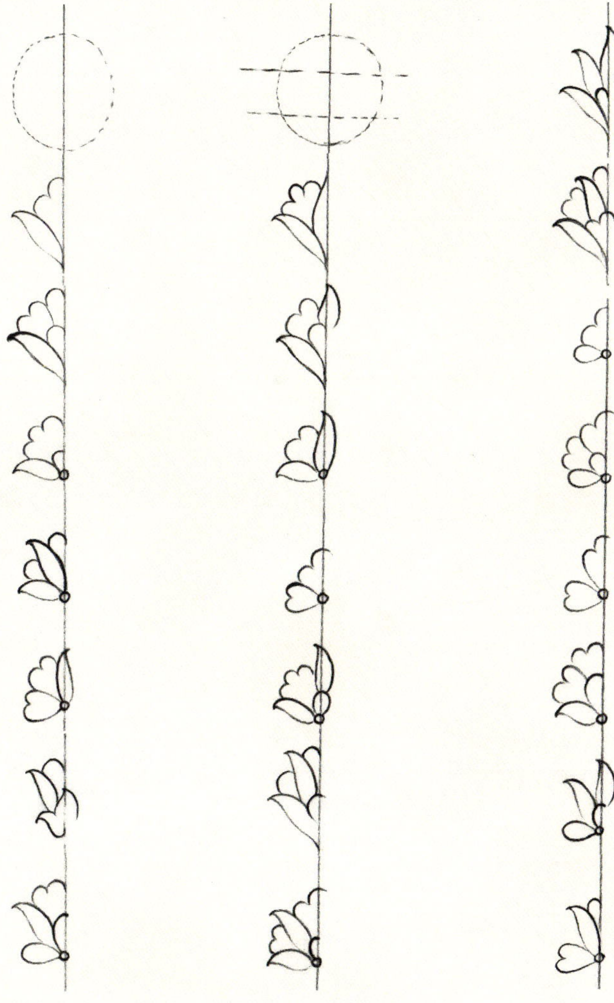

Figure 33 - Buds

section is broader. The reason for dividing the pattern into three parts is that the *khatai*s are examined in three sections. These are called the root, body, and crown leaves. Placing the flower in our pattern begins with the centrally located seed part. The seed is placed in the intersecting point of the lower straight line that cuts the width of the symmetry straight line. Later, taking the seed as center, the flower's root, body and crown leaves are put straight into the divided parts of the oval. First the vertical straight line is drawn on one side, and then folding the paper, the flower's symmetry is drawn on the other side of the straight line. Thus, the *khatai* drawing is completed (Figure 34).

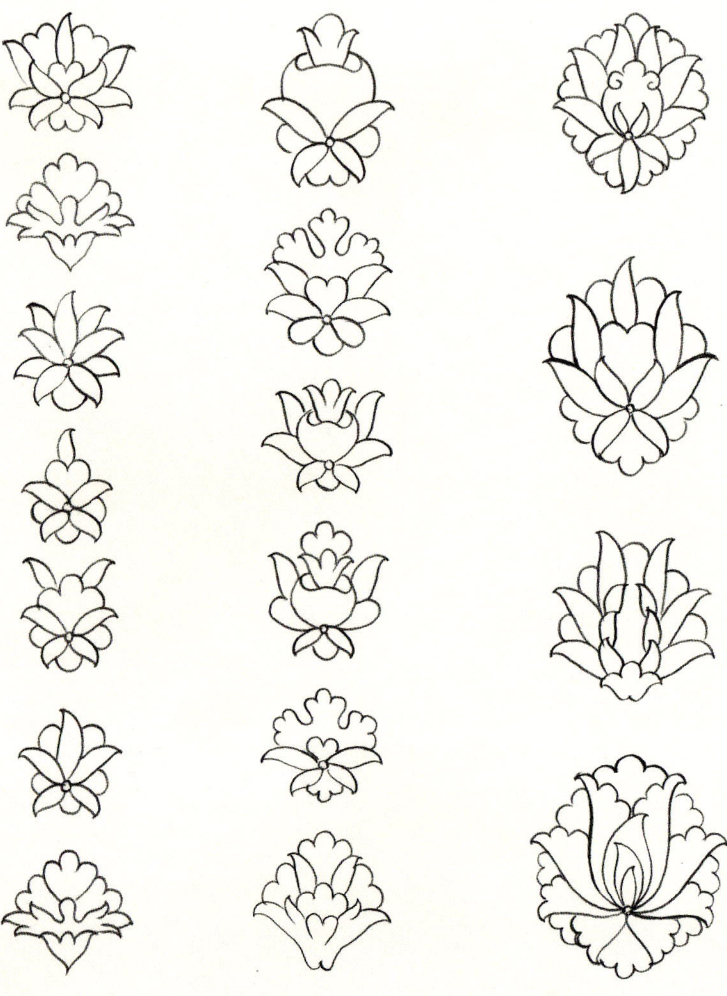

Figure 34 - Khatai drawings

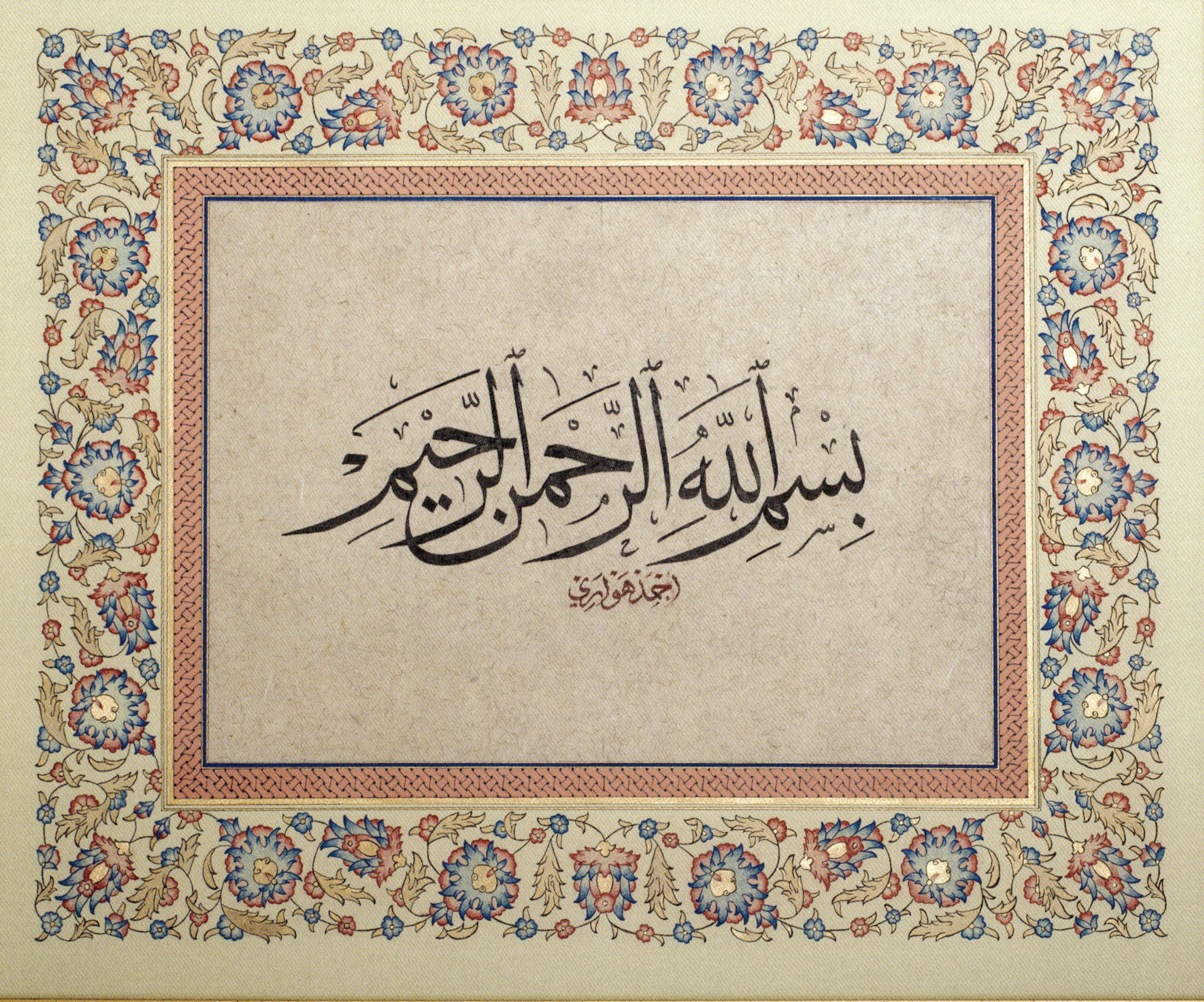

Arabic calligraphy of the Basmala surrounded by
the illuminated chain pattern and floral design by Cahide Kuş

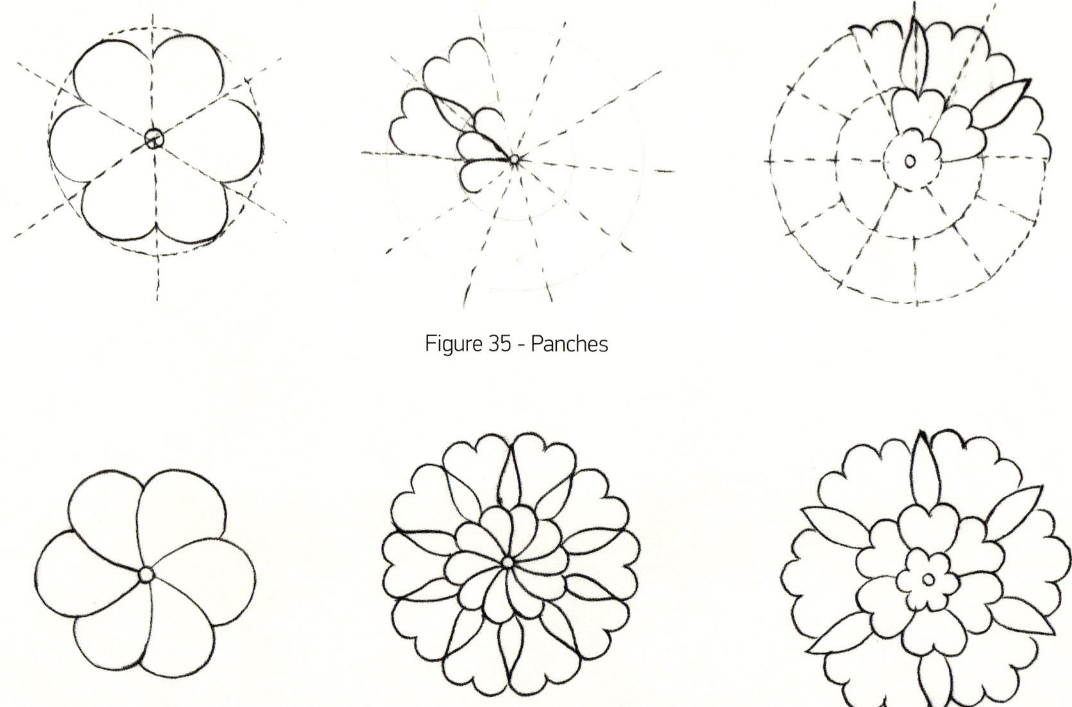

Figure 35 - Panches

While creating the design in illumination, central *khatai* motifs are begun by appointing the center; namely, they are put in the center points. Just as this floral design is used to designate the center, it can also be used in different places in the composition. Central *khatai*s are a birds-eye view of the whole flower (Figure 35). They are flowers that appear like daisies with petals overlapping one another. In the drawing of central *khatai*s, first a pattern is prepared. Because the pattern is round, the circle model is used in the drawing. These flowers, which are in layers opening outward from the inside, can be enlarged as much as we want. In order to maintain the proportion while drawing each layer, the pattern is broadened by using a circle larger than the previous one. According to the number of layers, these floral motifs are called two-layered, three-layered, and so on (Figure 36).

In the art of illumination we use sketch paper for design drawings. The reason for using sketch paper is that it is transparent and when we layer the flower or design we have drawn, we can copy its symmetry. While making all *khatai* drawings, we draw on one side of the paper the pattern we have prepared for drawing the design, and we use the other side of the paper to place a design in the pattern. Thus, when the drawing is finished, we can erase the pattern without spoiling the design on the back side of the paper.

Central Khatai Drawing Techniques

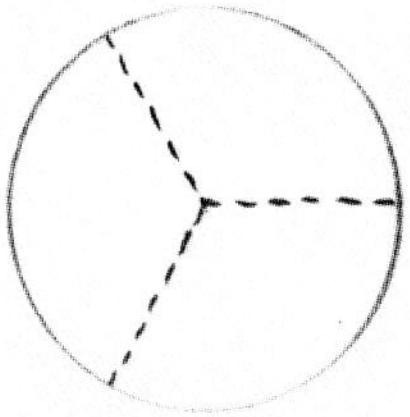

Panch with three petals

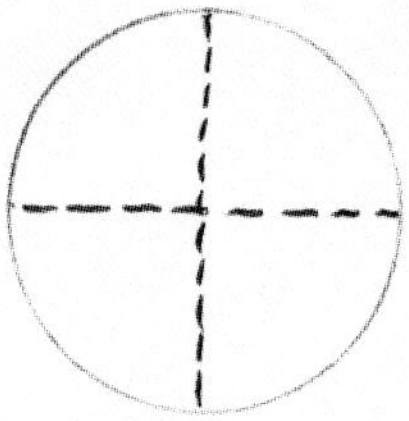

Panch with four petals

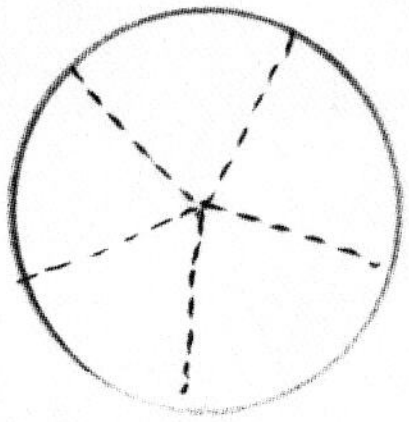

Panch with five petals

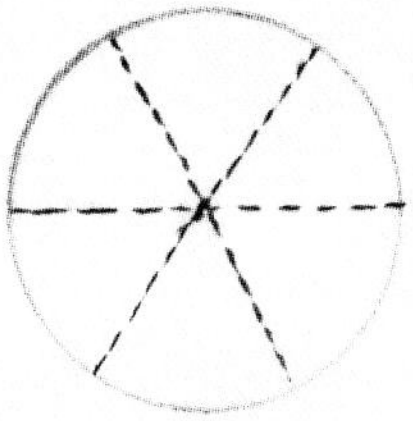

Panch with six petals

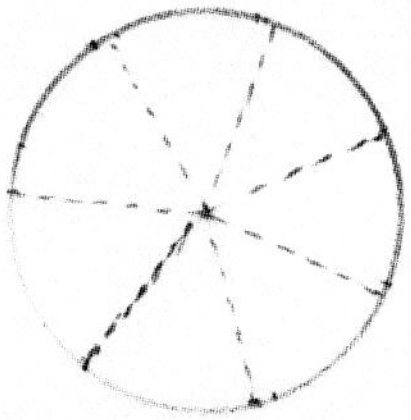

Panch with seven petals

Two-Layered Central Khatais

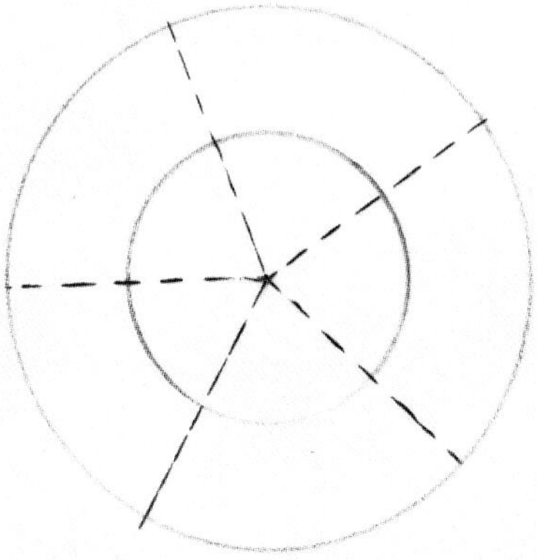

Central Khatai with five segments

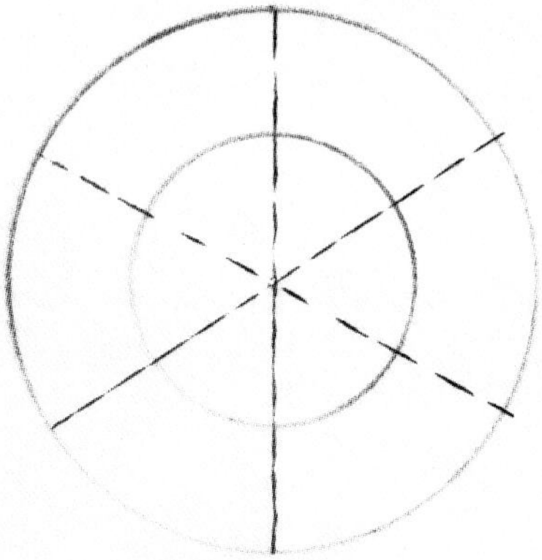

Central Khatai with six segments

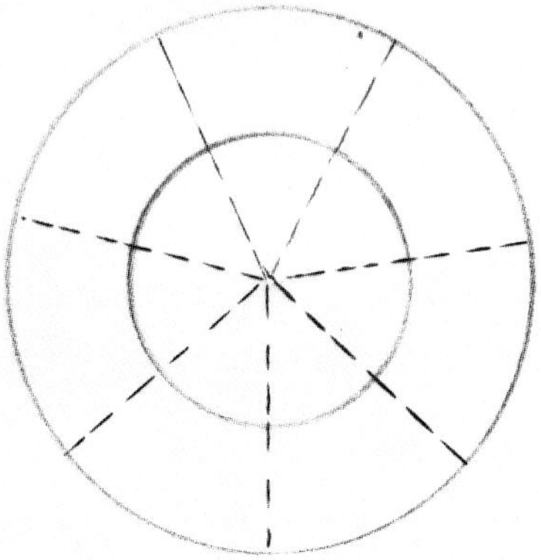

Central Khatai with seven segments

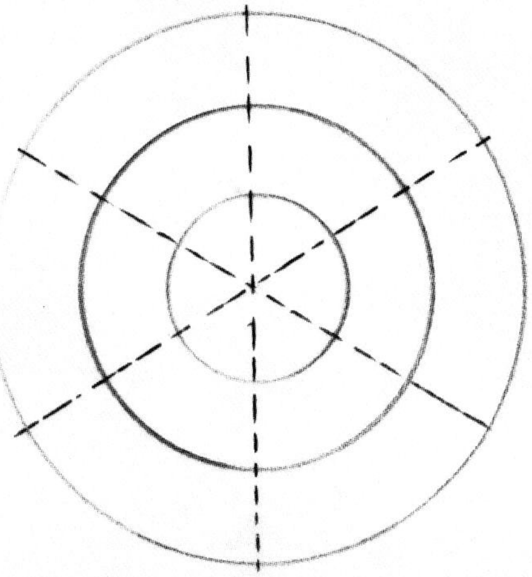

Figure 36 - Panch Types

Three-layered central Khatai with six segments

B. Composition Rules and Making the Design in Classic Ornamentation Arts

Placing the desired shapes on a surface in a style that is balanced and pleasing to the eye is called composition. It has been seen that from ancient times, people busy with art adhere to rules for making a beautiful and correct composition, and that they seek certain proportions. Here, the "Golden Mean" determined by the famous Roman architect Vitruvius is crucial for a balanced proportion. This balance rule was taken as a basis and applied in many Greek temples and especially in Egyptian pyramids. In addition, another ratio called the "Porte d' Harmonie," meaning "Harmony Door," was very widely accepted and applied by Western artists. In respect to the Harmony Door ratio being very easy and providing a result close to the Golden Mean, it is used widely today. This is a rectangle that results from a square being divided in the middle into two equal parts and adding to it a length equal to half the lower line of the square.[5]

In the art of illumination, a design is made that is suitable to the work that is going to be ornamented. If the panel to be ornamented has writing on it, a design giving priority to the writing is made. Just as when a person gets dolled up more than is necessary, their true expression is not reflected externally, if the adornment stands out more than the writing in a written work, the message of the writing will not be noticed. Whereas, in written works, even a single letter encompasses many meanings.

While an artist is creating a composition, she should know:

Why?

For what?

Where (Which material)?

How (Which technique)?

Which result she wants to obtain.[6]

After finding the right answers to all these questions, the area where the design will be applied is designated and, if the work is symmetric, usually one-fourth, but sometimes one-half of the area is taken as a base and the composition is made on the sketch paper (Figure 37).

---

5 Akar and Keskiner, *Türk Süsleme Sanatlarında Desen ve Motif* (Patterns and Motifs in Turkish Ornamentation Arts), p. 15

6 Özkeçeci and Özkeçeci, *Türk Sanatında Tezhip* (Illumination in Turkish Arts), p. 129

Jadwals (tabular lines) are the first stage of composing the illumination design. These lines in tabular form separate the calligraphy and illumination. In the process of manuscript decoration, the calligraphy is contoured with various types of chain patterns and borders so that the *jadwal* points become invisible. These ornamented chain patterns and borders contribute greatly to the esthetic of the work. The rich, ornate illuminations are made surrounding the *jadwals*.

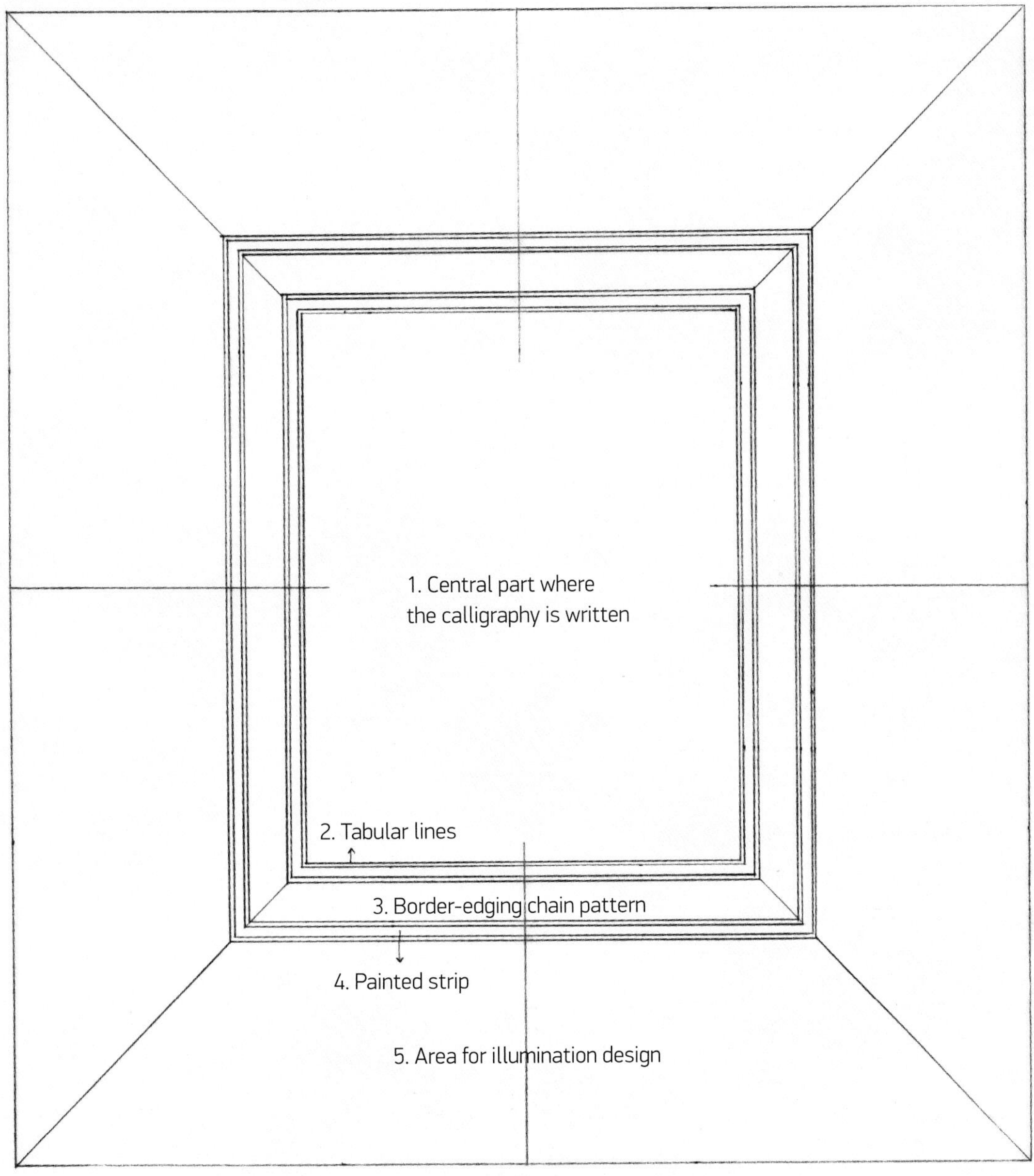

Figure 37 - Areas ornamented in illumination work

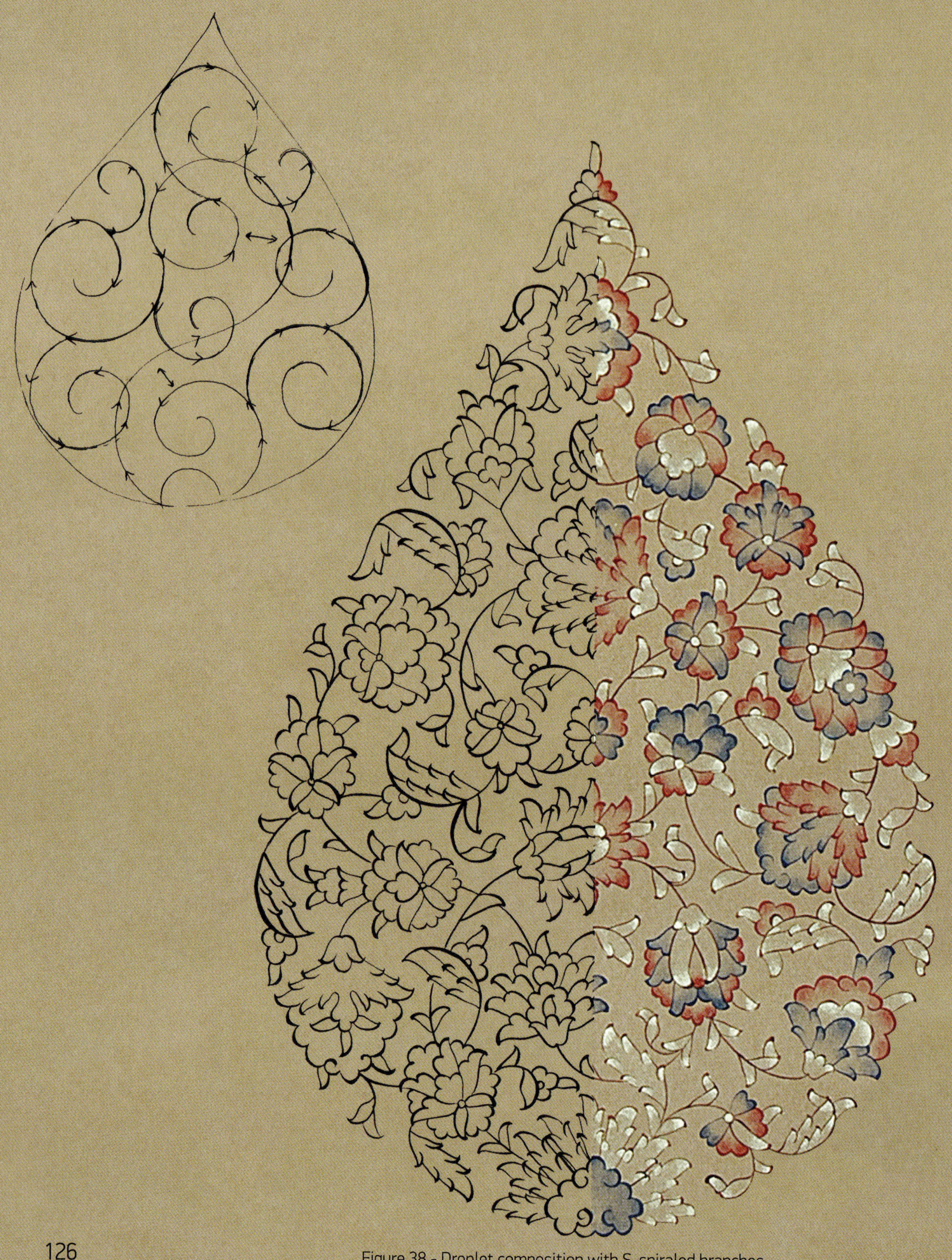

Figure 38 - Droplet composition with S-spiraled branches designed and illuminated by Sema Onat

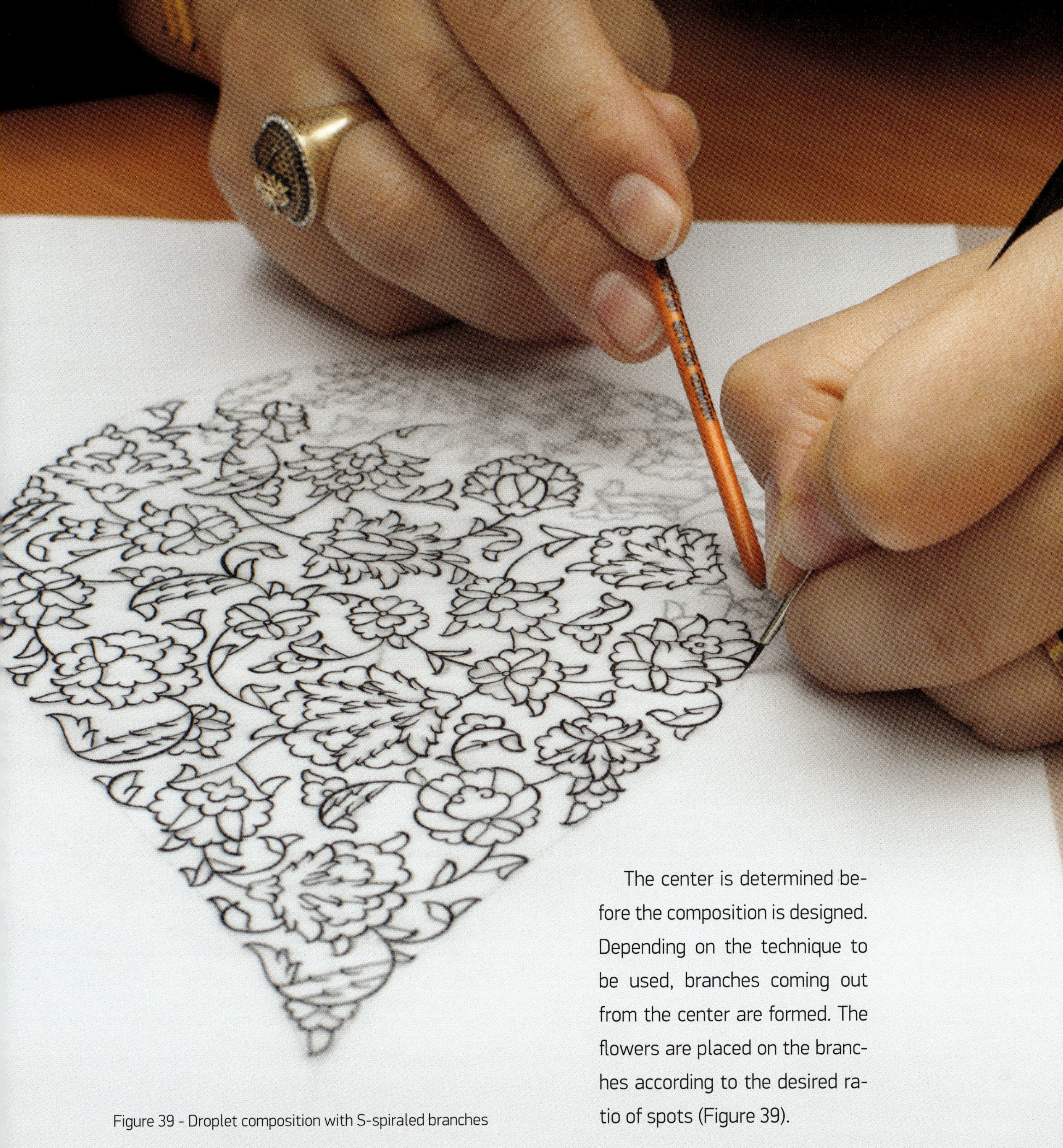

Figure 39 - Droplet composition with S-spiraled branches

The center is determined before the composition is designed. Depending on the technique to be used, branches coming out from the center are formed. The flowers are placed on the branches according to the desired ratio of spots (Figure 39).

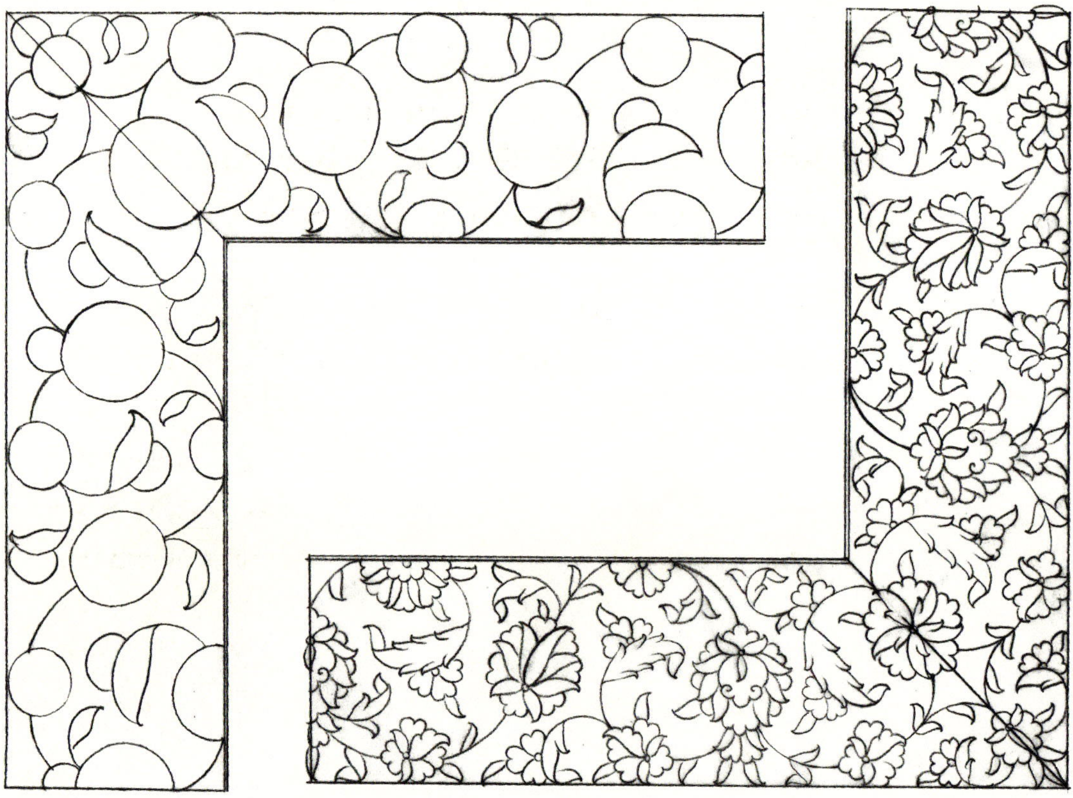

Figure 40 - Drawing one-fourth of the illumination design

At this stage, the sizes of the *khatai*s and *gonca*s to be used are made proportional. The main flowers are made large and secondary flowers are made smaller and distributed in accordance with the technique to be used. There is another matter that needs to be given attention during this stage. If the floral motifs are detailed, then detailed buds are used. If the flowers are not detailed, then plainer buds are used. *Khatai*s and *gonca*s are placed in the designated spots with suitable dimensions according to these rules. Leaf designs are placed at the end of the branches.

Finally, the empty spaces on the branches are completed with leaves in accordance with the design. Just as with the floral motifs, the matter of detail is taken into consideration in leaf drawing. As a result of these stages, one-fourth of the design has been formed (Figure 40).

The composition is completed taking into consideration the symmetry of the one-fourth complete part (Figure 41).

There are many techniques and methods in the formation of the composition. They are:

1. *Surgit* (Ad Infinitum) Technique
2. Single Thread Designs
3. Two-Thread Designs
4. Intersecting Designs
5. Touching Designs
6. Designs Suitable to the S Rule
7. Free Designs

Figure 41 - Completed design

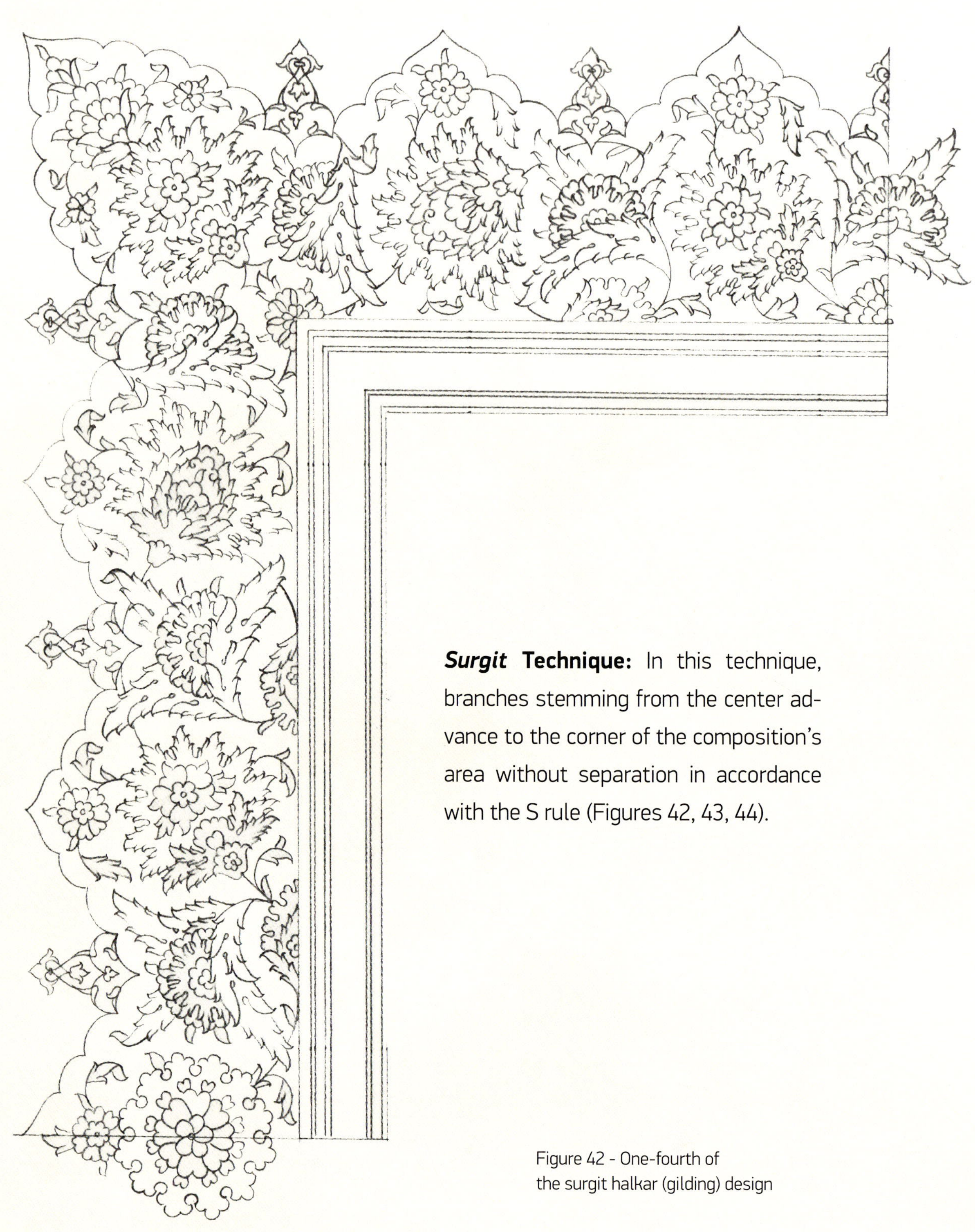

***Surgit* Technique:** In this technique, branches stemming from the center advance to the corner of the composition's area without separation in accordance with the S rule (Figures 42, 43, 44).

Figure 42 - One-fourth of the surgit halkar (gilding) design

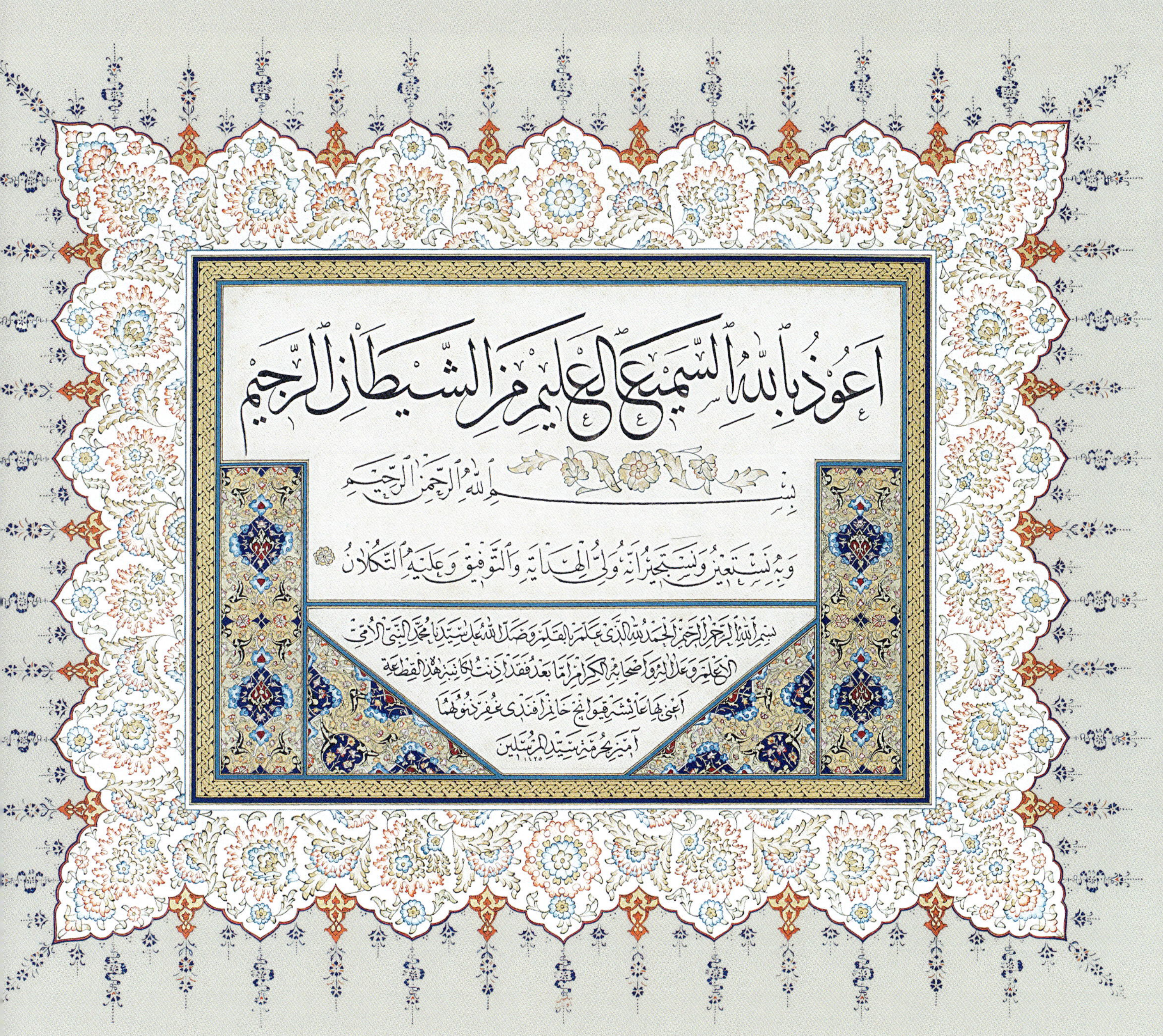

Illuminated surgit halkar (gilding) design with repeating Rumis and tigh work by Sema Onat

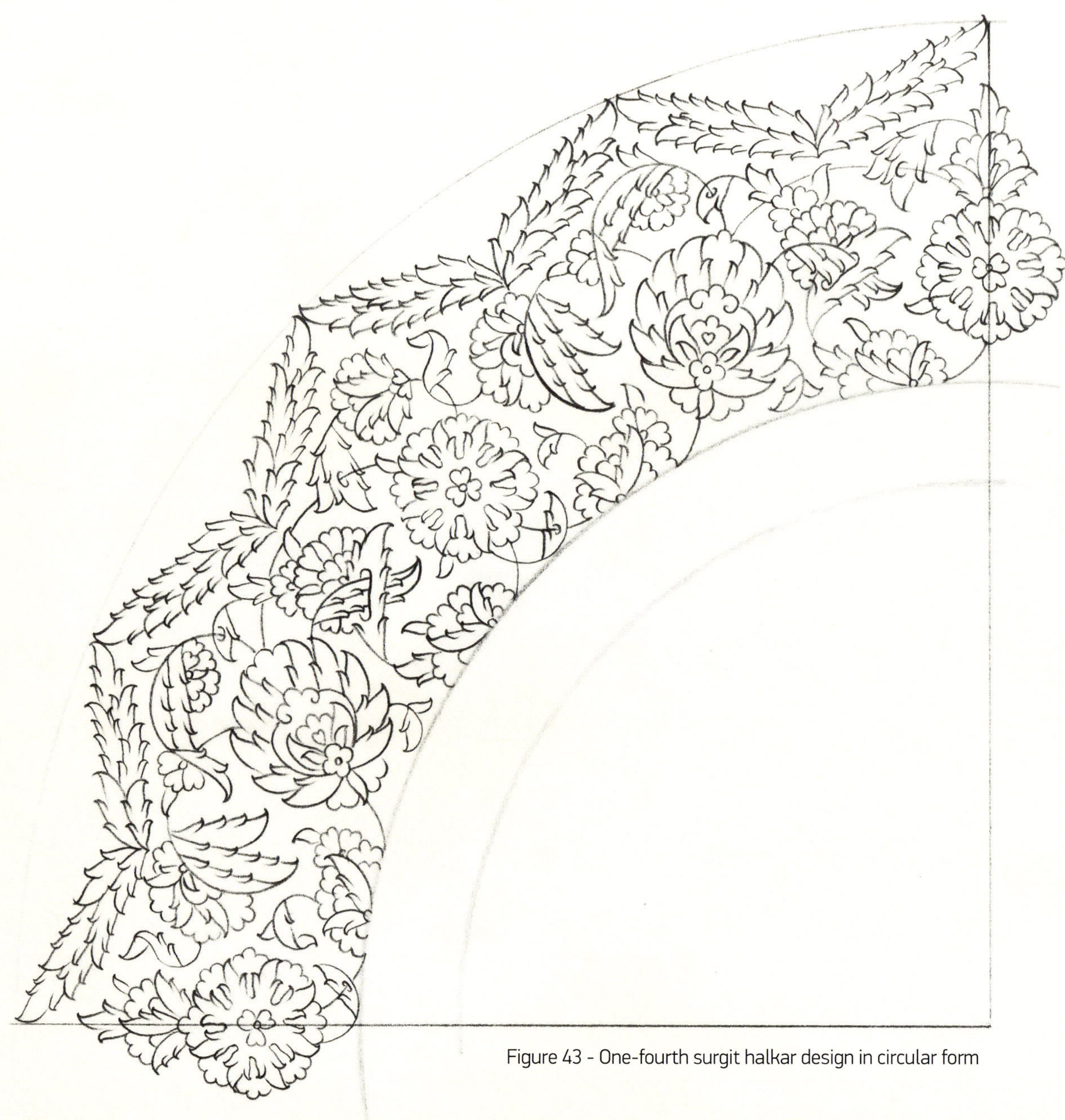

Figure 43 - One-fourth surgit halkar design in circular form

Illuminated surgit halkar (gilding) design by Sema Onat

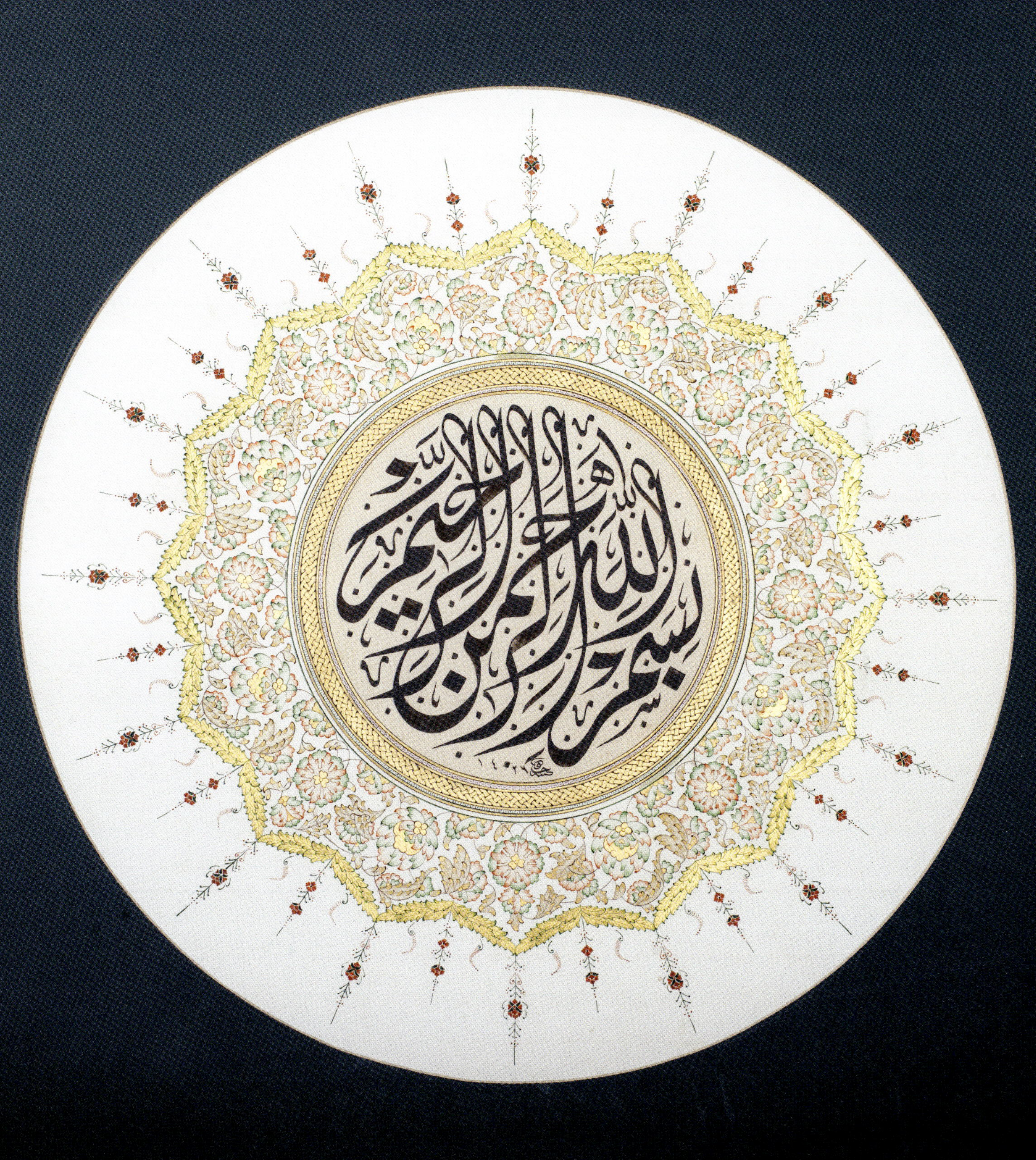
بسم الله الرحمن الرحيم

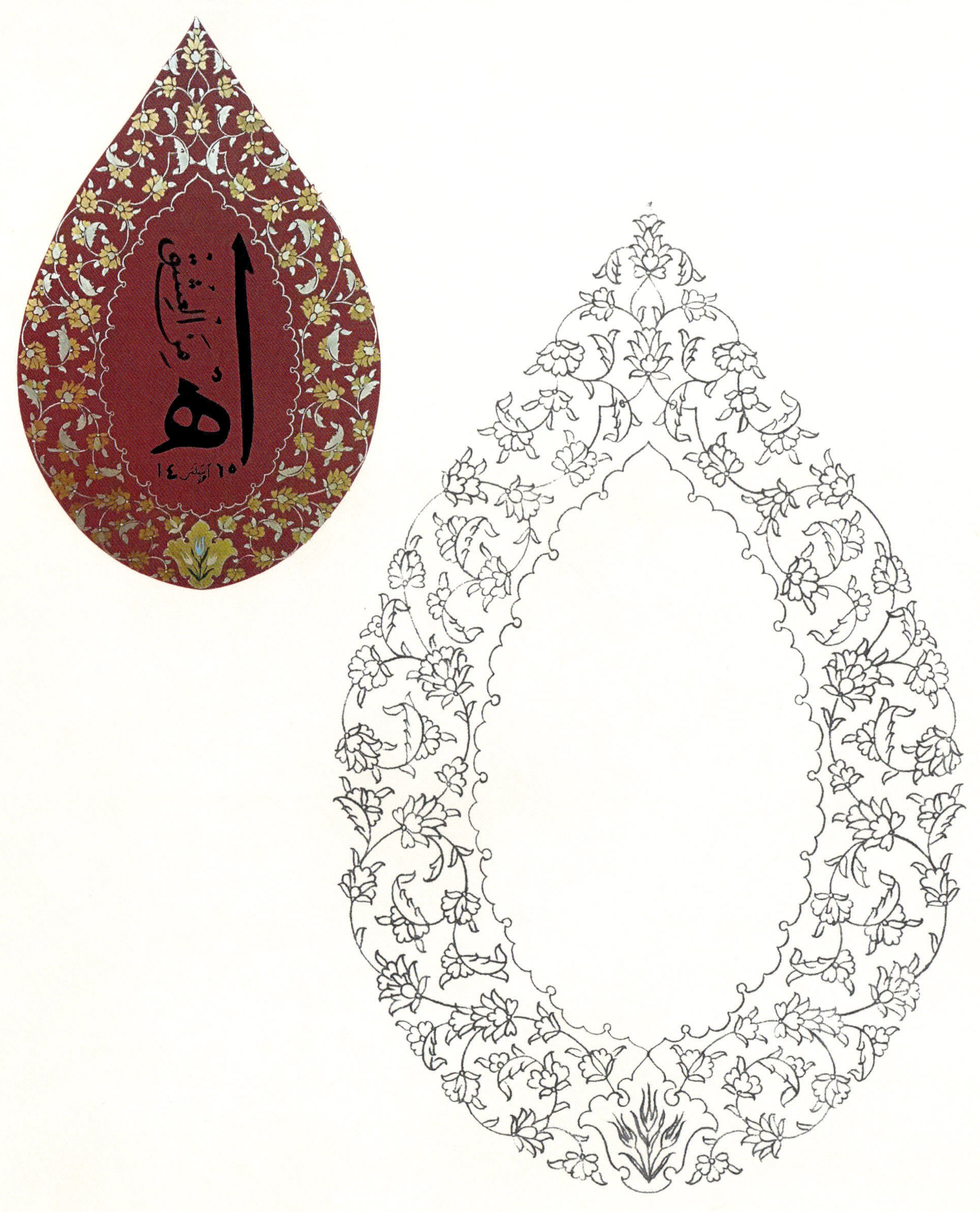

Figure 44 - Surgit halkar (gilding) with "S" spirals designed and illuminated by Sema Onat

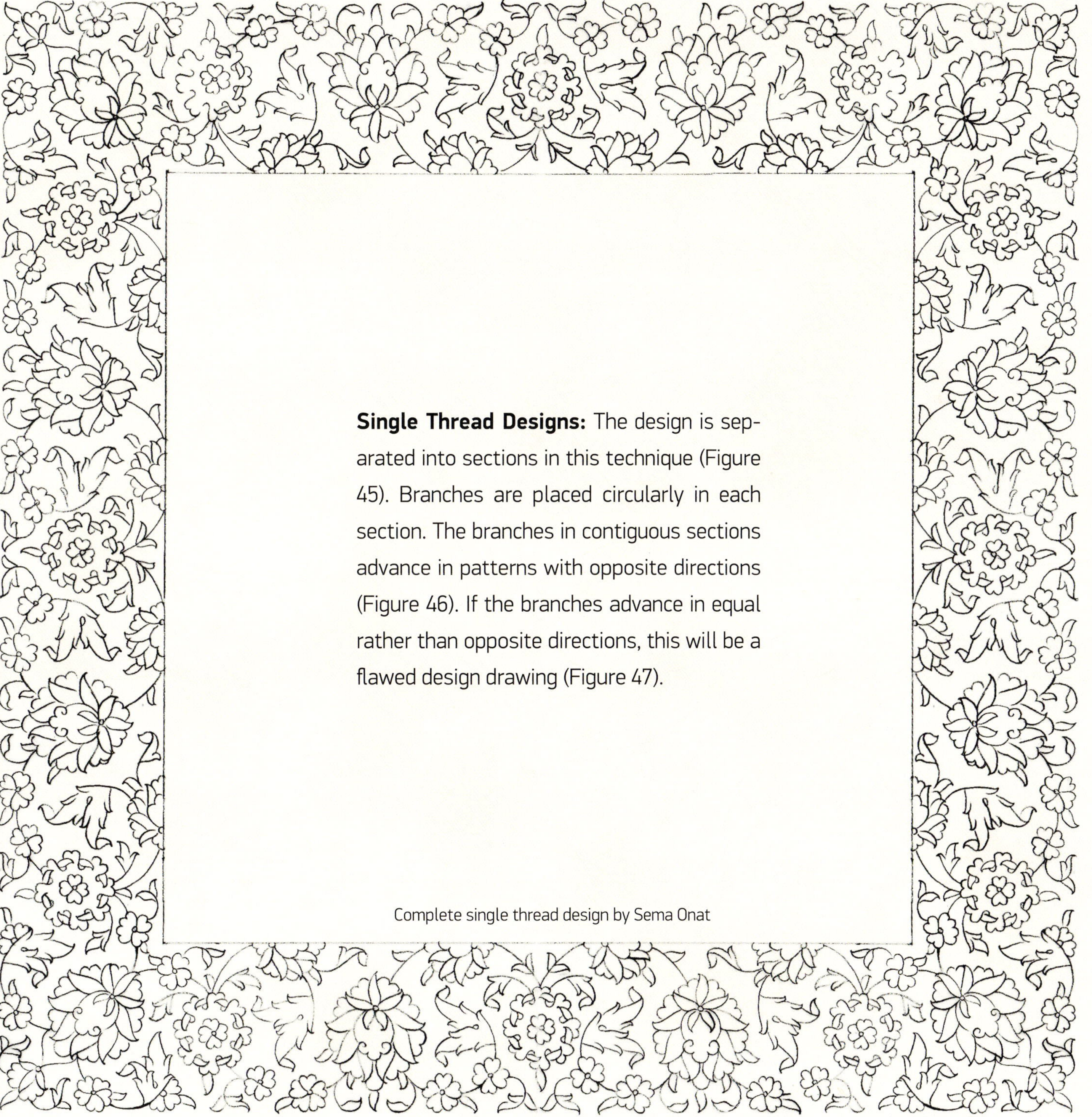

Single Thread Designs: The design is separated into sections in this technique (Figure 45). Branches are placed circularly in each section. The branches in contiguous sections advance in patterns with opposite directions (Figure 46). If the branches advance in equal rather than opposite directions, this will be a flawed design drawing (Figure 47).

Complete single thread design by Sema Onat

Figure 45 - One-fourth drawing of single thread design

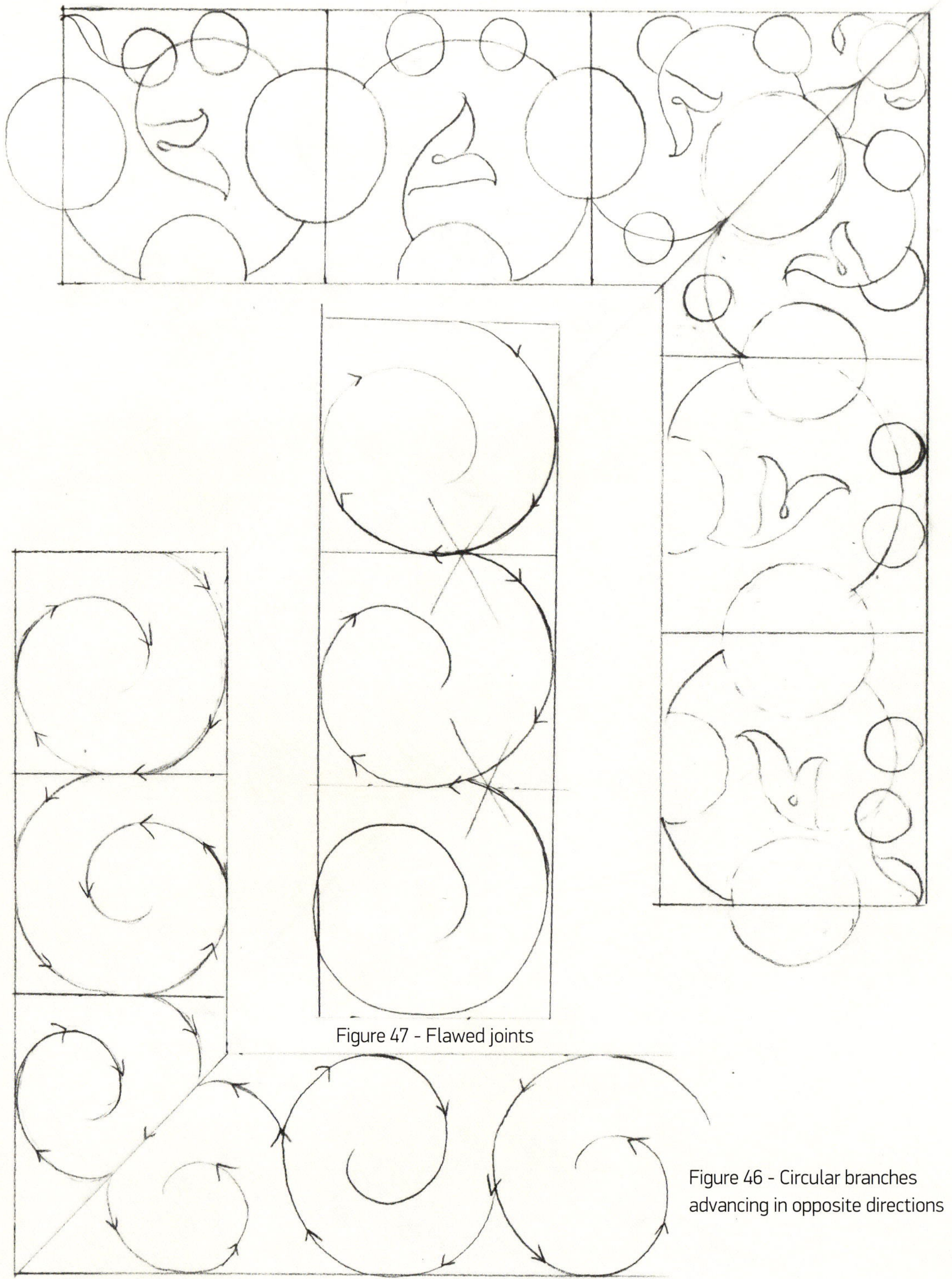

Figure 47 - Flawed joints

Figure 46 - Circular branches advancing in opposite directions

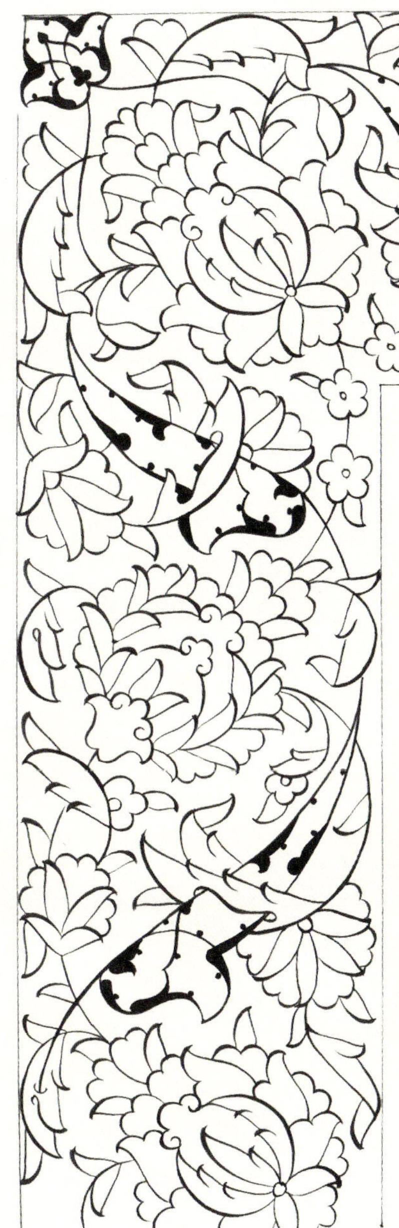

Figure 48 - One-fourth drawing of a two-thread design

Two-Thread Designs: In this technique, two different branches stem from the same center. One of the branches is a leaf and the other is a flower (Figure 48).

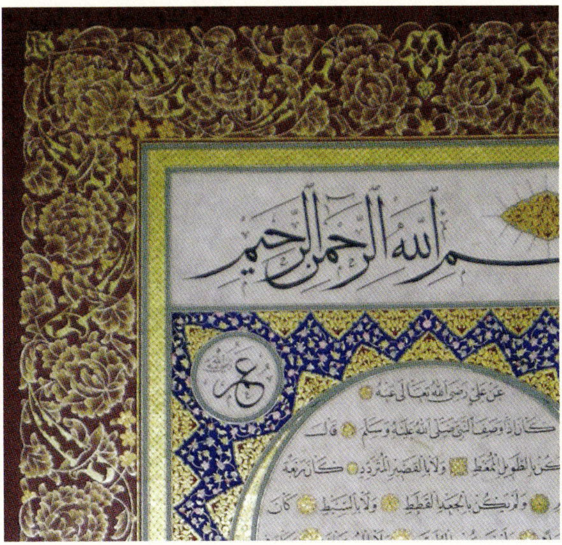

Detail from hilya work with two-thread design by Sema Onat

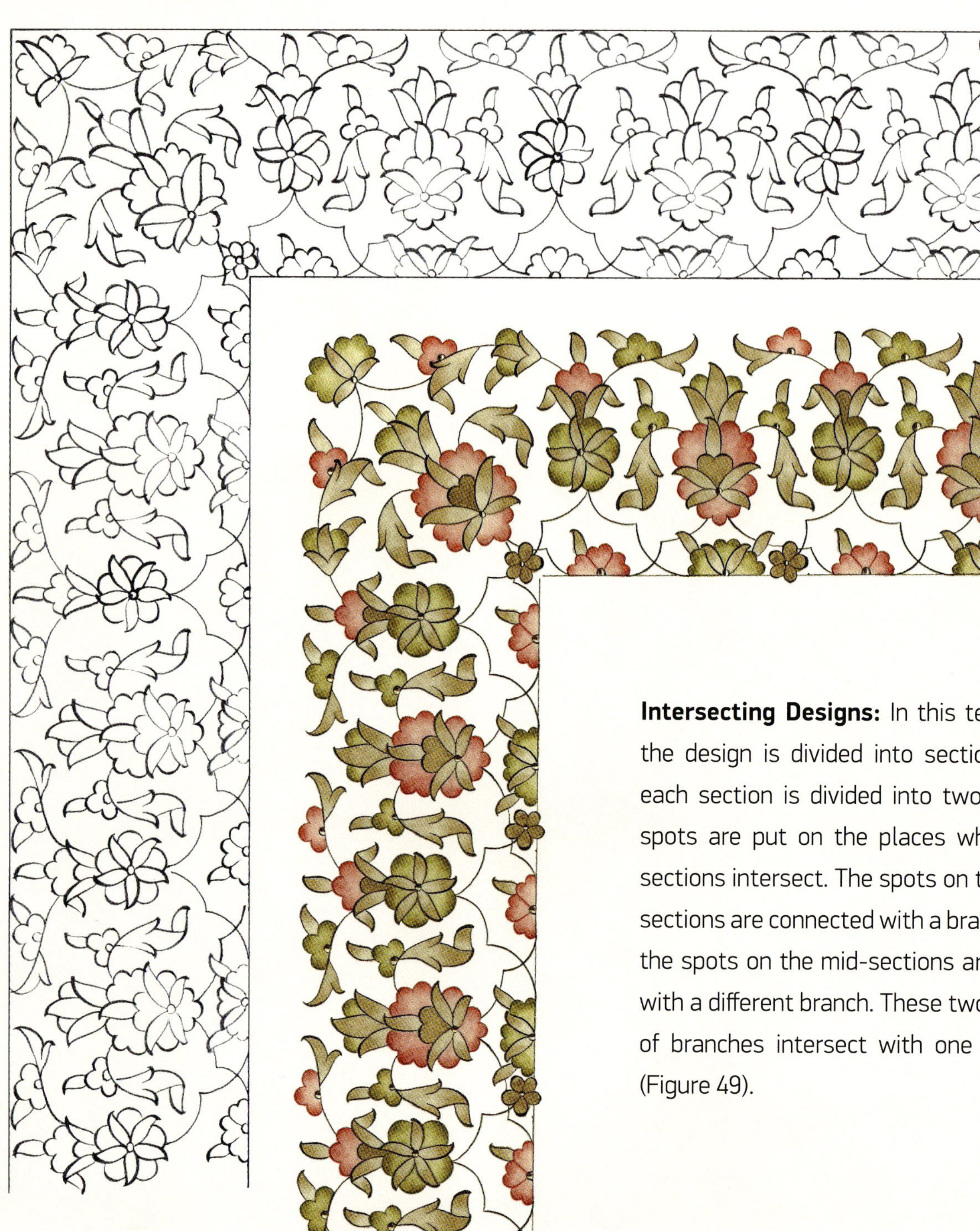

Figure 49 - One-fourth drawing of an intersecting design

Illuminated design

Intersecting Designs: In this technique the design is divided into sections, and each section is divided into two. *Khatai* spots are put on the places where the sections intersect. The spots on the main sections are connected with a branch, and the spots on the mid-sections are joined with a different branch. These two groups of branches intersect with one another (Figure 49).

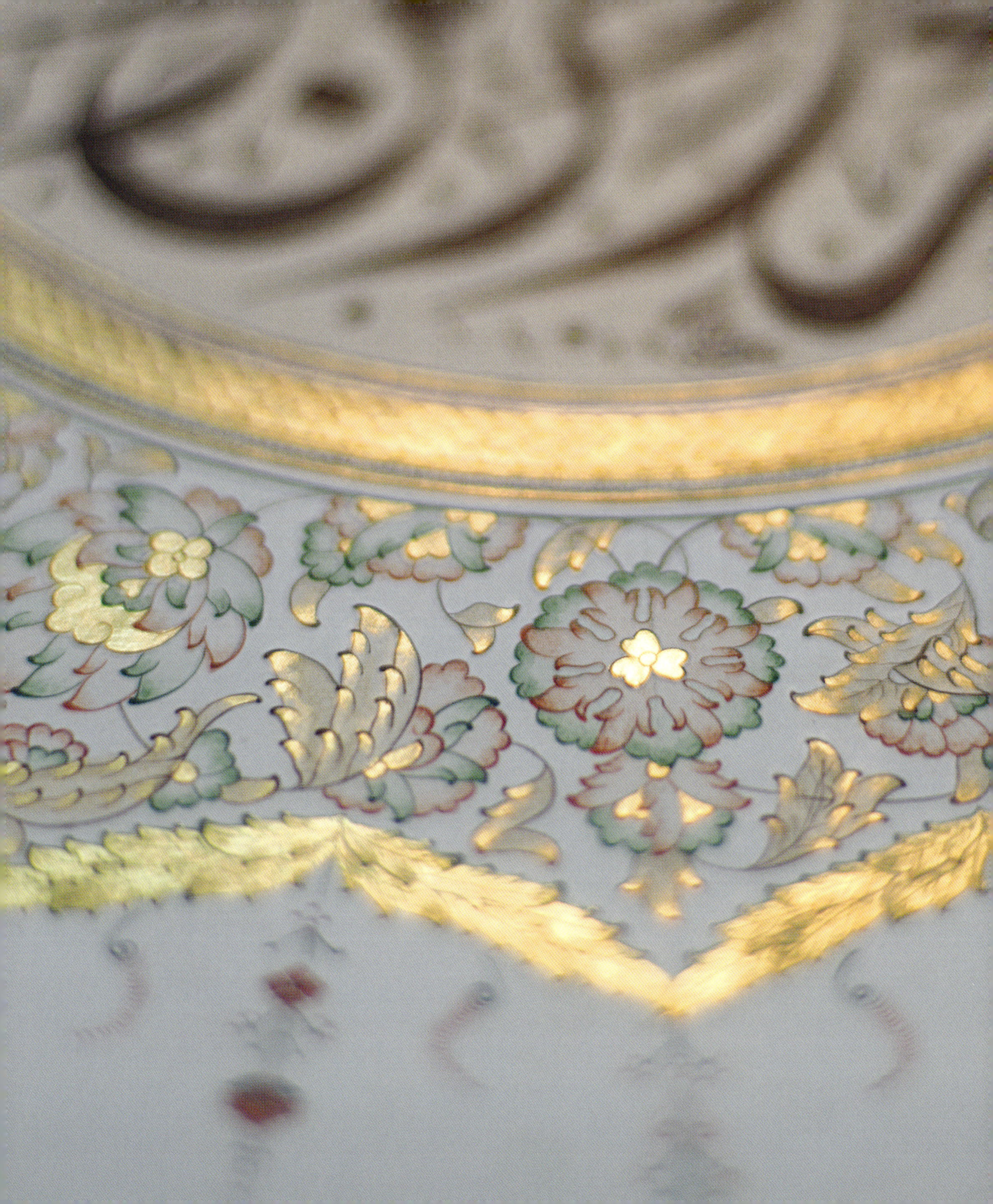

Touching Designs

The design is divided into sections in this technique. The branches are placed on the sections circularly and the contiguous sections are symmetrical with one another. For this reason, the branches in two sections touch each other (Figures 50, 51).

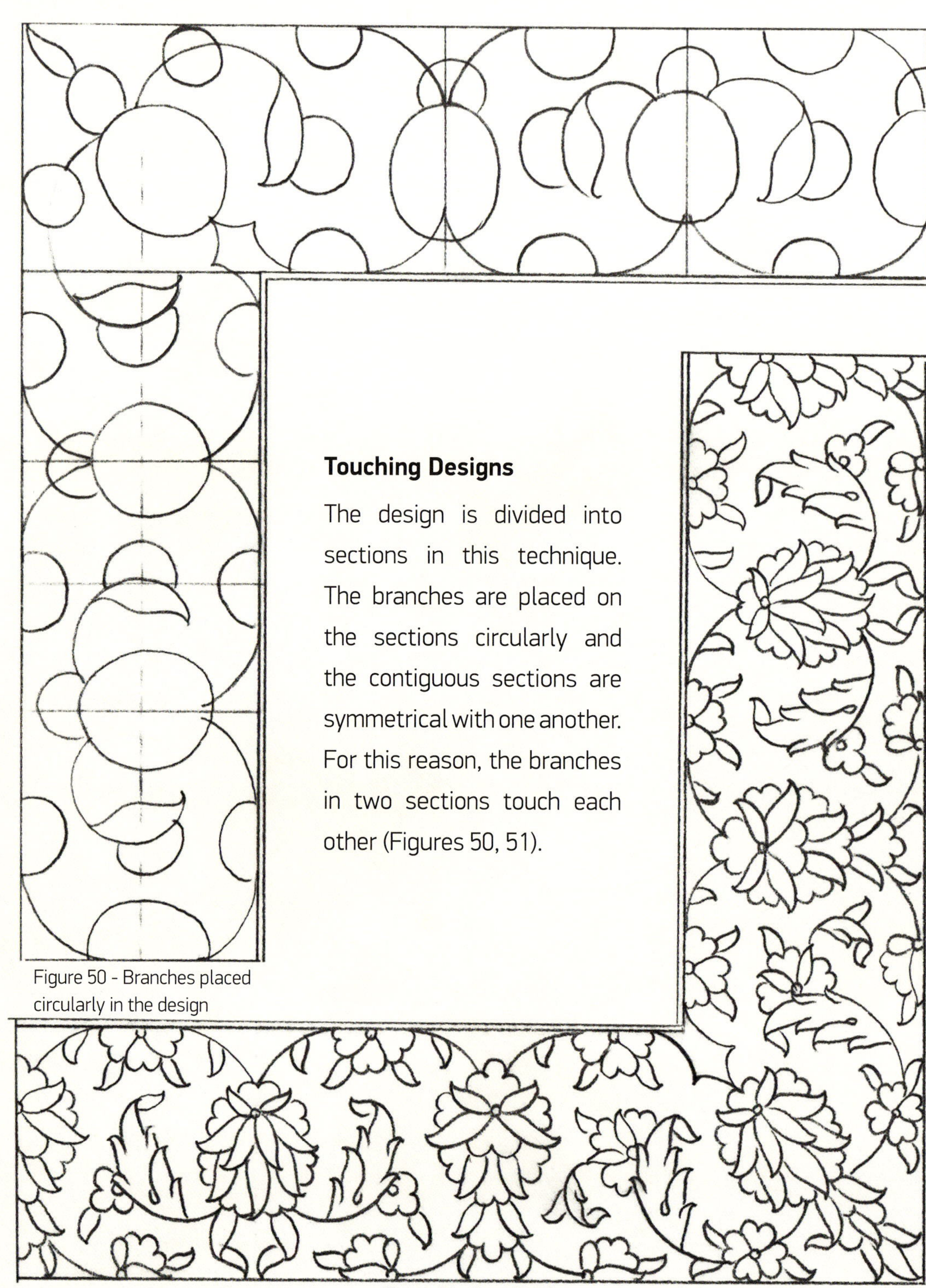

Figure 50 - Branches placed circularly in the design

Figure 51 - One-fourth drawing of a touching design

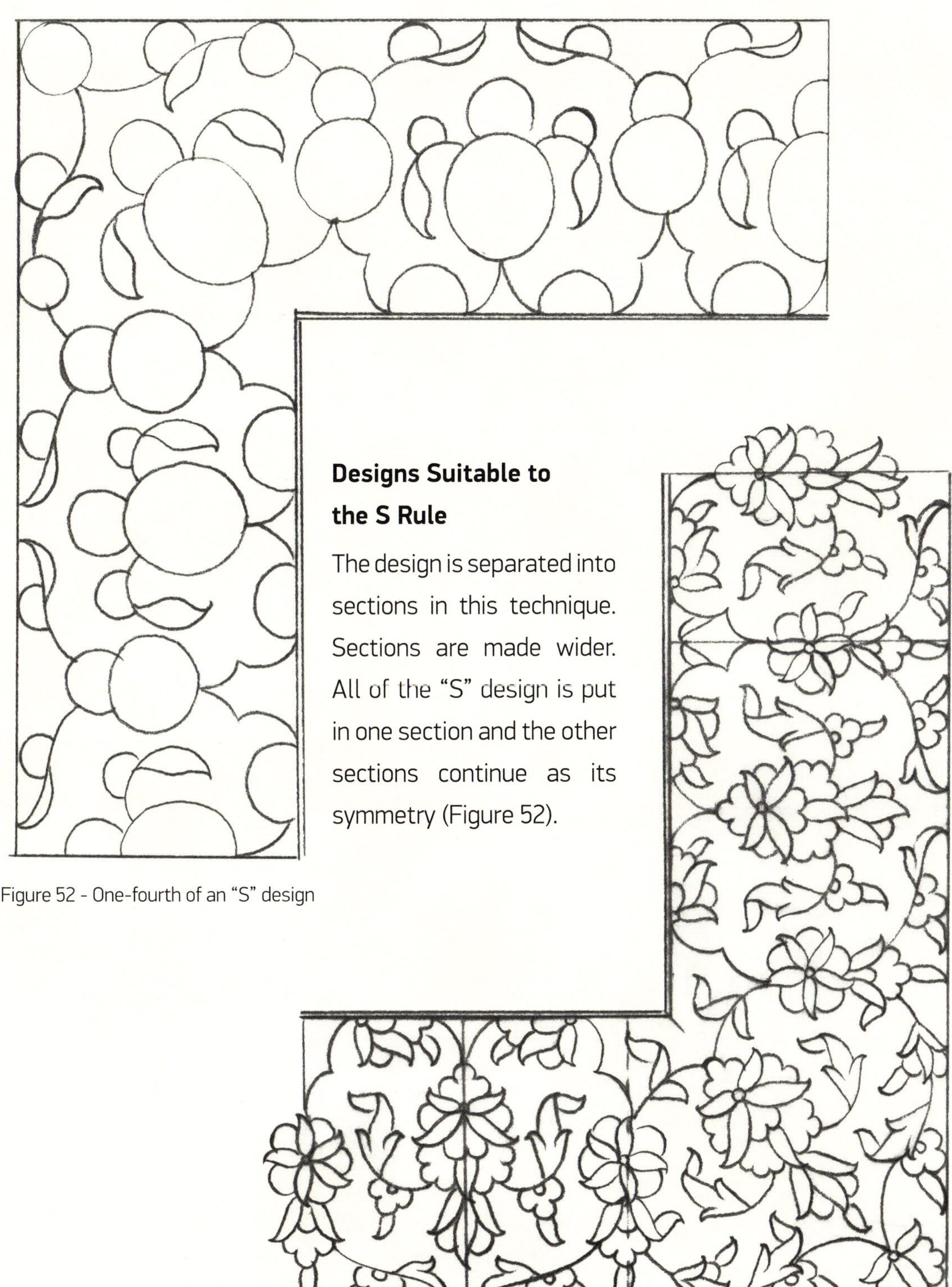

Figure 52 - One-fourth of an "S" design

Designs Suitable to the S Rule

The design is separated into sections in this technique. Sections are made wider. All of the "S" design is put in one section and the other sections continue as its symmetry (Figure 52).

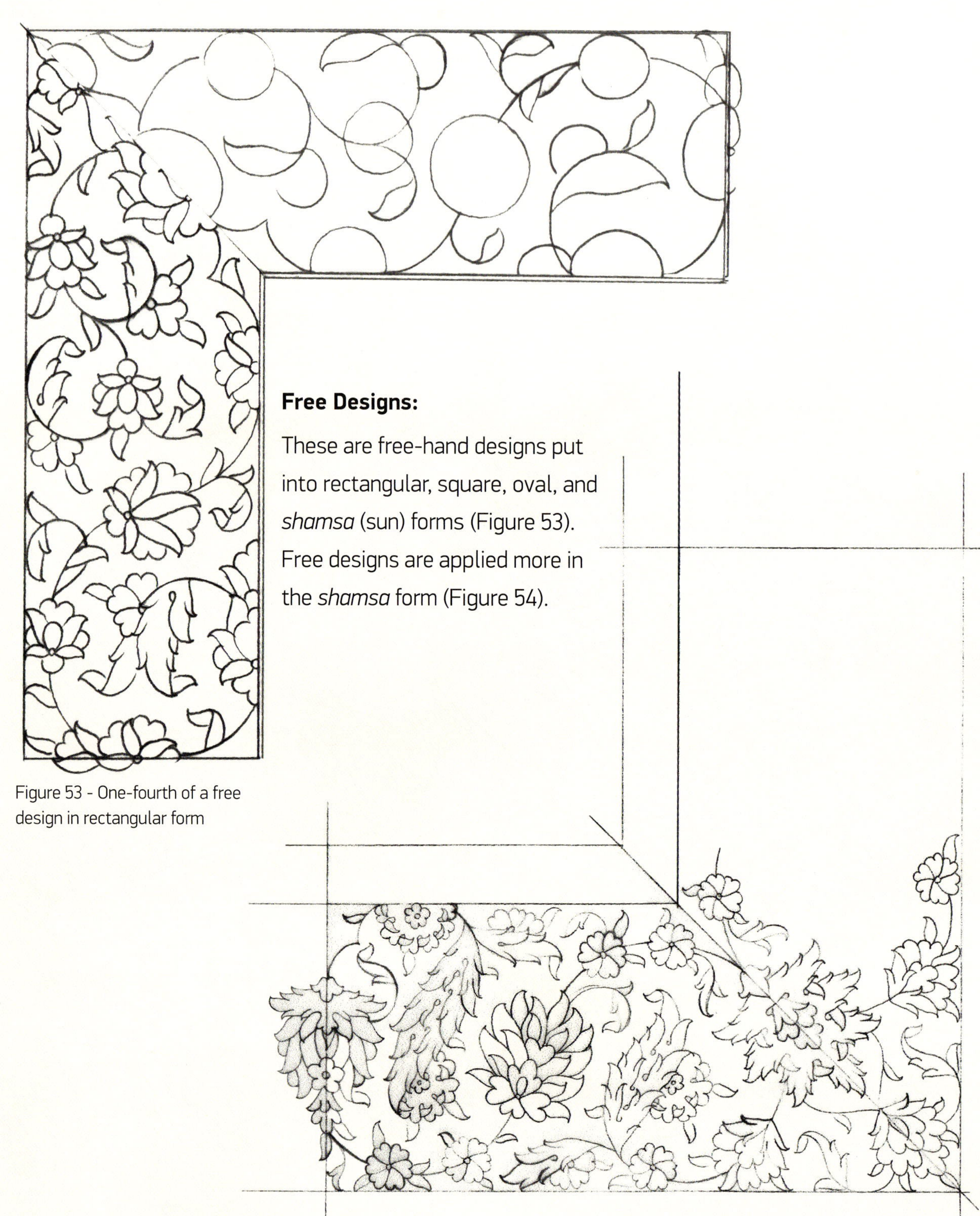

Figure 53 - One-fourth of a free design in rectangular form

Free Designs:

These are free-hand designs put into rectangular, square, oval, and *shamsa* (sun) forms (Figure 53). Free designs are applied more in the *shamsa* form (Figure 54).

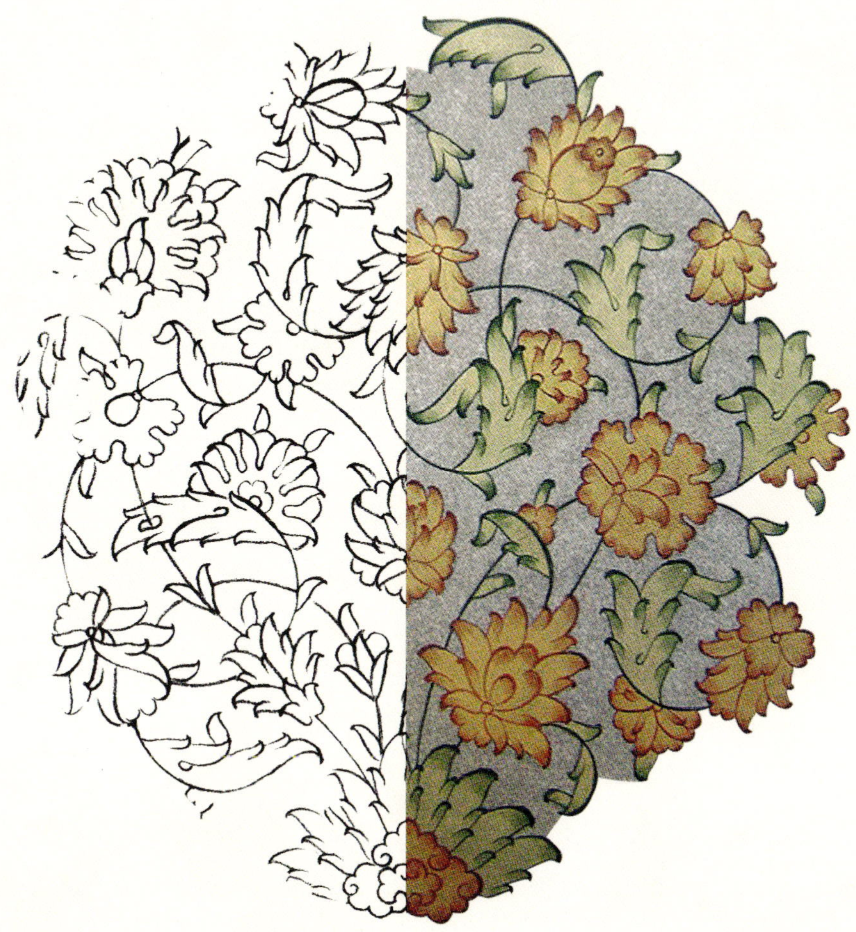

Figure 54 - Free-design in shamsa (sun) form

C. Transferring the Design

Completed on the sketch paper, the composition is put onto the surface where the work will be made. For this, the sketch paper where the design is drawn is turned backwards on the surface. The whole design is drawn over with a lead pencil. This is called “desen silkeleme” (transferring the design).

D. Painting the Design

As mentioned before, the task of painting in illumination begins with spreading gold on previously designated areas. After spreading the gold, the gilded branches and leaves are polished with a burnisher, and the places designated to be shiny in the background design are also polished. The next thing to be done is the painting of the motifs with various colors.

In classic illumination, motifs are painted in light colors and are distributed evenly. Ornamental lines are drawn to designate the outer limits of the motifs. Soot ink or commercial ink is used for these contour lines. In classic illumination, nuance is not made on these contour lines while it is made on the *halkar* (gilding) ornamentation. These contours can be drawn with gold on this type of gilding.

After this the surface is colored. In classic illumination, dark colors are preferred more as surface colors. Care should be taken so that the surface color does not have waves in it. Finally, the flowers are toned. The flowers on the gold surface can have their edges painted with a dark tone of their own color. Just as the edges of flowers can be toned on dark backgrounds, they can also be painted in the degradé style.

In painting the degradé style, three tones can be obtained from each color used. These tones are painted on motifs from the lightest to the darkest by decreasing the paint lines (Figure 55).

If *tigh* work is going to be made in the composition, after taking the measurements of the *tigh* areas, the design is made on sketch paper and transferred to the side of the work. Usually coloring *tigh*s is done with a brush using background tones.

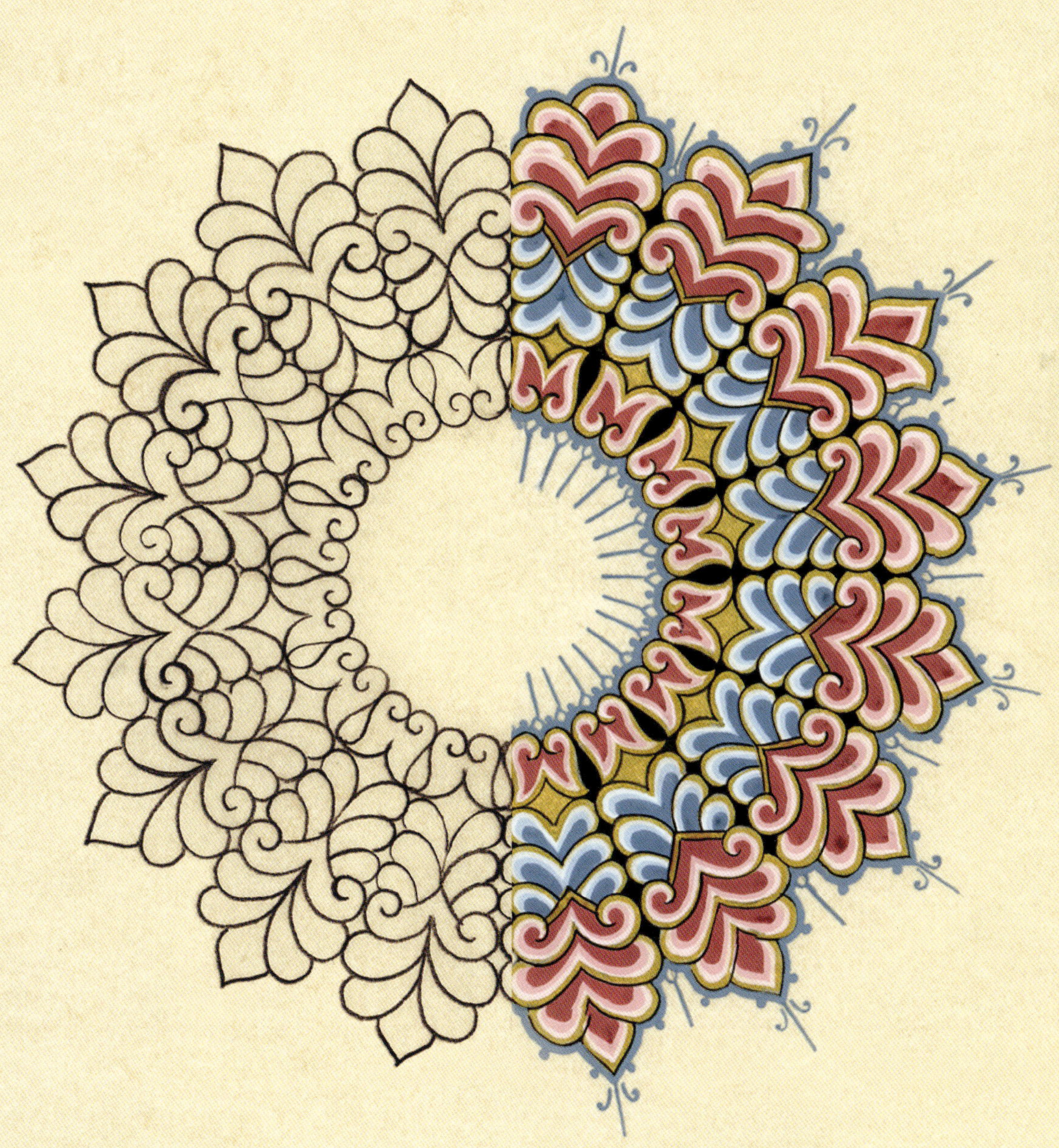

Figure 55 - Gradient colored munhani design by Sema Onat

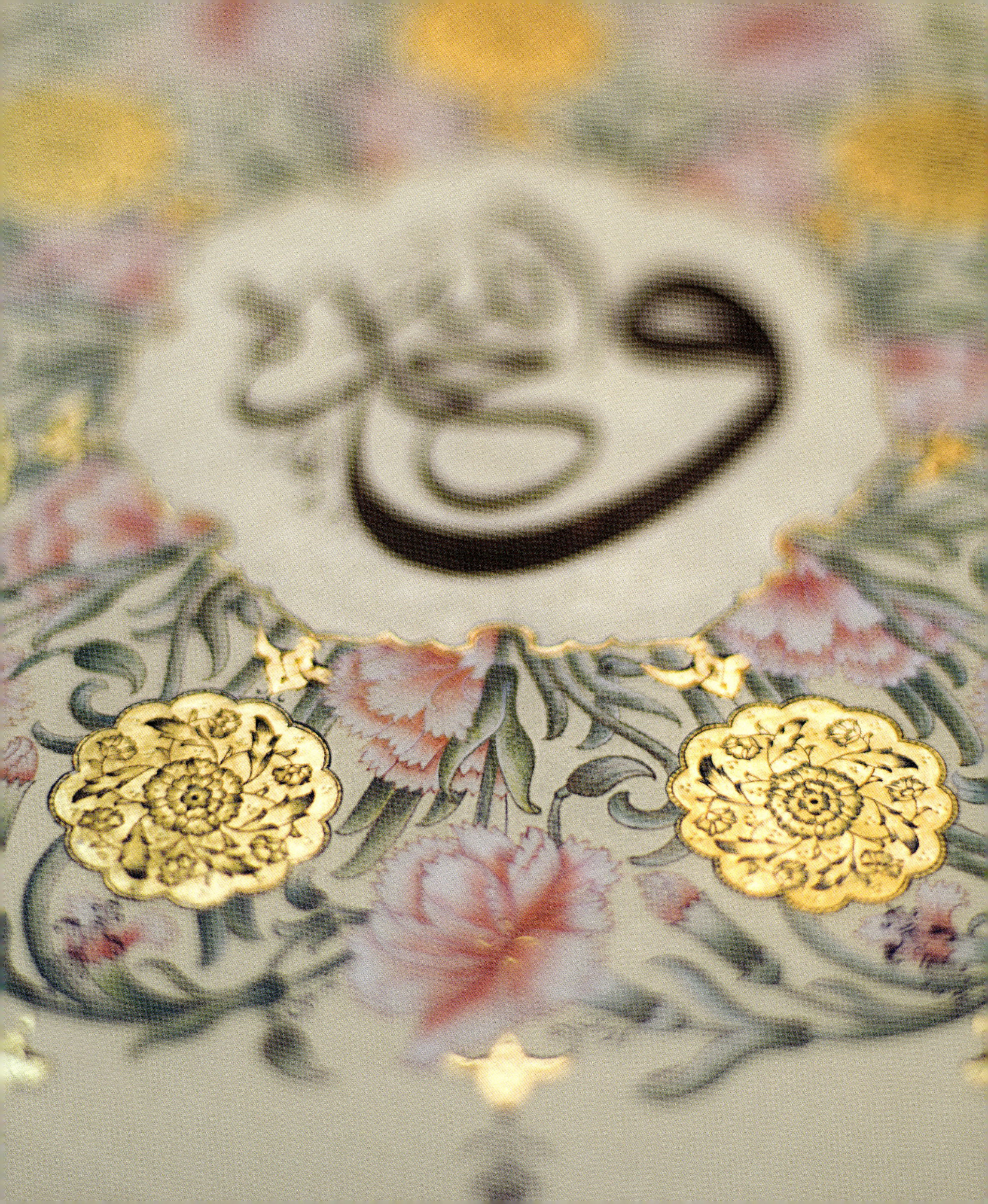

Part Six

General Forms Used in Illumination

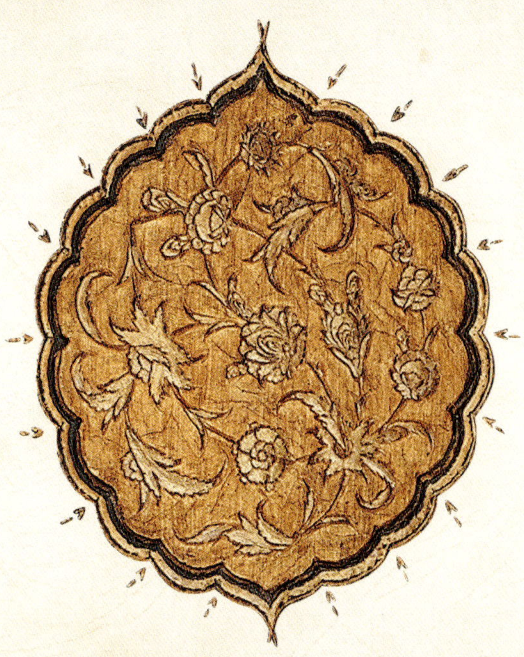

Figure 56a - *Shamsa* motif encircled with *tigh*s

A. Shamsa

They are oval and round forms. They are usually used on the bound covers and inner cover pages of handwritten works. There are examples of *shamsa* that only use gold or gold together with navy blue. *Shamsa* is a derivative of the sun (*shams*) motif. *Shamsa* designs symbolize the sun and light. Motifs called *salbak* can be added to the lower and upper parts of the *shamsa*. *Salbak*s are the same as one another and can be drawn tied to the *shamsa* or separate from it. *Shamsa* motifs can also be encircled with *tigh*s (Figure 56).

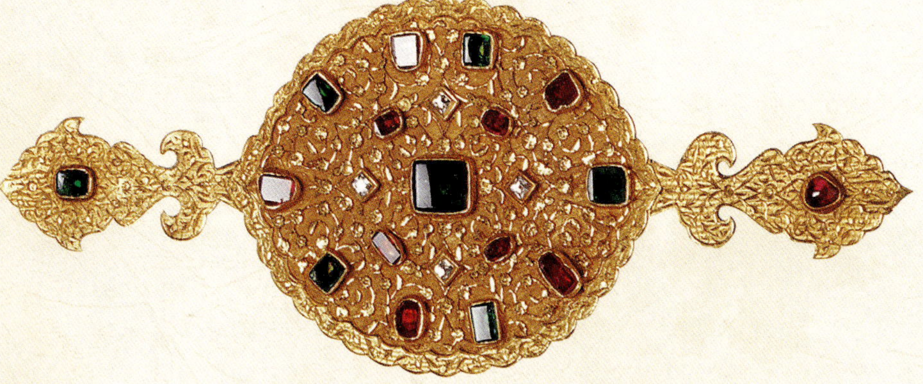

Figure 56b - *Shamsa* motif detail with *salbak*s

Elaborate illumination design applied to the Qur'an cover with magnificent craftsmanship. Topkapi Palace Museum

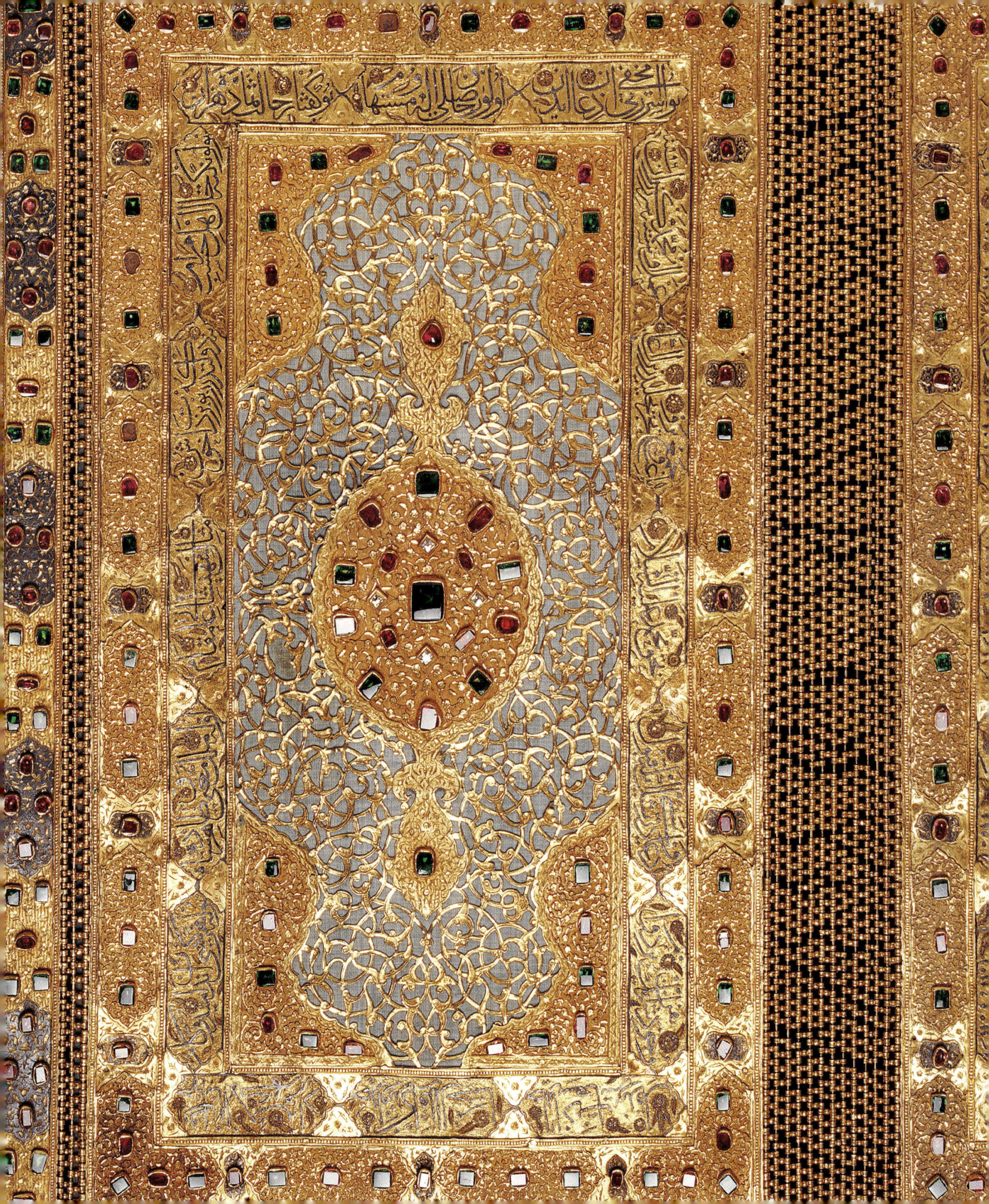

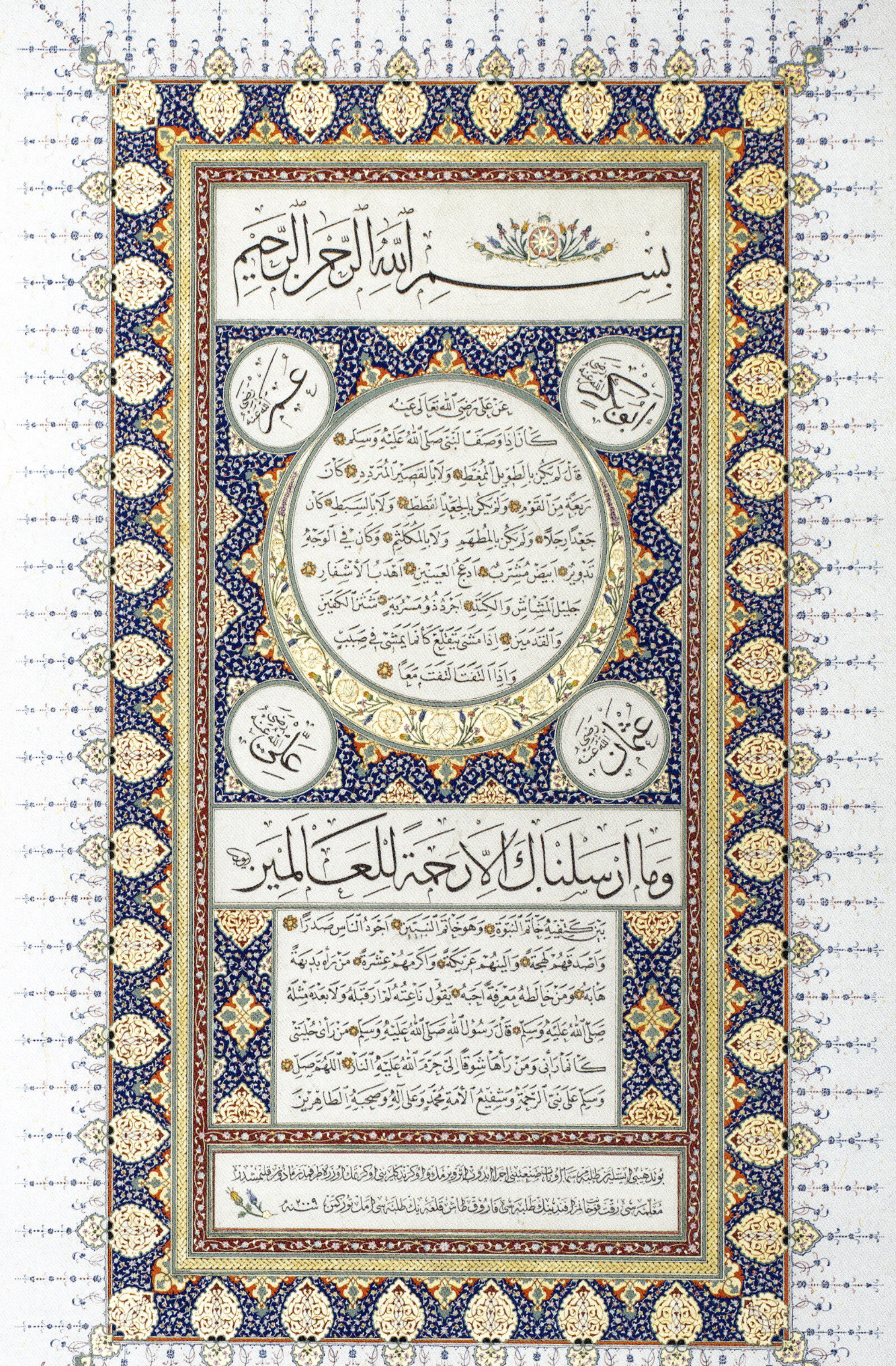

Figure 57 - *Hilya* wor
by Sema Onat

B. Hilya

Meaning adornment, ornamentation, beautiful attribute, and beautiful face, *hilya* is used to describe the Noble Prophet's physical characteristics and character traits. It is related that while Prophet Muhammad, upon him be peace and blessings, was very ill, when his daughter Fatima mentioned her sadness at not being able to see his face again, he said to his son-in-law Ali ibn Abi Talib, "Write my *hilya* so that it will be as if those who see it after me will have seen me."[8]

A classic *hilya* has the following sections:

1. Head Position (*Bash Maqam*): This is the top section where the Basmala is written. The ornamentation in the top position differs according to spaces. If the Basmala is written with the elongated (*kashida*) *sin* letter, the part where the letter *sin* extends is ornamented. If the Basmala is written with a cursive script (*thuluth*), the corners resting on the *jadwal* of the top position are adorned.
2. Central Part: This is the middle section of the *hilya*. It is usually in the form of a large circle. It is where the main writing is written. The names of the four rightly-guided caliphs are placed in the central part in small circles on the four sides of the text.
3. Crescent: In some *hilya*s the lower part of the round middle section is drawn as a crescent. Ornamentation is also made here.
4. Verse (*Ayah*): This is the section just under the middle section found in the form of a long rectangle. Here a verse describing the Noble Prophet is written.
5. Skirt: Here the continuation of the *hilya* text is written. The calligrapher's signature and the date are also put here.
6. *Qoltuq*: It is located on both sides of the skirt. These are sections richly adorned with illumination (Figure 57).

---

8 Özkeçeci and Özkeçeci, *Türk Sanatında Tezhip* (Illumination in Turkish Arts), p. 167

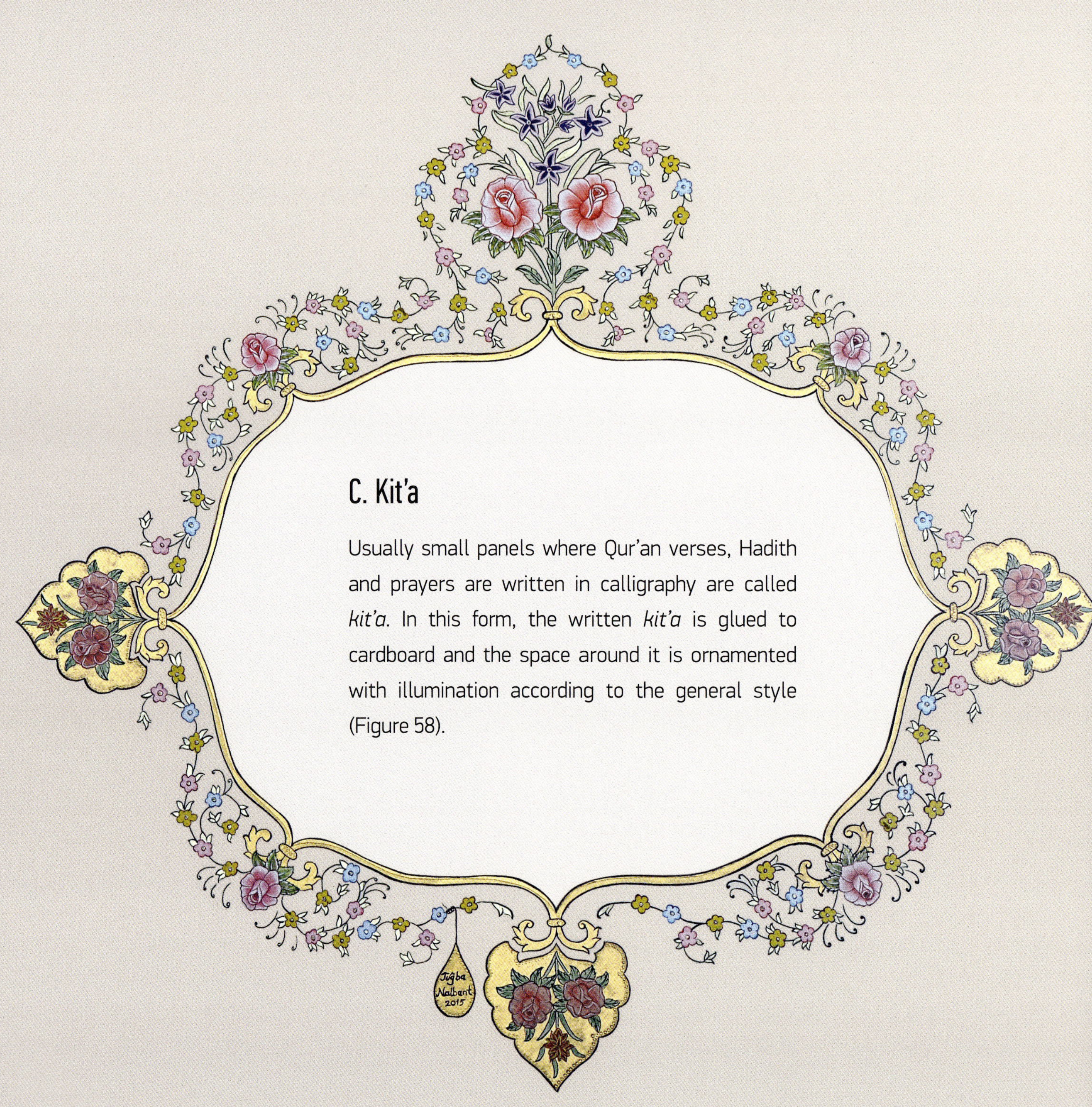

C. Kit'a

Usually small panels where Qur'an verses, Hadith and prayers are written in calligraphy are called *kit'a*. In this form, the written *kit'a* is glued to cardboard and the space around it is ornamented with illumination according to the general style (Figure 58).

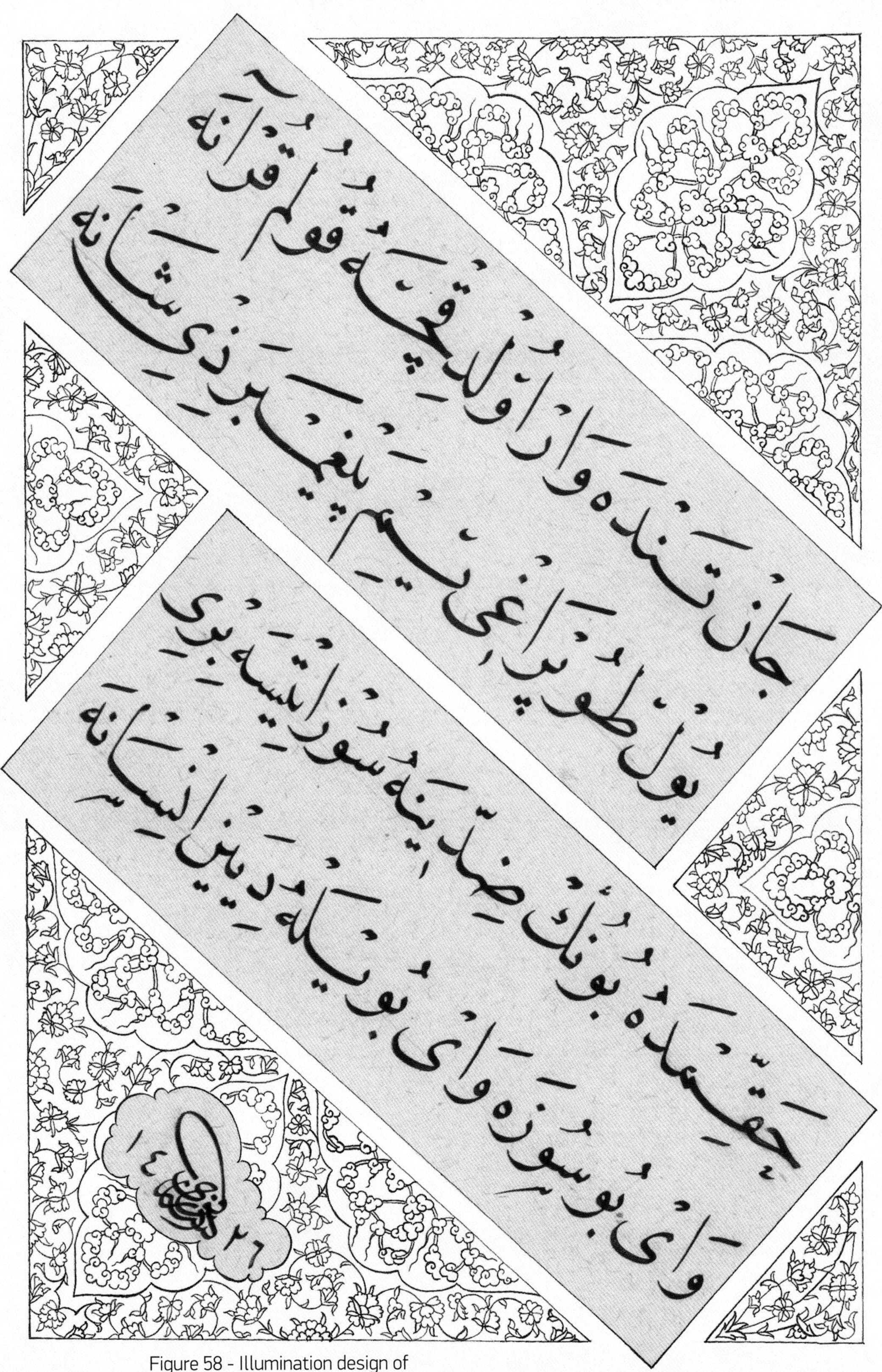

Figure 58 - Illumination design of
Mail (sloping) Kit'a by Sema Onat

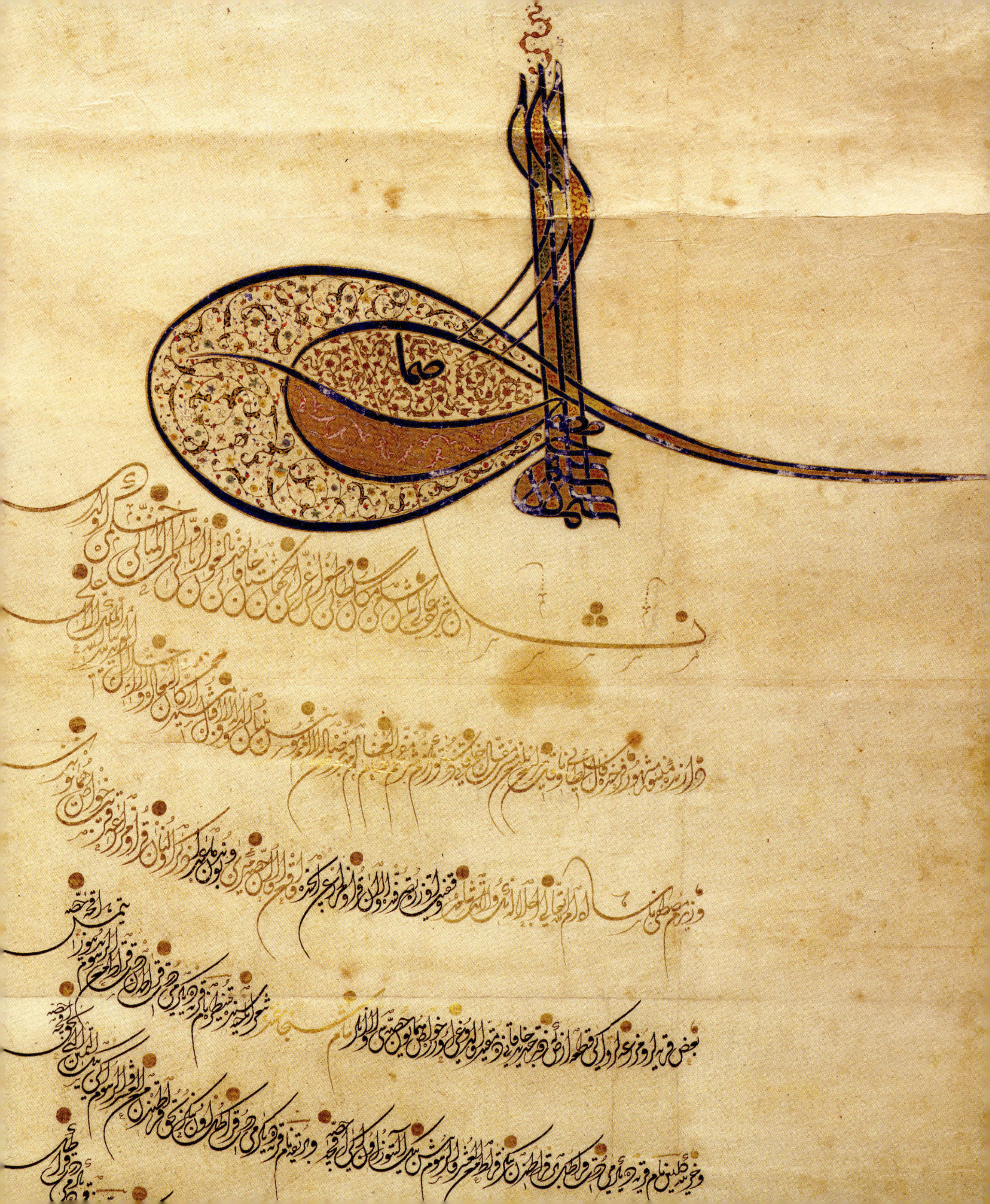

D. Ottoman Ferman (Edict)

The word "ferman" is derived from the Persian infinitive to order, command. The edict is a written decree given by the Ottoman sultan which contains commands that must be implemented. Very elaborate decorated versions were created for the imperial edicts that were also works of art in the long tradition of Ottoman illumination. Various kinds of calligraphy were used in the edicts during this period. The sections of the edicts that are illuminated are the head, including the artistic insignia of the sultan, lines, and stops.

il from Sultan Selim II's ferman, dated 1572

Sultan Mehmed IV's ferman: a classical Ottoman imperial edict written with the calligraphy of sloping lines

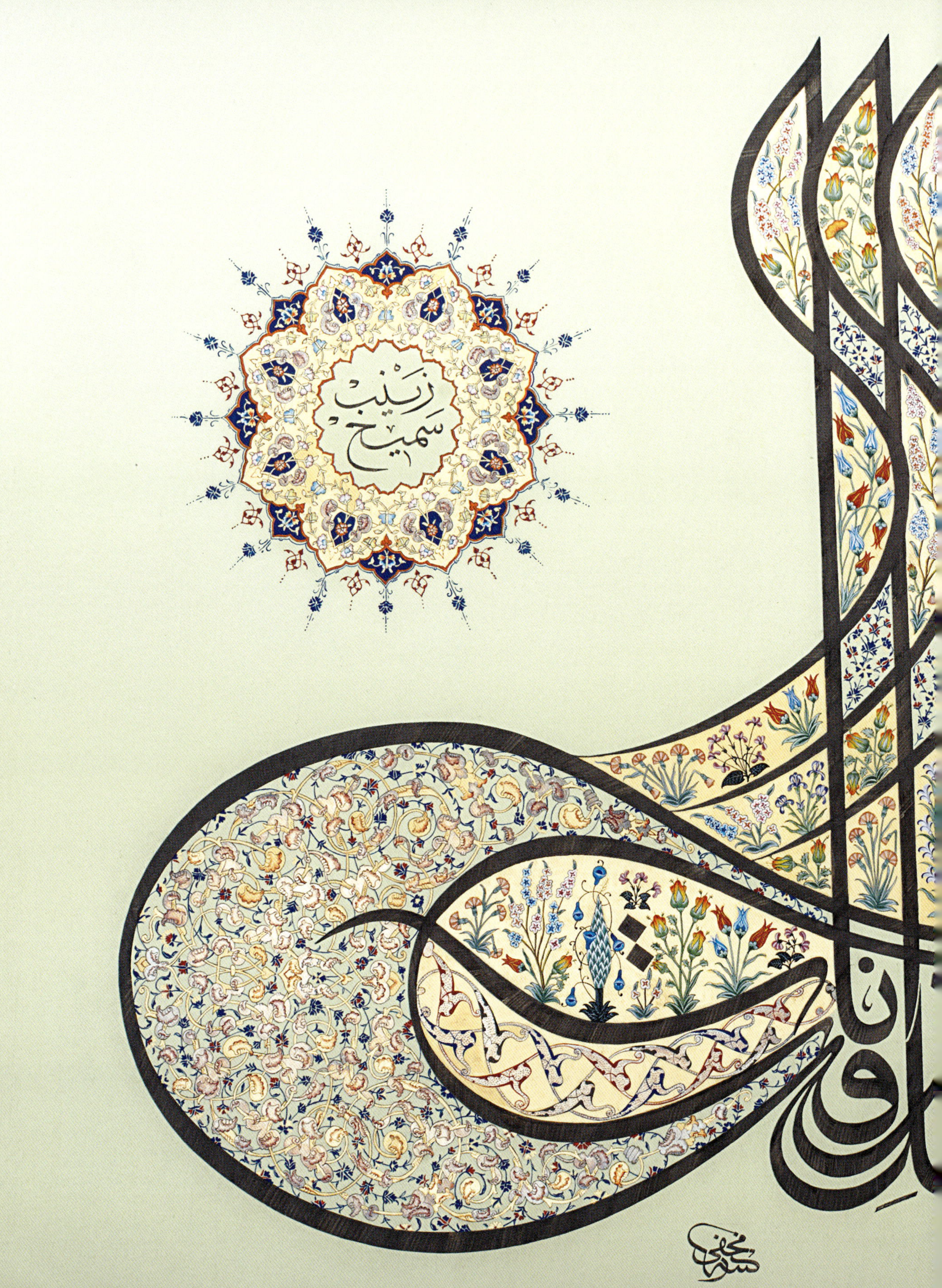
زينب
سميح

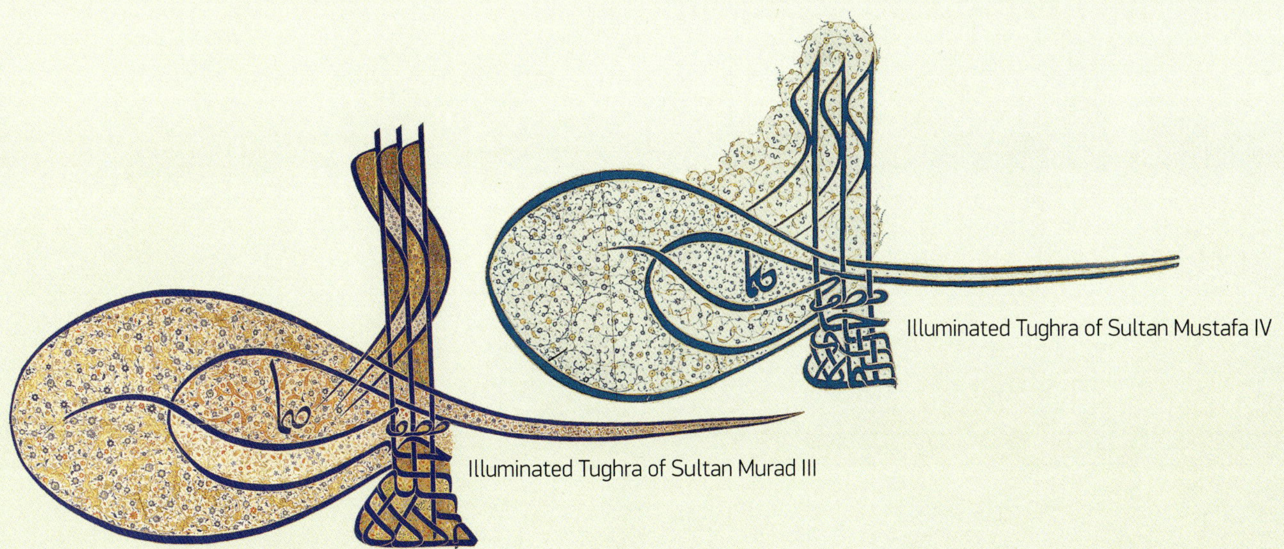

Illuminated Tughra of Sultan Mustafa IV

Illuminated Tughra of Sultan Murad III

E. Tughra (Insignia) of the Sultan

As a Turkish word, “tughra” means a special sign including the sultan’s name or the sultan’s signature. It is known that the *tughra* was first used by the second Ottoman Sultan, Orhan Bey. Flowers belonging to the Karamemi period are used in the ornamentation of the insignia. Sultan Suleyman the Magnificent and Sultan Mehmed the Conqueror’s insignias are among the *tughra*s with the most popular ornamentation. Today, the basmala and family insignias are also popularly written in the tughra form. The artist making the insignia is called a “tughrakash.”

Family insignia written in the tughra form, illuminated by Sema Onat

١٤٢٨

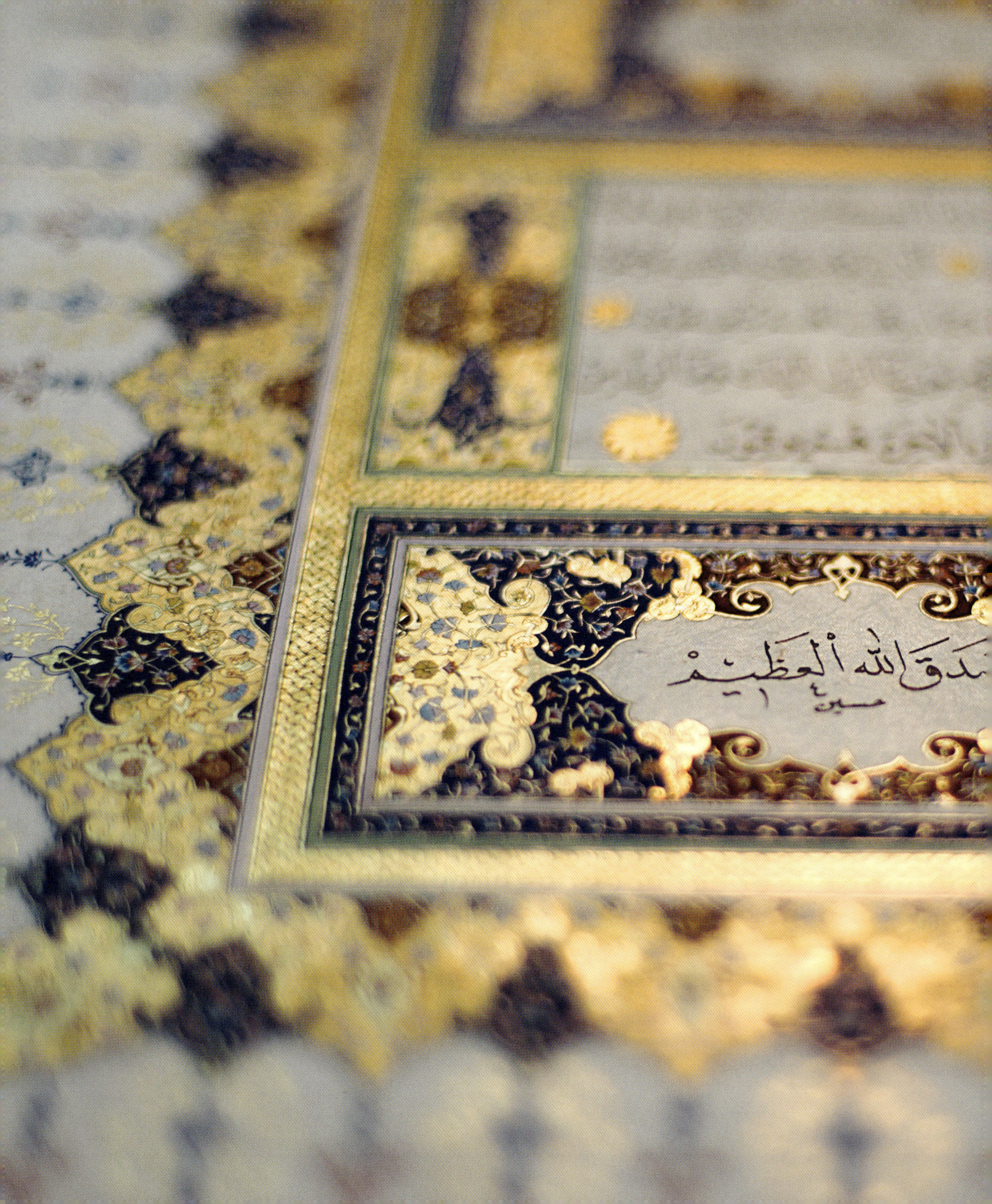
الله العظيم
حسين

Part Seven

Manuscript Illumination

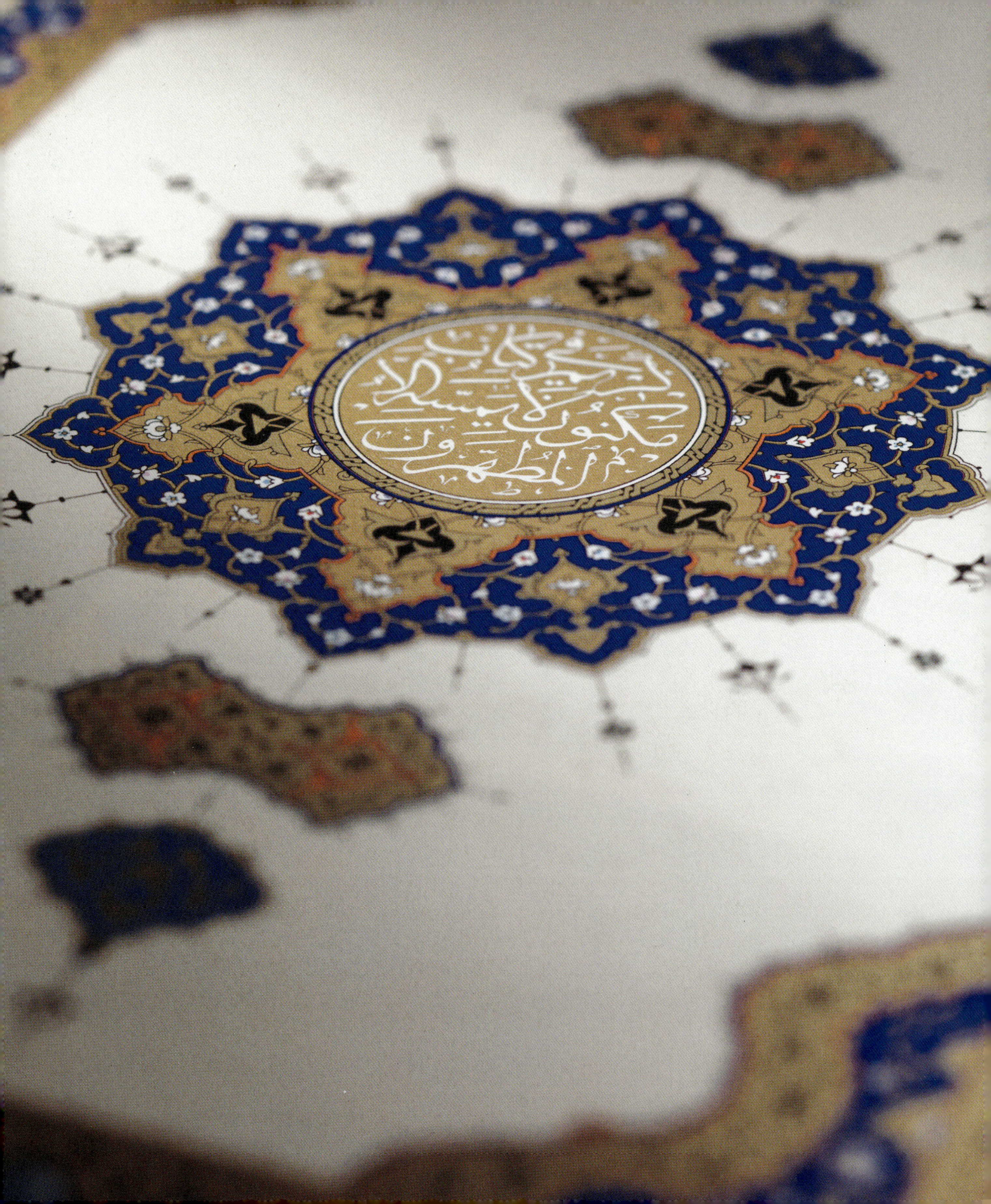
في كتاب مكنون لا يمسه إلا المطهرون

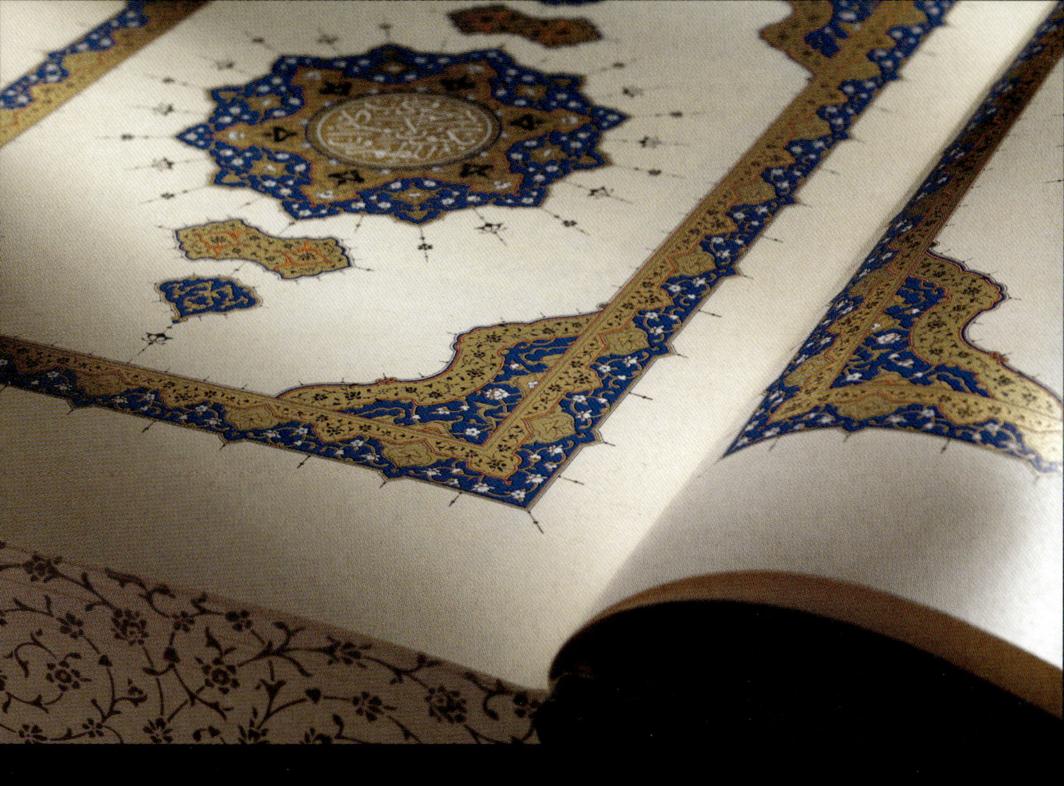

AREAS IN MANUSCRIPTS ORNAMENTED WITH ILLUMINATION

As a major part of Islamic book arts, illumination has been used extensively for the adornment of handwritten books. It is especially prominent in the ornamentation of Qur'an manuscripts. The illuminated Qur'an manuscripts display the amazing detail and richness of the text. A variety of elements within the manuscript have been commonly illuminated, including title pages, chapter headings, wide margins and borders.

A. *Zahriya* (Carpet) Pages: These are the title page of a handwritten book or the inner sides of a binding cover. These carpet pages face one another with no or little text and are completely covered with illumination.

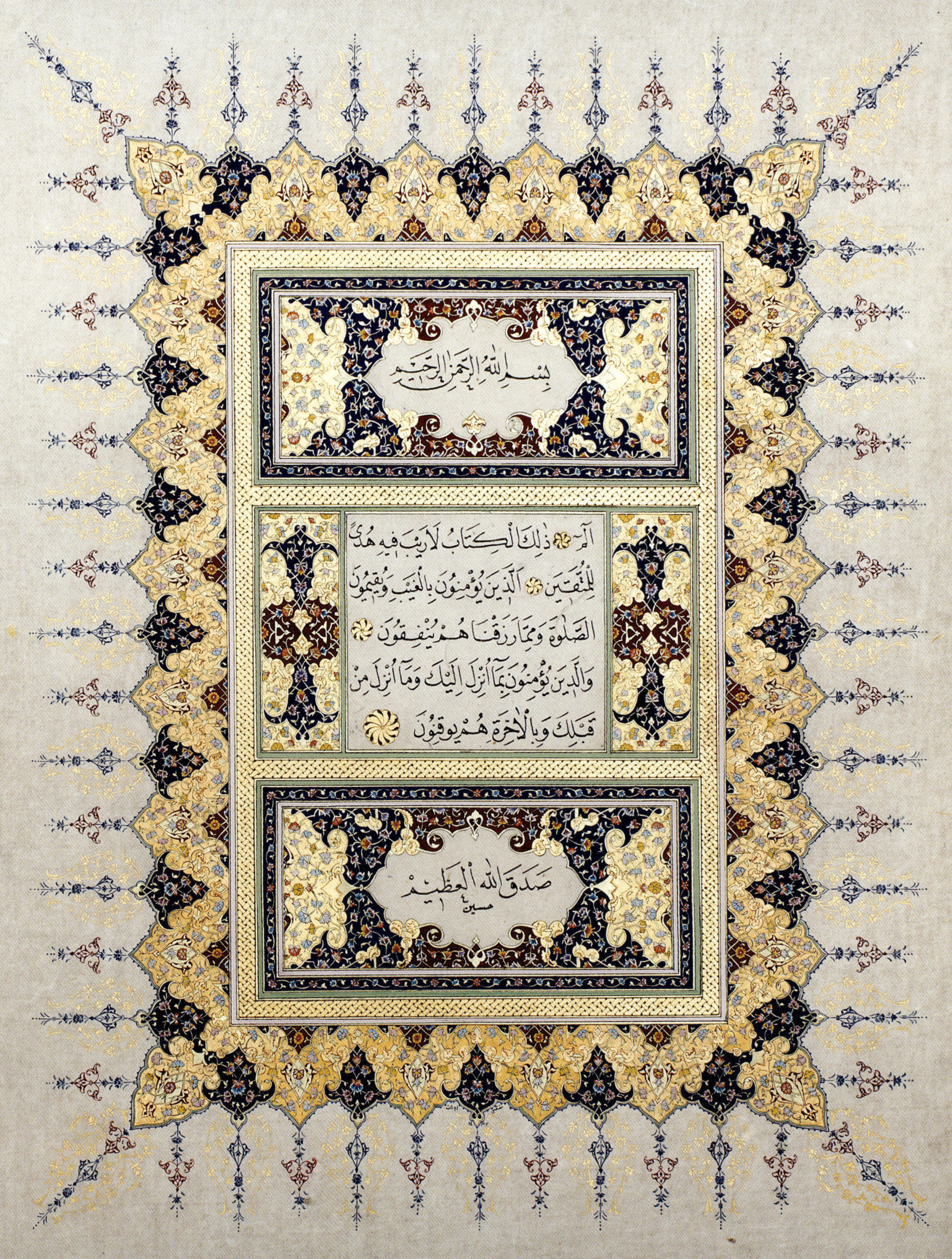

بسم الله الرحمن الرحيم
الم ذلك الكتاب لا ريب فيه هدى
للمتقين الذين يؤمنون بالغيب ويقيمون
الصلوة ومما رزقناهم ينفقون
والذين يؤمنون بما انزل اليك وما انزل من
قبلك وبالآخرة هم يوقنون
صدق الله العظيم

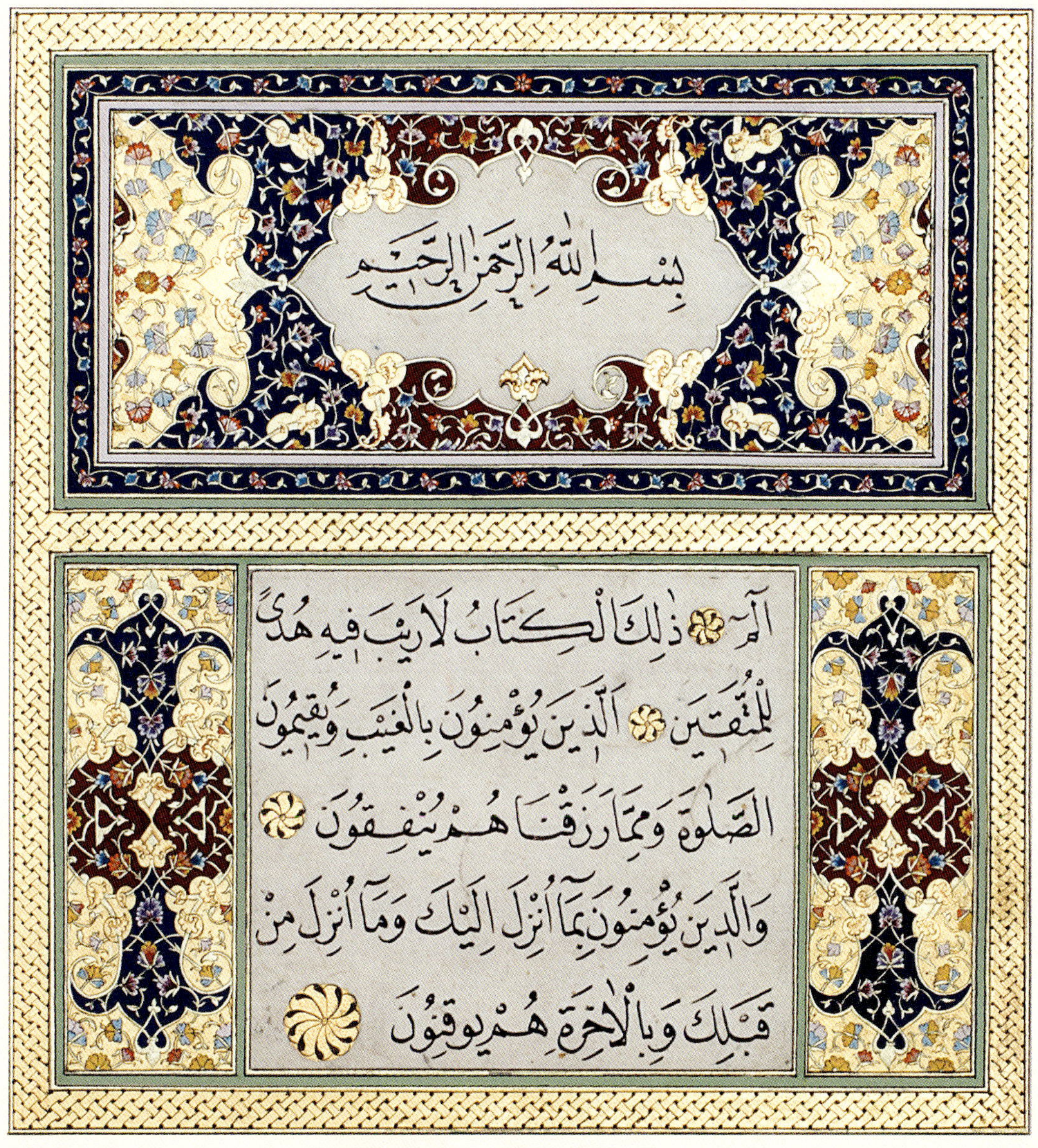

B. *Sarlawha* (The First or Main Chapter Heading): Immediately following the *zahriya*, it is the page where the manuscript begins. On this page the illumination stands out more than the writing and the most magnificent ornamentation of the period is used around this first (or main) chapter heading.

C. *Qoltuq* (Wide Margins): This is the empty space on the two sides of the writing. They are generally ornamented in a symmetrical way on spaces on both sides of the *sarlawha, mail qit'a* (the sloping line), and *surah*s in a way suitable to the general composition.

The left-side of the double page *sarlawha* illumination by Sema Onat

D. *Nuqtas* (Stops): These are flowers comprised of different motifs that are put at the end of verses. These verse dividers are also called *waqf*.

Various gold ornaments that mark the end of each verse

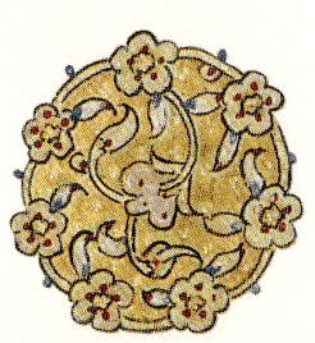

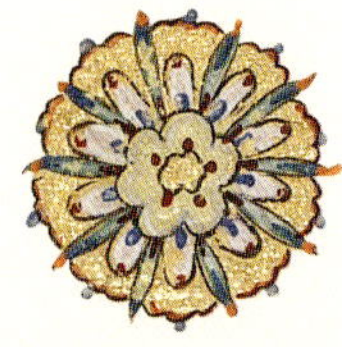

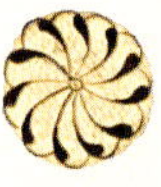

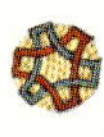

E. *Muqaddima* (Introduction): This is the introductory section of the book. Here the author states why he wrote the book, his name, and the date of writing.

F. *Khatima* (End) Pages: These are the last pages of a work. There are final prayers on these pages. The names of the calligrapher and illuminist, if any, are put on these pages.

G. *Guls* (Flower-shaped Ornamentation): These flower-shaped ornamentations are placed in specific places on pages of the Qur'an. *Sajda gul* is made during lines with the prostration of recitation (*sajda al-tilawa*); *hizb* (division) gul is every five pages; *juz* (fascicle) gul is on the first page of the fascicle; and *surah* (chapter) gul is at the beginning of Qur'anic chapters (Figure 59).

H. *Jadwal* (Tabular Lines): This is comprised of lines in tabular form to separate the writing and illumination. They are separated in turn with gold and color. They contribute to the esthetic of the work (Figure 60).

I. *Bayna's Sutur* (Between the Lines): This is ornamentation made between the wide line spacing of the writing. The spaces between the writing are sliced, encircled, and painted with gold. If the gold area is not very broad, a design is not made. Only dots are made with needle polishing. *Bayna's sutur* ornamentation can also be made in the space remaining between the lines with *rumi* and *khatai* motifs rather than gold.

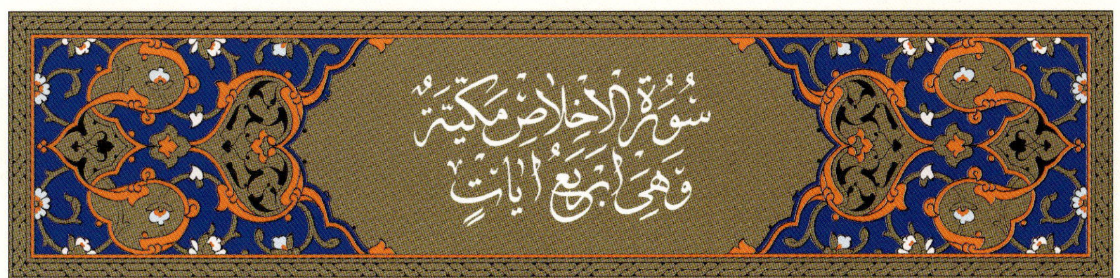

Rectangular *lawha*: Illuminating the blank spaces around the heading adds special magnificence and beauty to the text.

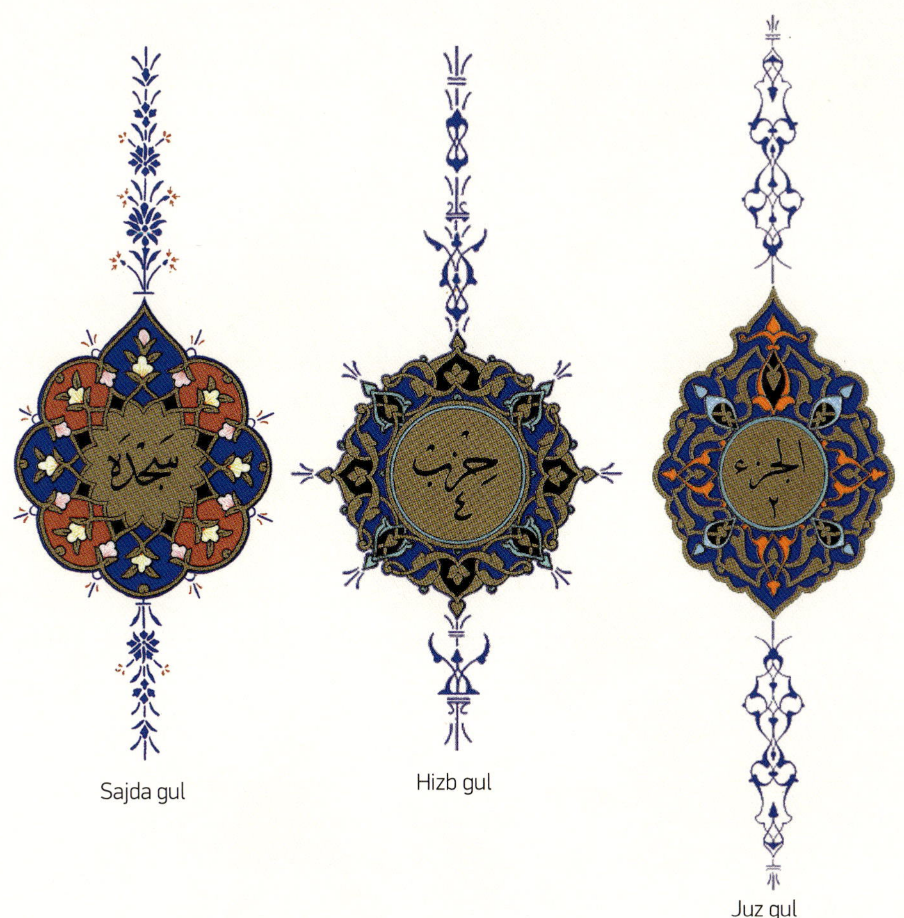

Figure 59 - Flower-shaped ornamentations used on pages of the Qur'an

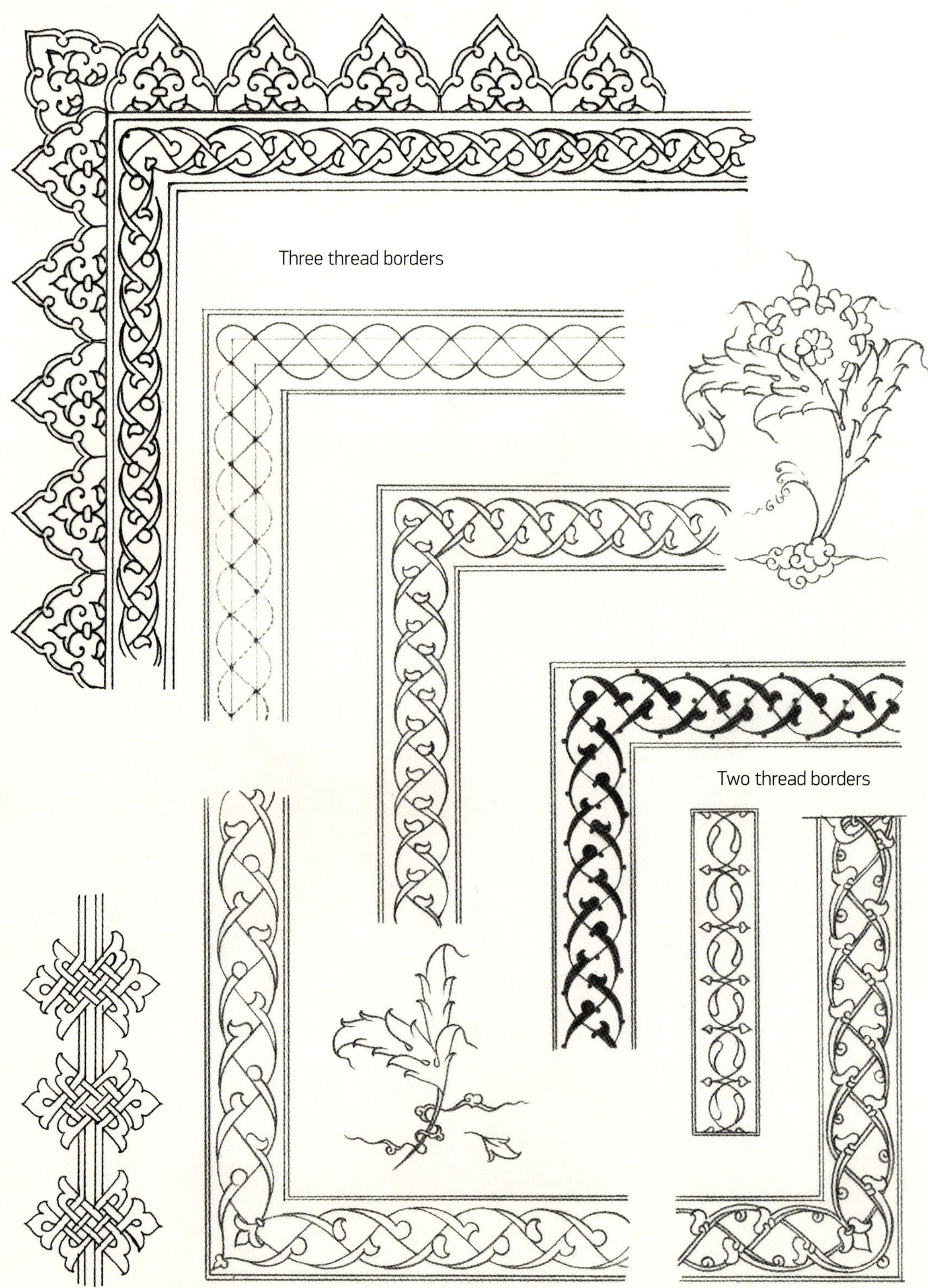

Figure 60 - Various border designs

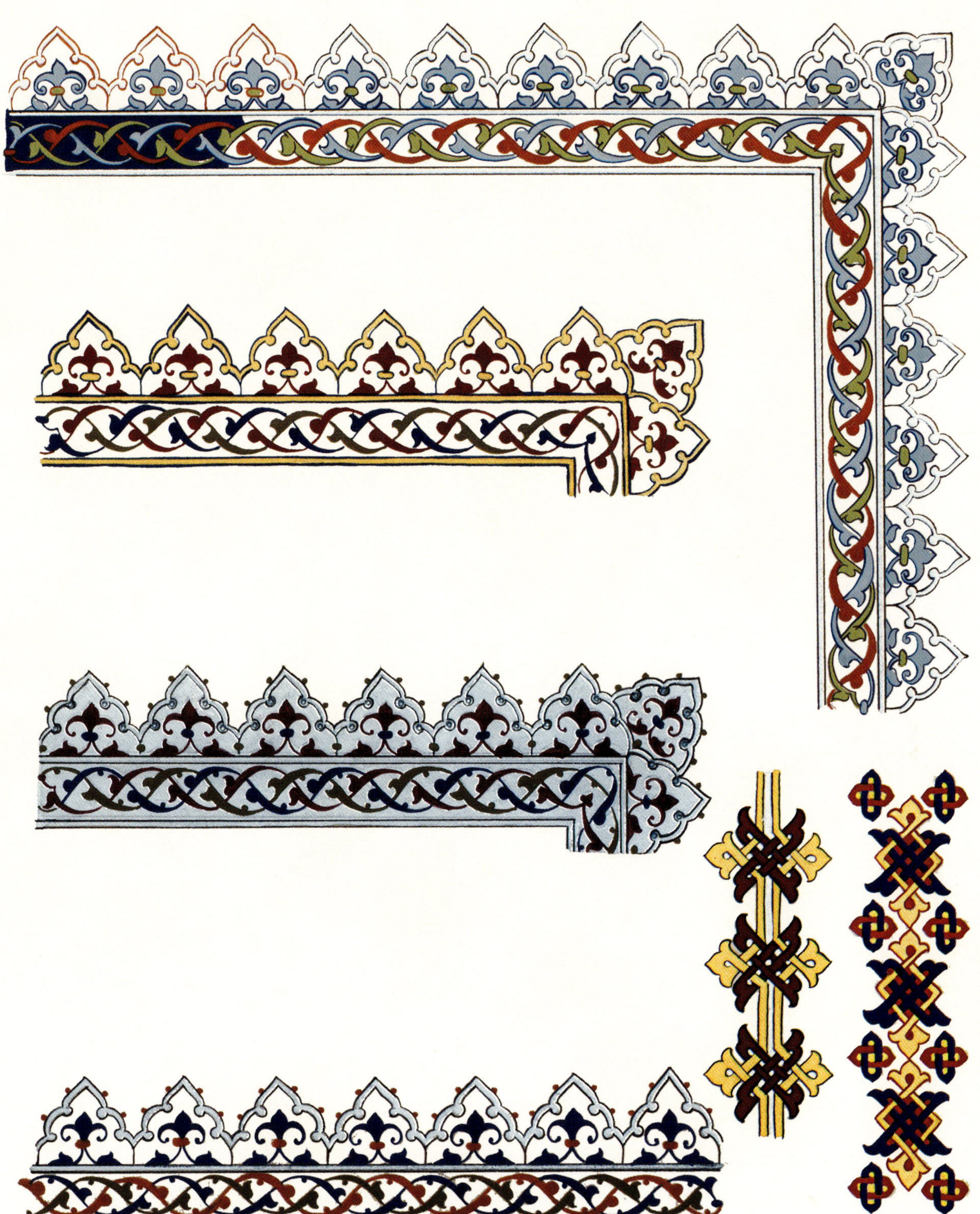

Illuminated border samples

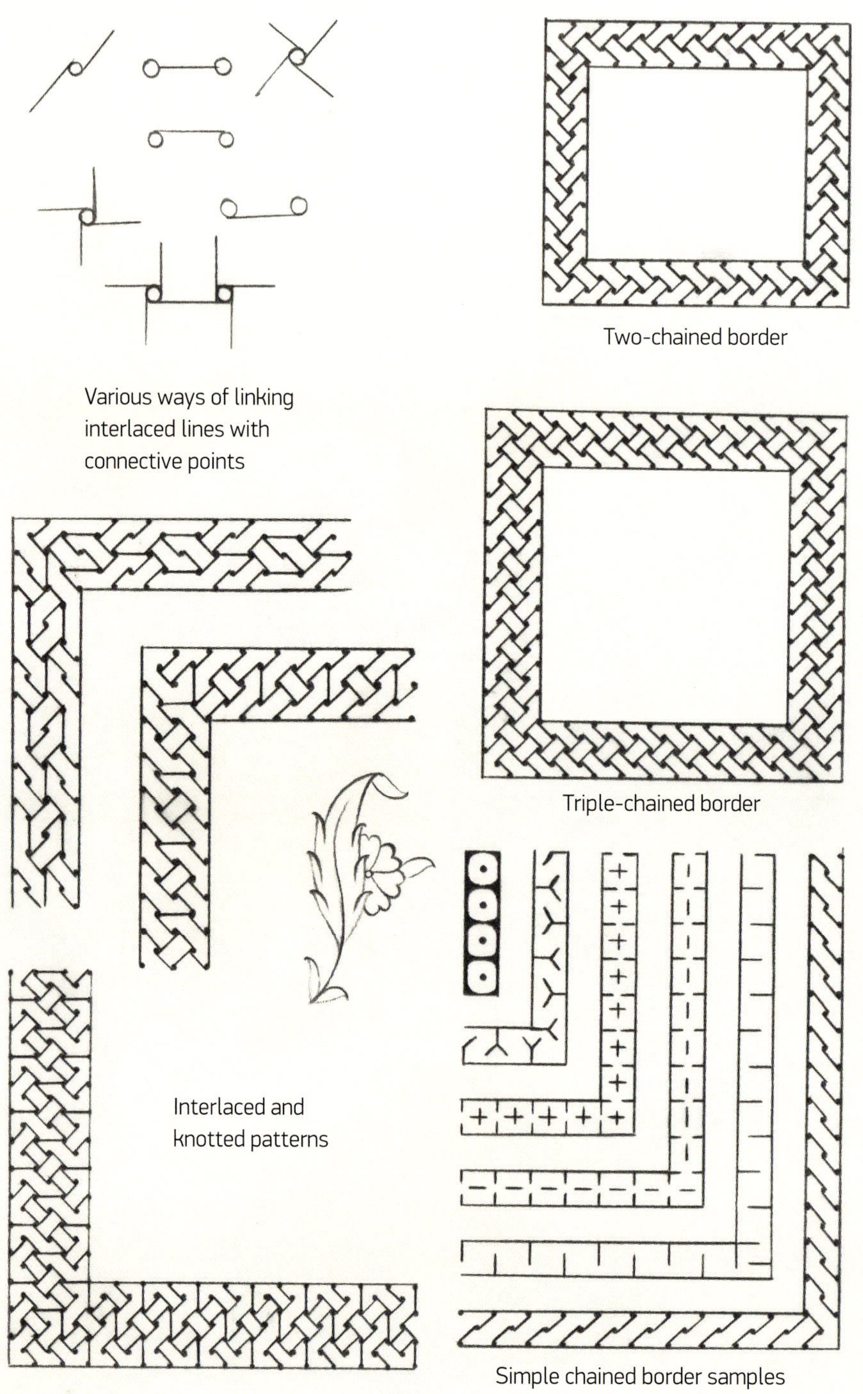

Figure 61 -Various types of chain patterns

J. Border-Edging-Chain Pattern: This kind of ornamentation consists of designs beginning at the end of the writing between the edge ornamentation area and the next section. The space left between the writing and the design is one millimeter *jadwal* gold, two millimeters of colorful edging; then gold is applied to the seven-eight millimeter chain pattern area remaining in the middle. If color is applied to the chain pattern part remaining in the middle, gold is used for the edging (Figure 61).

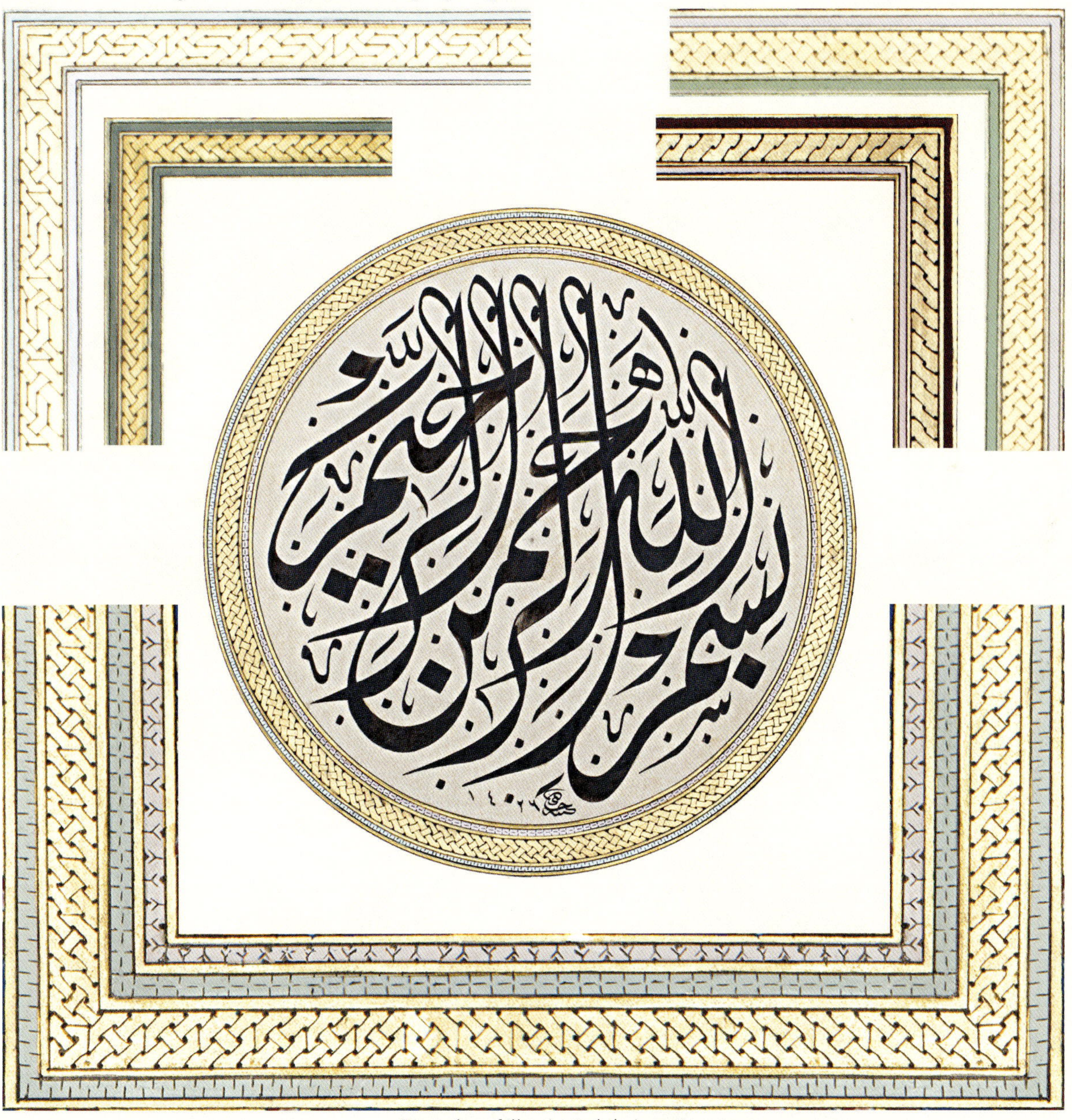

Examples of illuminated chain patterns

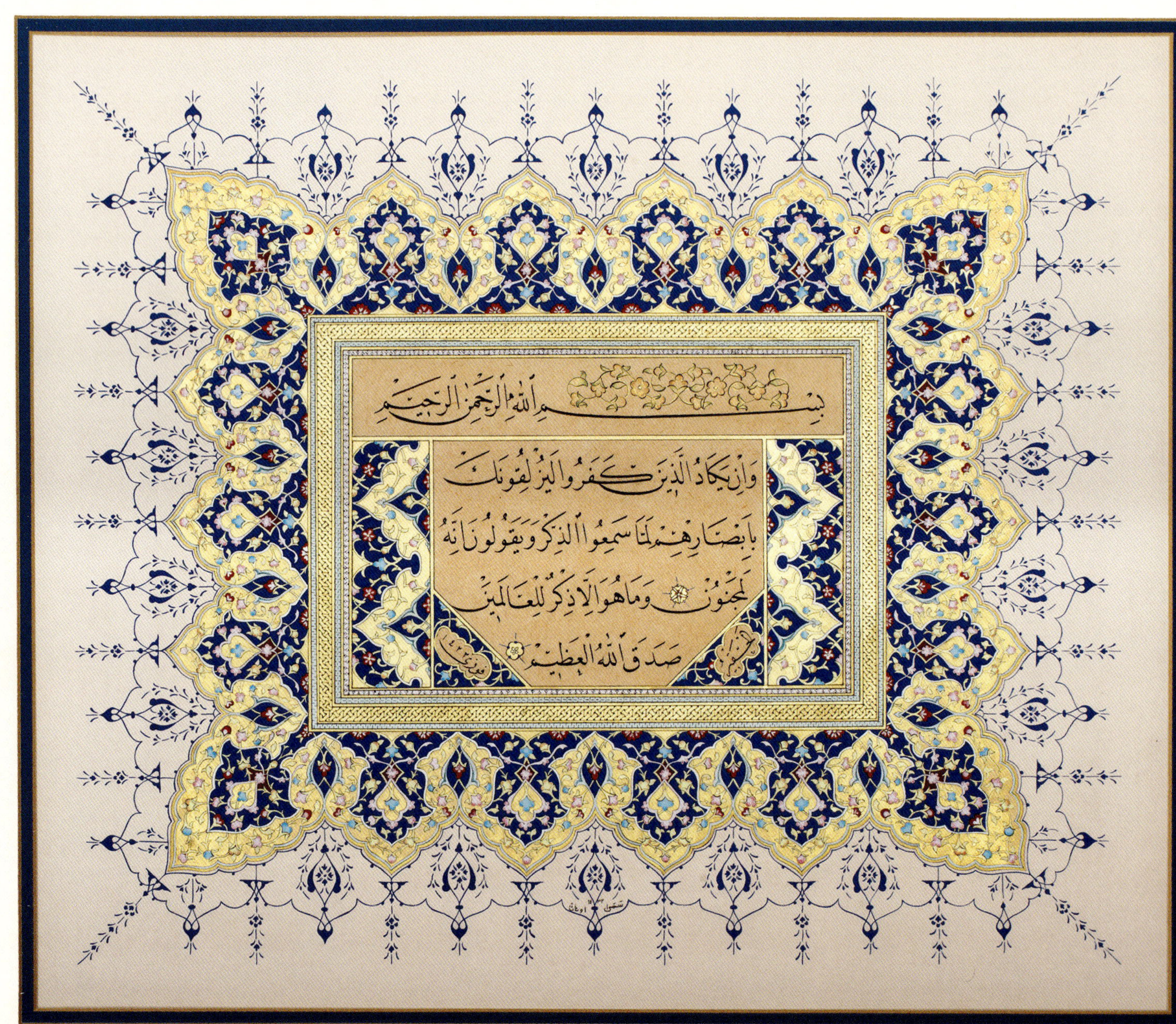

Classical illumination work by Sema Onat

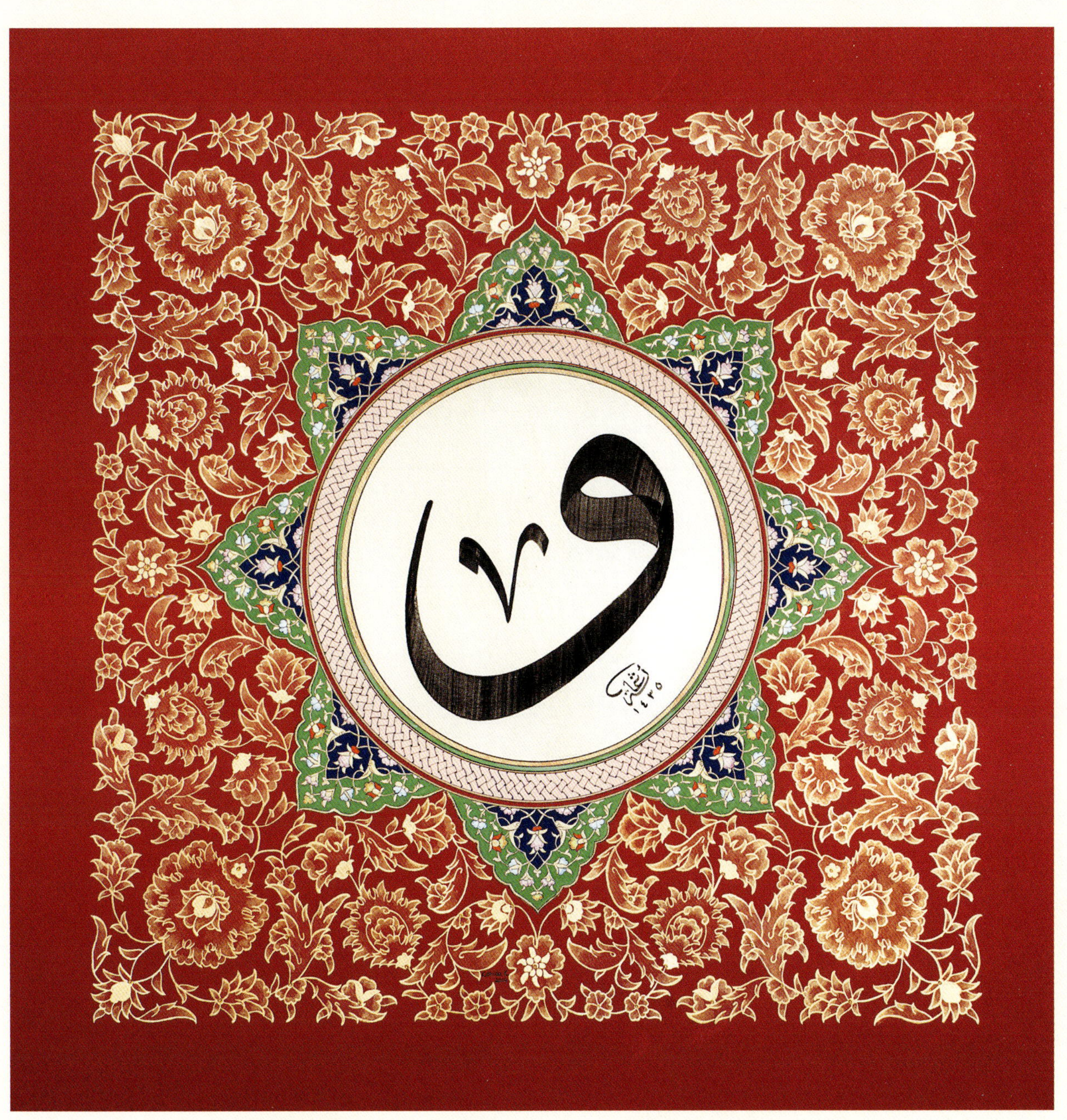

Classical illumination work by Cahide Kuş

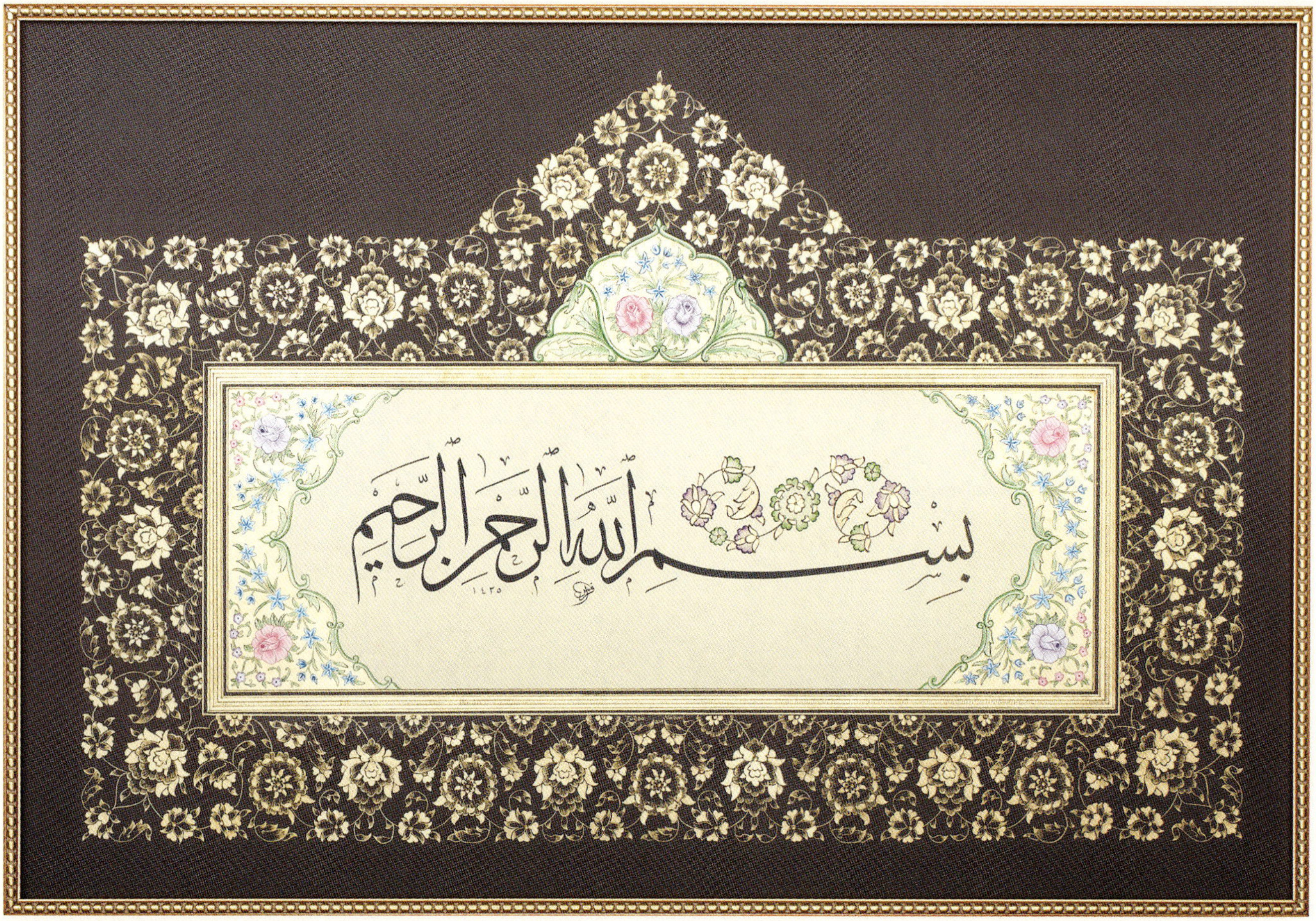

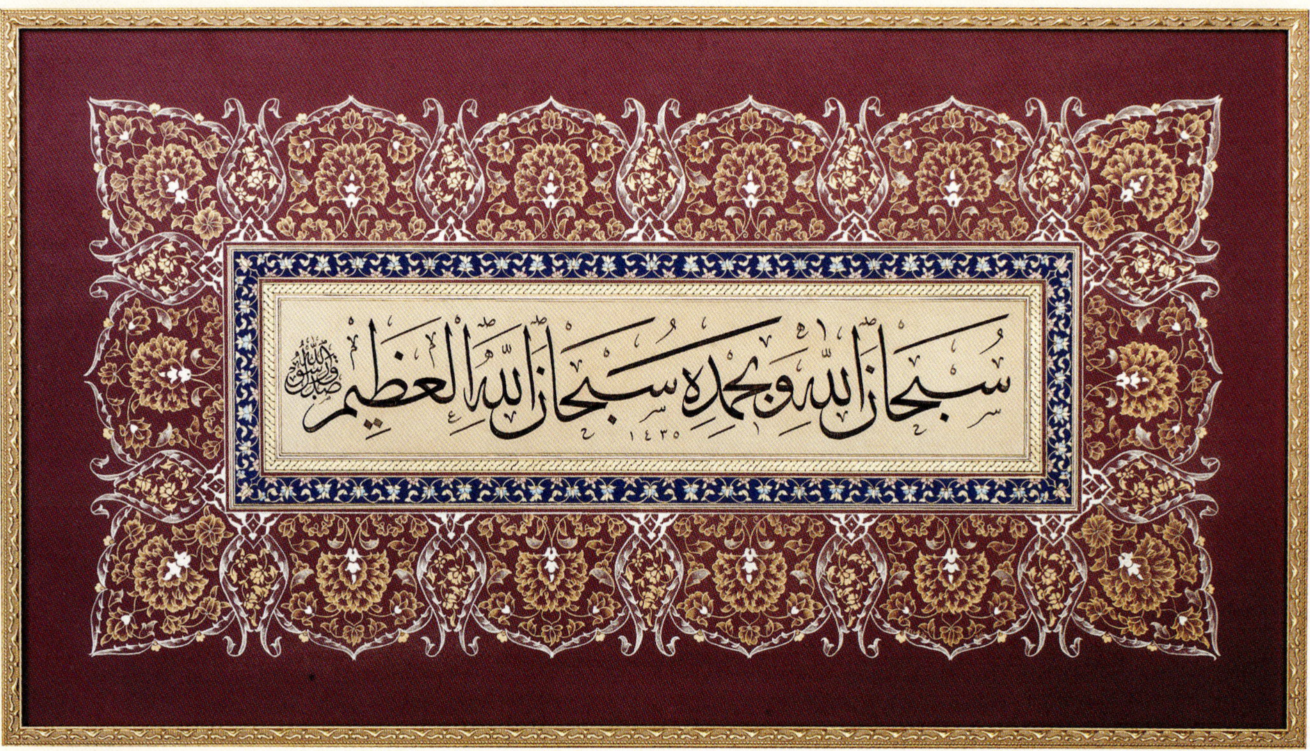

Classical illumination works by Sema Onat

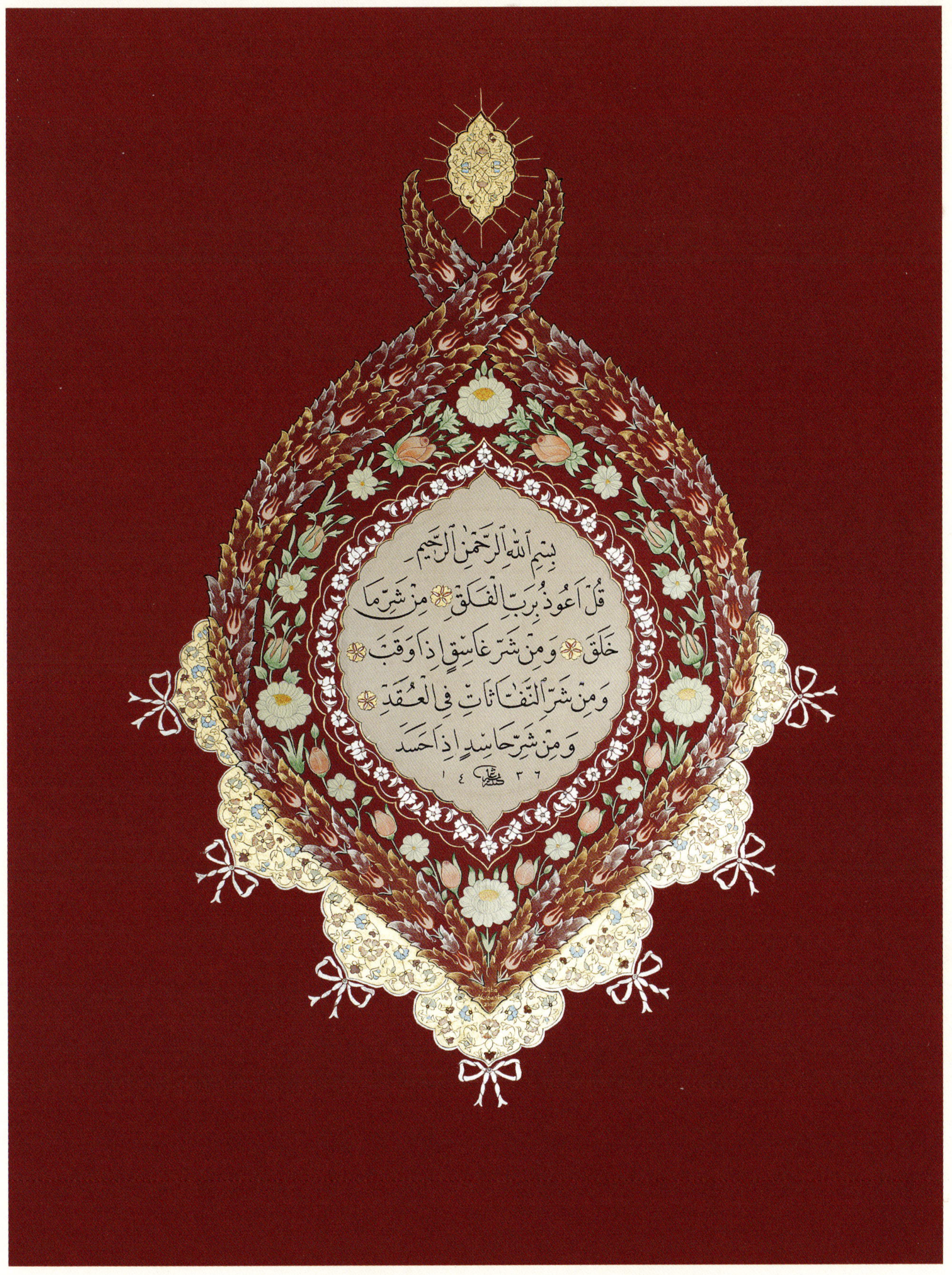

Classical illumination with Halkar and floral motifs by Tuğba Nalbant

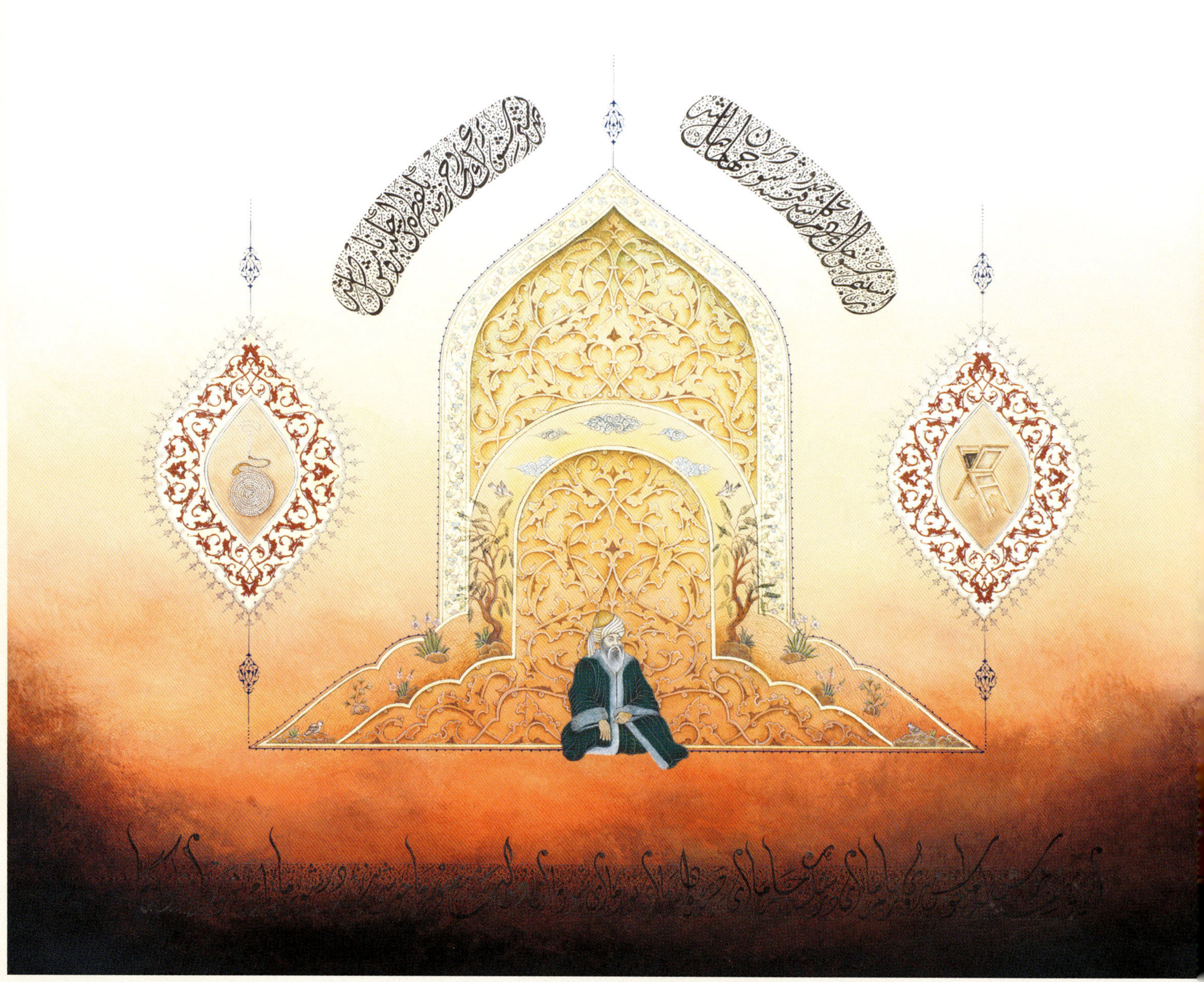

Miniature work with segmented Rumi motifs and illuminated borders by Sema Onat

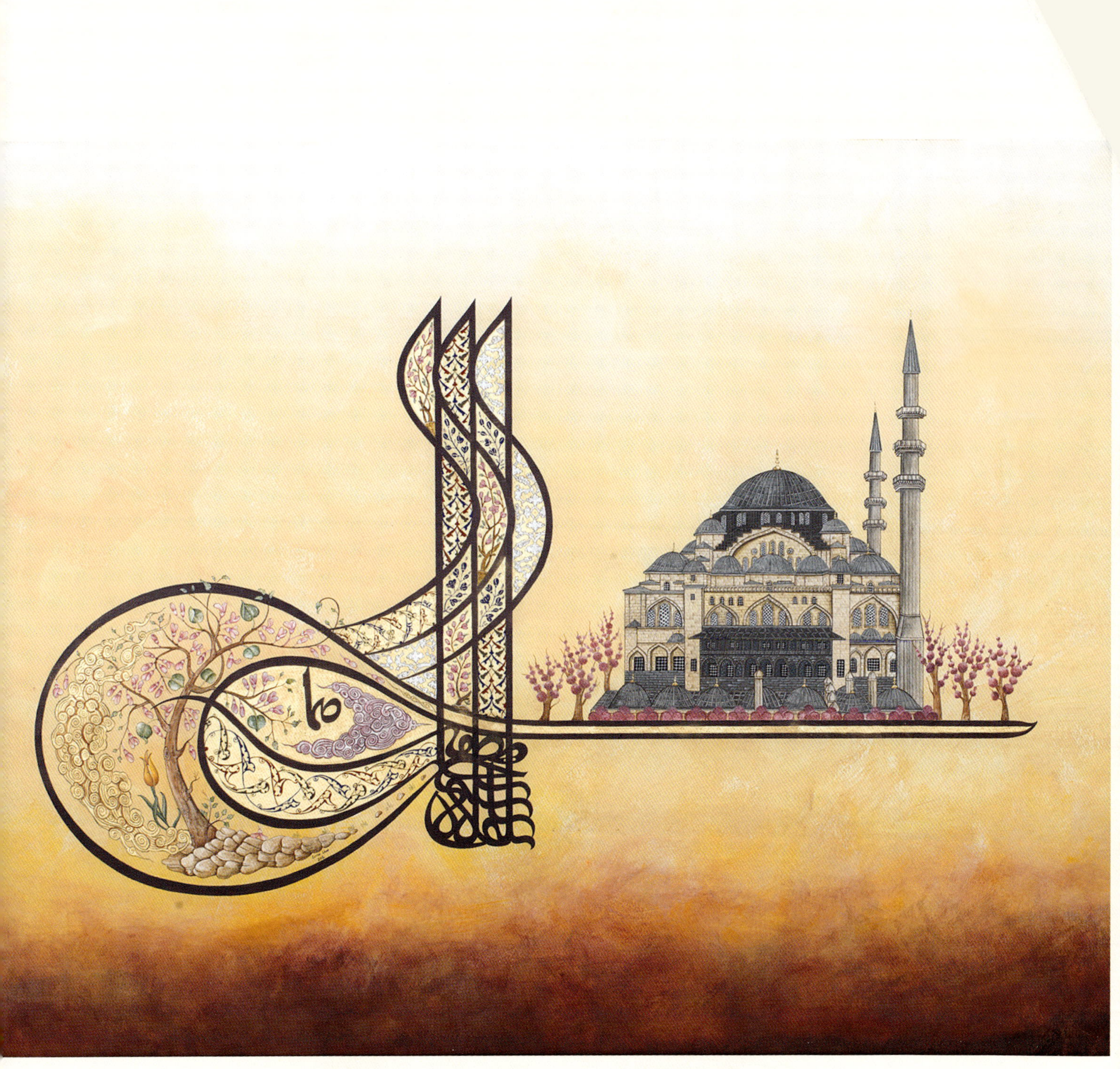

Miniature of a mosque and a tughra having Rumi motifs by Sema Onat

Sources

Akar, Azade and Keskiner, Cahide. *Türk Süsleme Sanatlarında Desen ve Motif* (Patterns and Motifs in Turkish Ornamentation Arts), Tercüman Gazetesi: Istanbul, 1978.

Birol, İnci. *Klasik Devir Türk Tezyini Sanatlarında Desen Tasarımı* Çizim *Tekniği ve* Çeşitleri (Design Pattern Drawing Techniques in Turkish Ornamentation Arts during the Classical Period), Kubbealtı Akademisi Kültür ve Sanat Vakfı Publication: Istanbul, 2008.

Demiriz, Yıldız. *Osmanlı Kitap Sanatında Doğal* Çiçekler (Naturalist Flowers in the Ottoman Book Arts), Yorum Sanat Baskı: Istanbul, 2005.

Duran, Gülnur. *Ali* Üsküdari*: Tezhip ve Rugani* Üstadı, Çiçek *Ressamı* (Ali Üsküdari: Master Illumination Artist, Flower Painter), Kubbealtı Akademisi Kültür ve Sanat Vakfı Publication: Istanbul, 2008.

Keskiner, Cahide. *Türk Süsleme Sanatlarında Stilize* Çiçekler *Hatai* (Stylized Flowers in Turkish Ornamentation Arts), Turkish Ministry of Culture Publication: Ankara, 2000.

Özen, Mine Esiner. *Türk Tezhip Sanatı* (Turkish Illumination Art), Gözen Kitap ve Yayınevi: Istanbul, 2003.

Özkeçeci, İlhan and Özkeçeci, Şule Bilge. *Türk Sanatında Tezhip* (Illumination in Turkish Arts), Yazıgen Publishing: Istanbul, 2014.